UNLOCKING SUCCESS IN ICT 2022 MENTORSHIP

THE SMART MONEY GUIDE TO THE FULL ICT DAY TRADING MODEL

The market is always teaching you something, so be a student of the game.
-ICT

by **LumiTraders**

Title: Unlocking Success in ICT 2022 Mentorship: The Smart Money Guide to The Full ICT Day Trading Model by LumiTraders

For permissions, please contact:

LumiTraders

Twitter: @LumiTraders

www. LumiTraders.com

info@lumitraders.com

Published by LumiTraders

First Edition: 2023

ISBN: 9798862884296

Design and Typesetting: Darya Filipenka

Editing: Elisabeth Morgan Thompson

Disclaimer: The information provided in this book is for educational and informational purposes only. It is not intended to be a substitute for professional advice. The author and publisher disclaim any liability for any decisions made based on the information provided in this book.

The information and concepts presented in this book are solely my interpretation of ICT (Inner Circle Trader) concepts, which were originally authored and created by Michael J. Huddleston (Inner Circle Trader). It is important to clarify that I do not claim ownership of these concepts and recognizes Michael J. Huddleston as their original source. SMC (Smart Money Concepts) and ICT concepts are synonymous and originate from the same author, Michael J. Huddleston.

Unlocking Success in ICT 2022 Mentorship: The Smart Money Guide to The Full ICT Day Trading Model by LumiTraders

LUMI
TRADERS

Table of Contents

Disclaimer

The contents of this book are intended for educational purposes only. This book does not provide financial advice, nor does it make any specific recommendations for financial decisions.

The information and concepts presented in this book are solely my interpretation of ICT (Inner Circle Trader) concepts, which were originally authored and created by Michael J. Huddleston (Inner Circle Trader).

For a more comprehensive and detailed understanding of these concepts, it is recommended that readers refer to Michael J. Huddleston's original work available on his YouTube channel (The Inner Circle Trader) and Twitter.

The concepts discussed in this book may also be taught elsewhere and may have been given different names.

It is important to clarify that I do not claim ownership of these concepts and recognizes Michael J. Huddleston as their original source. SMC (Smart Money Concepts) and ICT concepts are synonymous and originate from the same author, Michael J. Huddleston.

Readers are urged to exercise their own judgment and seek professional financial advice when making investment or trading decisions. I am not responsible for any financial actions or decisions made by readers based on the information contained herein. My purpose is solely to provide educational insights and perspectives on these concepts, and any implementation of these ideas is done at the reader's own discretion and risk.

Unlocking Success in ICT 2022 Mentorship by **Darya Filipenka**
Edited by **Elisabeth Morgan Thompson**

Introduction

My name is Darya. I present LumiTraders community. Inspired by Michael, I have decided sharing my knowledge, and doing my best to help simplify ICT concepts for newer traders.

Michael Huddleston, also known as Inner Circle Trader, is a legendary forex trader, the "father of smart money" and a proponent of the "conspiracy theory" that trading markets are not free, and all prices are controlled by a market maker.

With a wealth of knowledge spanning 33 enlightening chapters, this book is your roadmap to becoming a savvy trader.

In this extensive mentorship book, you'll embark on a journey that delves into the very heart of trading, from the fundamental concepts to the advanced strategies employed by seasoned traders. Chapter by chapter, you'll explore the following key areas:

- **Chapters 1 through 3** provide a solid foundation, introducing you to intraday trading, price action, trade setup elements, and the critical concept of liquidity in trading.

- **Chapters 4 to 11** dive deep into the nuances of market structure, London session insights, order flow analysis, and various trading patterns such as the Three Drives Pattern and ICT Killzones.

- **Chapters 12 to 15** focus on daily biases, consolidation hurdles, economic calendar events, and precision market structure techniques.

- **Chapters 16 to 22** reveal multiple setups within trading sessions, intermarket relationships, and the impact of major events like FOMC and NFP on your trading decisions.

- **Chapters 23 to 30** introduce you to strategies related to new week/day openings, liquidity voids, and utilizing the institutional perspective in your trading.

- **Chapters 31 to 33** take you to an even higher level, discussing central bank dealers' ranges, high-probability day trade setups, and quarterly shifts

Throughout this book, you'll also find valuable insights on using various techniques, from economic calendar events and daily templates to institutional perception and core content block types.

With each chapter building upon the knowledge gained in the previous one, you'll gradually become proficient in navigating the intricacies of intraday trading.

By the time you reach the final chapter, you'll have a well-rounded understanding of how to make informed trading decisions, manage risks effectively, and capitalize on opportunities in the ever-evolving world of financial markets.

The "Unlocking Success in ICT 2022 Mentorship: The Smart Money Guide to The Full ICT Day Trading Model by LumiTraders" is not just a book; it's your mentor, guiding you through the maze of smart money trading concepts and equipping you with the skills and knowledge needed to excel in this dynamic field. Whether you're a novice looking to start your trading journey or an experienced trader seeking to refine your strategies, this guide is an invaluable resource that will empower you to navigate the markets with confidence and precision.

By the end of this book, you will have a solid foundation in the Inner Circle Trader concept and be equipped with the knowledge and skills you need to navigate the complex world of institutional order flow analysis and achieve your financial goals. Whether you are trading for income, growth, or speculation, this book will provide you with the tools you need to succeed in the world of Inner Circle Trading. Let's get started!

LumiTraders ✅
@LumiTraders

Elisabeth
@no_hay_calor

@lumi_traders

@no_hay_calor

lumitraders.com

General Terminology

AD (A/D) - - - - - - - - - - - - - - - - - - Accumulation and/or Distribution
ADR - Average Daily Range
AKZ - Asian Kill Zone
AMD - Accumulation, Manipulation, Distribution
BB - Breaker Block
BE - Break-Even
BG - Breakaway Gap
BISI - Buyside Imbalance Sell Side Inefficiency
BMS - Break of Market Structure
BoS - Break of Structure
BPR - Balanced Price Range
BSL - Buyside Liquidity
CE - Consequent Encroachment
CBDR - Central Bank Dealers Range
DD - Drawdown
DH/DL - - - - - - - - - - - - - - - - - - - Daily High / Daily Low
DOL - Draw on Liquidity
EQH/EQL - - - - - - - - - - - - - - - - - Equal Highs / Equal Lows
FVG - Fair Value Gap
HH - Higher High
HL - Higher Low
HOD - High of Day
HOW - High of Week
HRLR - High Resistance Liquidity Run
HTF - Higher Time Frame
IFVG - Inversion FVG
IOF - Institutional Order Flow
IOFED - Institutional Order Flow Entry Drill
IPDA - Interbank Price Delivery Algorithm
ITH - Intermediate-Term High
ITL - Intermediate-Term Low
KZ - Kill Zone
LC - London Close
LCKZ - London Close Kill Zone
LH - Lower High
LL - Lower Low
LO - London Open
LOD - Low of Day
LOW - Low of Week
LOKZ - London Open Kill Zone
LRLR - Low Resistance Liquidity Run
LTF - Lower Time Frame

LTH	Long-Term High
LTL	Long-Term Low
LQ	Liquidity
LV	Liquidity Void
MB	Mitigation Block
MG	Measuring Gap
MM	Market-Maker
MS	Market Structure
MMXM	Market Maker Buy/Sell Model
MSS	Market Structure Shift
MT	Mean Threshold
NDOG	New Day Opening Gap
NFP	Non-Farm Payroll report
NMO	NY Midnight Opening Price
NYO	New York Open
NYOKZ	New York Open Kill Zone
NWOG	New Week Opening Gap
OB	Order Block
OF	Order Flow
OP	Opening Price
OTE	Optimal Trade Entry
PA	Price Action
PDH	Previous Day High
PDL	Previous Day Low
PO3	Power of Three
RB	Rejection Block
RDRB	Redelivered Rebalanced PD Array
RR (R/R, R:R)	Risk/Reward ratio or Reward/Risk ratio
RHO	Return to Origin or Return to OB
SB	Silver Bullet
SIBI	Sellside Imbalance Buyside Inefficiency
S&D	Seek and destroy
SH	Swing High
SL	Stop Loss
SMT	Smart Money Tool
SMT DIV	SMT Divergence
STH	Short-Term High
STL	Short-Term Low
TA (T/A)	Technical Analysis
TF	Time Frame
TP	Take-Profit
TS	Turtle Soup
TZ	Time Zone
VI	Volume Imbalance

Chapter 1

Introduction to Intraday Trading and Price Action

Intraday trading, also known as day trading, involves buying and selling financial instruments within the same trading day. Unlike long-term position trading, intraday trading focuses on taking advantage of short-term price fluctuations to make quick profits.

Position Trading	Swing Trading
Long-term: Monthly Intermediate: Weekly Short-term: Daily	Long-term: Daily Intermediate: 4h Short-term: 1h
Short-term Trading	**Day Trading**
Long-term: 4h Intermediate: 1h Short-term: 15m	Long-term: 1h Intermediate: 15m Short-term: 5m

Why choose intraday trading over other trading styles? Here are some advantages to consider:

1. Quick Decision-Making: Intraday traders are able to make quick decisions based on real-time market data. This allows them to capitalize on short-term market movements and potentially generate profits within a single trading day.

2. Flexibility: Intraday trading offers flexibility in terms of time commitment. As an intraday trader, you can choose the hours that suit your schedule and still actively participate in the market.

3. Lower Capital Requirements: Intraday trading can be done with smaller capital compared to long-term position trading. This is particularly true when trading micro accounts or using leveraged products like CFDs.

The Demo Account Approach

One of the key aspects of becoming a successful trader is gaining experience and honing your skills. This is where a demo account can be incredibly valuable. A demo account allows you to trade in a simulated environment using virtual money, providing you with a risk-free opportunity to practice your trading strategies and familiarize yourself with the platform.

When you use a demo account, you have the opportunity to learn and apply analysis concepts without the pressure of real financial risk. This can help you develop a solid foundation of knowledge and skills that will ultimately make you a better trader.

Some traders may feel overwhelmed by the vast amount of information available to them. A demo account allows you to focus on specific trading models or concepts, helping you avoid analysis paralysis and allowing you to make more informed decisions.

Why Some Traders Struggle with Demo Trading

While demo trading offers numerous benefits, it is not without its challenges. Understanding these challenges can help you navigate them effectively and make the most of your demo trading experience.

One common challenge traders face when using a demo account is maintaining discipline. It's important to treat your demo account as if it were a live account, following your trading plan and sticking to your strategies. This discipline will carry over into live trading and contribute to your long-term success.

Another challenge is the temptation to rush into live trading without sufficient practice and preparation. A demo account allows you to gain experience and build confidence before risking real money. It's crucial to take the time to learn and understand the concepts and strategies before transitioning to live trading.

Some traders may question the effectiveness of demo trading, believing that the skills and strategies learned in a simulated environment may not translate well to live trading. However, this skepticism can be addressed by understanding the purpose and approach of demo trading.

Demo trading allows you to test and refine your trading strategies in a controlled environment. By consistently achieving positive results in your demo trades, you can gain confidence in your abilities and increase the likelihood of success in live trading.

9

It's important to remember that the primary goal of demo trading is not to make money, but rather to learn and practice. The profits or losses you make in a demo account may not accurately reflect what you would experience in a live account. Instead, focus on refining your skills and strategies. To make the most of your demo trading experience, it's important to approach it with a commitment to learning and following instructions.

Pay close attention to the concepts and strategies being taught and strive to understand them visually. Avoid overcomplicating your analysis and focus on key levels and indicators that make sense to you. Simplifying your approach can lead to better decision-making.

Remember that demo trading is a stepping stone to live trading. Use this opportunity to gradually build your skills and confidence, just as you would progress through different levels of education. With time and consistent effort, you can develop the necessary skills to trade successfully in live accounts.

Remember, practice makes perfect, and demo trading provides the perfect platform for that practice.

The Advantages of Short-Term Trading

Short-term trading, also known as intraday trading, involves making quick decisions and capitalizing on short-lived market opportunities.

One of the key advantages of intraday trading is the ability to take advantage of frequent setups. Unlike longer time frames, where setups may be scarce, intraday trading provides ample opportunities for traders to identify potential trades. ICT emphasizes that by learning how to take 5 handles (a measure of price movement) out of a market like the E-mini S&P, traders can gradually build their trading skills and profits.

Additionally, he highlights the accessibility of intraday trading. Even if traders do not have the capital to trade full-sized contracts, they can opt for micro accounts. This flexibility allows traders to start with smaller initial margins and gradually scale up their trading activities.

Applying Intraday Trading Techniques to Different Time Frames

Intraday trading techniques can be applied to various time frames, providing traders with the flexibility to adapt their strategies to different market conditions. While ICT primarily focuses on intraday trading, he assures us that the concepts he teaches can be scaled up to longer time frames. ICT emphasizes the importance of visually understanding the concepts he teaches, enabling traders to simplify their analysis and focus on key elements that make sense.

Improving Understanding of Price Action

The ultimate goal of this mentorship is to improve our understanding of price action. ICT assures us that we will learn concepts that repeat frequently in the market, allowing us to identify setups with common characteristics. While the setups may not be identical, ICT encourages us to trust our familiarity with similar patterns.

It is important to note that this mentorship is not about providing trade setups. Instead, ICT will draw our attention to potential setups before they occur, allowing us to study them and apply the concepts they teach. This approach emphasizes the importance of discipline and personal responsibility in trading.

Throughout this mentorship, ICT aims to guide us from being yearners to becoming structured learners. By following the process and dedicating ourselves to learning, we can progress from understanding the concepts to implementing them effectively and becoming earners in the trading world.

Realistic Expectations and Individual Growth

Trading is a unique and personal experience that requires individuals to grow and go through a learning process. It is important to manage your expectations and understand that becoming a successful trader takes time and effort. As our mentor, ICT cannot speed up this process for us, but he is optimistic about our potential.

It is important to recognize that not everyone will be able to effectively implement the strategies and techniques ICT teaches. Some individuals may try to take shortcuts or believe that certain steps are not necessary. **However, it is vital to understand that failure to follow the recommended actions may result in reduced results.**

Remember, trading is both the easiest and sometimes the most challenging thing you will ever do. It requires dedication, discipline, and a willingness to learn and adapt.

Commitment and Discipline in Trading

In the world of trading, commitment and discipline are key factors that can greatly impact your success.

When you graduated from University, you have already demonstrated your ability to understand complex ideas and follow instructions. The same level of discipline and commitment is required in trading. It is important to approach trading with a mindset of continuous learning, practice, and adherence to the principles taught.

ICT mentions the concept of "analysis paralysis" and how it can hinder traders' decision-making process. This is a common challenge faced by many traders, especially those who are just starting out. To overcome this, it is crucial to follow instructions and complete assigned tasks diligently.

Trading is not something that can be approached casually. It requires focus, attention, and the ability to prioritize your time effectively. Understanding the challenges of balancing trading with other responsibilities will help you develop strategies to manage your time efficiently and ensure that you are able to fully commit to your trading journey.

In order to succeed in trading, discipline and commitment are paramount. ICT highlights the importance of respecting the sharp edges of the knowledge and tools provided. This serves as a reminder that trading is not a game or a hobby, but a serious endeavor that requires discipline and responsibility.

Chapter 2

Elements To A Trade Setup

Micro contracts allow traders to trade with a smaller amount of capital, making it more accessible for those who may not have the resources to trade full contracts.

In the context of futures index trading, a micro contracts can be an excellent starting point for honing your trading skills and gaining experience in the market.

While there are various trading strategies out there, it is important to note that this mentorship will not focus on high-frequency trading strategies. Instead, we will explore a more comprehensive approach to futures index trading, emphasizing the importance of understanding market structure, identifying setups, and executing trades with precision.

Remember, as we progress through this mentorship, it is crucial to engage in backtesting and trial-and-error to refine your trading skills. Consistency and the ability to find profitable moves in the market are key goals to strive for. So, let's dive into the world of futures index trading and explore the exciting opportunities it presents!

ELEMENTS OF A TRADE SETUP
Important thing to do, calibrate your TradingView account or any other platforms towards the NY time zone. Everything related to time in in this ICT mentorship 2023 is referred to the NY time zone.
The best time to execute trades is between 8:30 and 11:00 in the NY trading session.
High frequency trading algorithms execute their trades on the 1–5m. This is based on the given market structure on that moment of time.
These are the elements you should look out for when it comes to a trade setup: • You want to see a run on liquidity either on Buyside or Sellside Liquidity. • You want to see a shift in market structure by breaking a short term high/low. • You enter a trade in a FVG. • You should target liquidity or imbalances.
By using the Fib extension tool in TradingView, you can identify if you are in premium or in discount: • Above the 50% level → Premium market. • Below the 50% level → Discounted market.

Analyzing Weekly Candle Movements and Swing Highs/Lows

Weekly candle movements can provide valuable insights into the market bias and help traders make informed trading decisions.

Here are a few key points to consider:

1. **Foundation of a Trading Model:** Weekly candle movements form the foundation of a trading model. We need to have a clear understanding of what we are looking for in order to identify profitable setups. The goal is to find setups that are not limited to small price movements but have the potential for larger gains.

2. **Independent Thinking:** We should aim to develop independent thinking and not rely on black box systems or signal services. By understanding the rules and processes of analyzing weekly candle movements, we can become self-sufficient and make trading decisions based on their own analysis.

3. **Clean and Precise Charts:** Analyzing weekly candle movements allows us to have clean and precise charts, free from unnecessary noise and distortion.

Understanding Swing Highs and Lows on the Daily Chart

Swing highs and lows on the daily chart are important indicators that help us identify potential reversal points and determine the strength of a trend. Here are some key points to understand:

1. **Imbalance and Efficient Pricing:** Swing highs and lows represent areas of imbalance in the market. A swing high occurs when the price reaches a peak and starts to decline, indicating a potential reversal from a bullish trend. Conversely, a swing low occurs when the price reaches a trough and starts to rise, indicating a potential reversal from a bearish trend. These imbalances need to be efficiently priced and booked by the algorithm.

2. **Precision and Delivery:** Swing highs and lows demonstrate precision and delivery in price movements. Each candle's high to low range represents an inefficiently delivered price move.

3. **Learning from Mistakes:** It's important to acknowledge that we will not always make perfect decisions. There will be times when trades are left on the table or mistakes are made. However, by consistently analyzing swing highs and lows and learning from past experiences, traders can improve their decision-making process and increase their chances of success.

How to Use Weekly Candle Movements and Swing Highs/Lows in Trading Decisions

Now that we understand the significance of weekly candle movements and swing highs/lows, let's explore how to use these indicators to make informed trading decisions. Here are a few strategies to consider:

1. **Identifying Reversal Points:** By analyzing swing highs/lows, we can identify potential reversal points in the market. This can help them determine when to enter or exit a trade, maximizing their profit potential.

2. **Confirming Market Bias:** Weekly candle can provide insights into the overall market bias. By analyzing the size, direction of weekly candles, we can confirm whether the market is bullish or bearish. This information can guide their trading decisions and help them align with the prevailing trend.

3. **Setting Stop Loss and Take Profit Levels:** Swing highs and lows can be used to set effective stop loss and take profit levels. Traders can place their stop loss orders above swing highs in a bearish trend and below swing lows in a bullish trend. This helps to minimize losses and protect profits.

So, by incorporating these strategies into their trading approach, we can leverage the power of weekly candle movements and swing highs/lows to improve their trading outcomes.

Remember, practice and experience are key to mastering these techniques. Analyzing weekly candle movements and swing highs/lows requires patience, discipline, and a commitment to continuous learning.

Institutional Swing Points

There are mainly 2 types of institutional swing points, namely stop runs and failure swings. These are the most powerful and most dynamic.

<u>Stop Runs:</u> The market trades to a key level or just short of it – but fails to immediately react indicating another run deeper before a reversal. After the reversal – the opportunity is best taken when the short-term Market Structure breaking point is retested. First run on stops in an intermediate term price swing is ideal – smart money will look to unseat the aggressive trailing stops.

Stop run or turtle soup - highest, most probable trading condition, you want to be looking for this one.

- The market trades to a key level or just short of it - but fails to immediately react - indicating another run deeper before a reversal.

- After the reversal - the opportunity is best taken when the short-term Market Structure breaking point is retested.

Identifying high liquidity levels is important for successful trades using the Turtle Soup. It is not enough to simply trade above any old high or below any old low.

Analyzing charts to spot old highs with high liquidity:

- Look for order blocks: Order blocks are areas on the chart where there is a significant concentration of orders. These areas often indicate high liquidity levels.

- Identify fair value gaps: Fair value gaps occur when there is a price difference between the current market price and the fair value price. These gaps can provide insights into liquidity levels and potential market movements.

- Consider higher time frames: Analyzing higher time frames, such as 15-minute or 1-hour charts, can give us a broader perspective on liquidity levels. Look for patterns and confluences across multiple time frames to strengthen your analysis.

- Pay attention to relative equal lows: Relative equal lows occur when the market reaches similar price levels multiple times. These lows indicate a potential support level and can be used as a reference for selling above old highs.

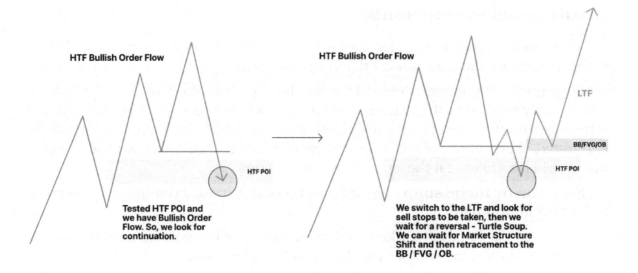

HTF Bullish Order Flow

HTF POI

Tested HTF POI and
we have Bullish Order
Flow. So, we look for
continuation.

HTF Bullish Order Flow

LTF

BB/FVG/OB

HTF POI

We switch to the LTF and look for
sell stops to be taken, then we
wait for a reversal - Turtle Soup.
We can wait for Market Structure
Shift and then retracement to the
BB / FVG / OB.

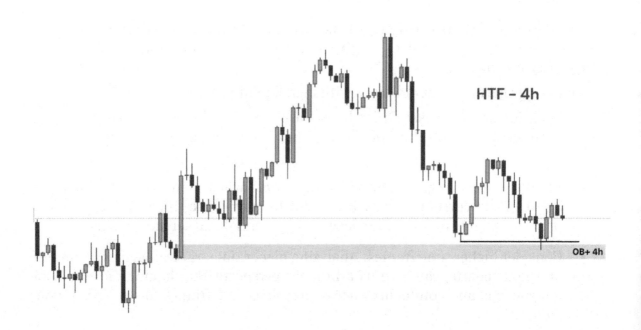

HTF – 4h

OB+ 4h

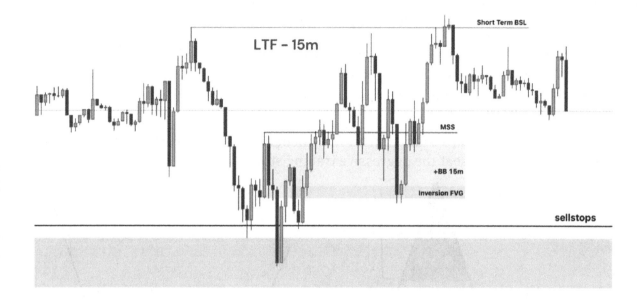

This is one of the most powerful, significant price patterns and you need to learn the characteristics about where it forms. ICT loves this pattern because he can see when it's forming. He can see when it's just falling short of a level and where price will go to anticipate one more drive lower/higher.

It's important that you have the institutional reference points marked out on your chart so that you can anticipate these patterns unfolding before they actually do. Otherwise you'll be surprised by these things. And second, you have to go into your own charts looking for this so that you learn to trust the institutional reference points as in points where price actually goes to reverse.

What is this pattern? Market makes a higher high, fails (false break above old high/ below old low), then break down and has a rejection at the highs.

In a selling scenario: generally the market will rally up to resistance or down to support (so a PD array like a bearish OB, Breaker, liquidity voids, MB, (fair value) gap or an old low or high low previous day or week) it will first fail to reach that level and break a little lower and then it rallies higher above the STH. That short term high will get many traders caught. When we see price hover below a key institutional reference point, we anticipate price trading to them to the point or a little bit into them.

Defining Institutional Swing Points:

The market trades to a key level or just short of it - but fails to immediately react - indicating another run deeper before a reversal.

After the reversal - the opportunity is best taken when the short-term Market Structure breaking point is retested.

First run on stops in a Market in an intermediate term price swing is ideal - smart money will look to unseat the aggressive trailing stops.

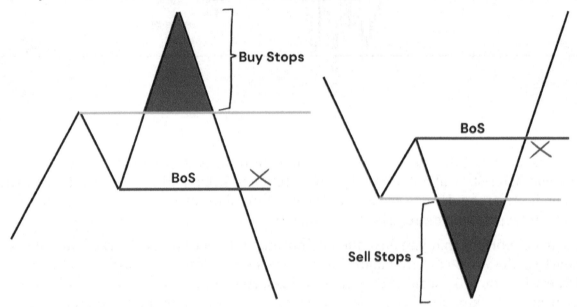

The red triangle often becomes the wick. We don't want price to hang around there, we want an immediate reaction away (V-shape).

How to trade this?

- Like an institutional trader and sell right at the top as price trades through the STH/STL. When you anticipate this pattern to form, you'll have your highest probable entries for all your set-ups because it's the deepest discount buy/ deepest premium sell. It will feel scary to sell above an old high or buy below an old low but that's because you haven't practiced enough. You haven't seen the effects of looking at institutional order flow from a HTF perspective. You have to practice and build confidence.

- You can wait for price to make a market structure break and buy/sell when price returns to the breaker with the stop at or above the high/low (red triangle). We already had a stop run so there's no reason for that high/low where your stop is to get taken out.

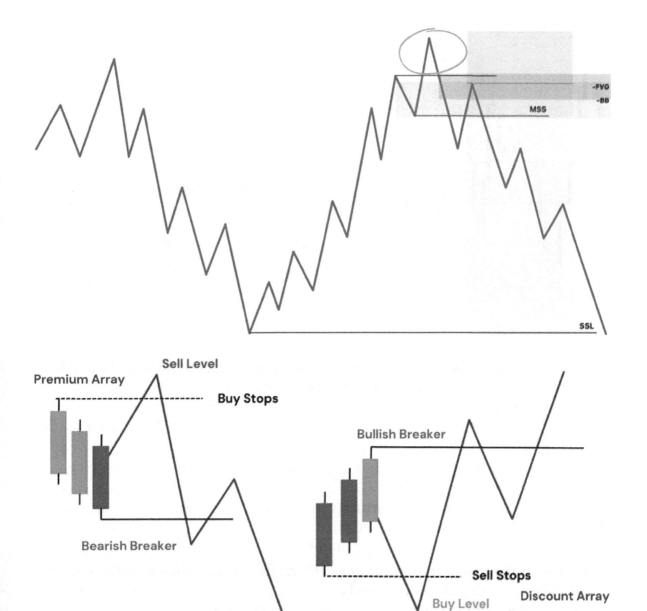

-FVG
-BB
MSS
SSL

Premium Array
Sell Level
Buy Stops
Bearish Breaker

Bullish Breaker
Sell Stops
Buy Level
Discount Array

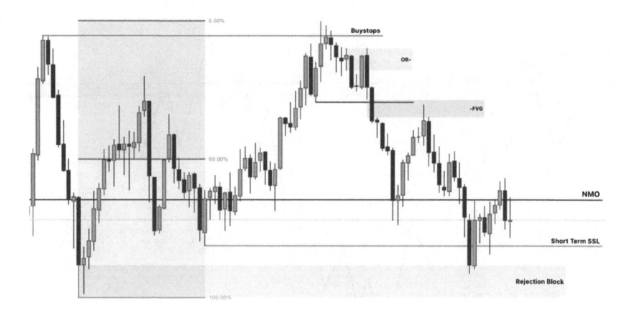

Failure Swing

<u>Failure Swings:</u> The market trades through a key level initially but fails to immediately continue – after rejecting the new price level – the market retraces only to attempt to stage another drive to retest the new price level. After the reversal, the opportunity is best taken when the initial key level is retested or after a market structure breaking point retested.

We aim for breaker swing points, but they don't always occur. We don't know if it will give a breaker before we get the swing failure. If the stop run/turtle soup doesn't occur, we still have a trading opportunity in the form of a failure swing pattern. The blue line is a PD array. You want to see price move away from it aggressively (V-shape) and try to come down/up again but fail and break a short-term low/high.

- The market trades through a key level initially but fails to immediately continue - after rejecting the new Price Level - the market retraces only to attempt to stage another drive to retest or overtake the new Price Level.

- After the reversal the opportunity is best taken when the initial key level is retested. Or after a Market Structure breaking point is retested.

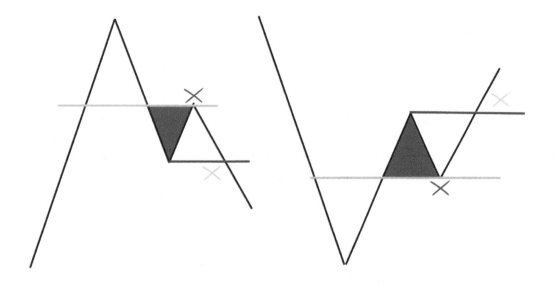

Stop Hunts and Market Manipulation

Stop hunts, also known as stop-loss hunting or market manipulation, are a common occurrence in financial markets. They refer to deliberate actions taken by large market participants to trigger stop-loss orders placed by other traders. This manipulation creates a temporary spike in price, causing these stop-loss orders to be executed, and often resulting in a rapid reversal of the market.

The impact of stop hunts can be significant. Traders who have placed stop-loss orders at specific price levels to limit their losses find themselves being forced out of their positions due to the sudden market movement. This can lead to increased volatility and can create opportunities for those who initiated the stop hunts to profit from the subsequent price reversal.

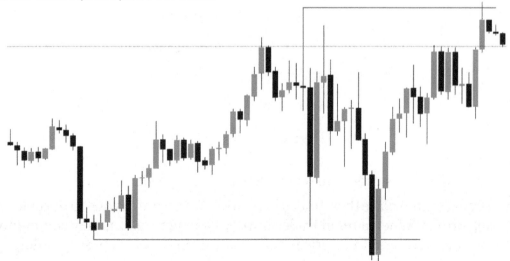

Chapter 3

Introduction to Liquidity in Trading

Liquidity is the lifeblood of the markets. Liquidity is what allows anyone to buy or sell for a profit, or a loss. It is what creates opportunity in the markets. While liquidity may not hold much significance for a retail trader, it is of paramount importance to big players who must carefully consider it in order to execute positions successfully. In an illiquid market, there are few buyers and sellers, and trades may take longer to complete, and prices can be more volatile.

What does "liquidity" refer to in our trading?

In the trading market, we can categorize participants into two primary groups. While some arguments might suggest the presence of three or more groups, I'll simplify it into two main categories.

The first group comprises central banks, algorithms, and institutions. The second group consists of retail traders in the US.

The influence over market funds is primarily held by the first group. When this group aims to manipulate the market, they require willing buyers who would buy assets at the specific prices they intend to target.

For instance, if their goal is to decrease the price by $250, they need individuals ready to buy from them at that designated price point.

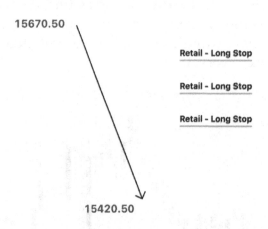

[credit to @menda_crypto]

Why do retail traders choose to buy or sell at these specific areas?

Retail traders often place their trades in relation to these areas due to the placement of their stop orders. When a retail trader initiates a long position, they commonly set a stop order that triggers if the price reaches a certain level. This stop order, when activated, effectively closes the long trade, and simultaneously opens a short trade. This occurrence is referred to as a "long stop" and the resulting short trade contributes to what is known as "Sell Side Liquidity (SSL)."

Conversely, when retail traders enter a short position, they establish a short stop. Once this short stop is reached, it triggers a long trade, leading to what is termed "Buy Side Liquidity (BSL)."

In essence, these trading decisions are often influenced by the positioning of stop orders, creating liquidity through the automatic opening of opposing trades when certain price levels are reached.

The first group consistently engages in price manipulation to shape the perception of retail traders. They often create scenarios where retail traders perceive the market as bearish when the banks are actually aiming to accumulate buy positions. Similarly, these banks manipulate the perception of retail traders into believing the market is bullish precisely when they intend to gather sell positions.

Let's start with some statistics: over 90% of retail traders end up losing money. Trading is a zero-sum game, where money is not created but rather taken from losers and handed to winners. To ensure you're on the winning side, it's crucial to understand who the losers and winners are.

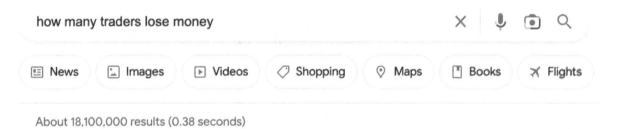

Anyone who starts down the road to becoming a trader eventually comes across the statistic that 90 per cent of traders fail to make money when trading the stock market. This statistic deems that over time 80 per cent lose, 10 per cent break even and 10 per cent make money consistently. Mar 8, 2023

In trading, the losing party often comprises retail traders, while the winning party usually consists of bigger, wealthier players. This is where liquidity comes into play. Understanding liquidity can help you make informed trading decisions and align yourself with the winning side.

Liquidity, derived from the term "liquid," refers to the ability of assets to flow or be easily exchanged. In an economic context, assets that can be readily converted into cash are known as "liquid assets." For instance, owning a house may not be considered highly liquid as it cannot be easily used for purchasing goods. However, you can increase your liquidity by selling your house for cash, which is why the term "liquidating" is used. When you liquidate your portfolio, you exchange less liquid assets for more liquid ones, with cash being the most liquid asset. Therefore, when someone is liquidating, they are essentially exchanging assets for cash.

To help you better understand what liquidity is, I have drawn some simple diagram. It illustrates why we refer to certain levels as "liquidity". The point is not that the models themselves are liquidity, but that when a certain price model appears, liquidity is attracted at key levels and price points.

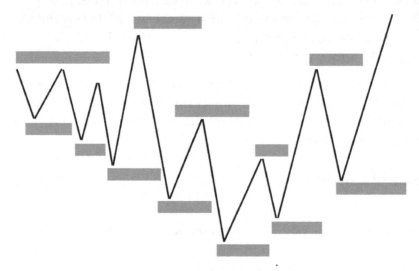

In the figure above, the zones marked in blue are the places where liquidity accumulates. This is where most trading systems place buy, sell and stop loss orders.

So what is the use of liquidity for us traders? Good question. Liquidity helps us determine where the price is likely to go next. You can learn to trade only using one liquidity levels. It's not difficult, but the risks and potential profits will not be so attractive. In order to get a high-quality trading idea, using the liquidity, you need to apply the market structure on the HTF, order blocks and Premium/Discount zones (we will talk about it later in this book). This helps to understand what kind of liquidity will attract the price and where we should enter into the trade and where we should exit.

Have you ever wondered why some cryptocurrencies or certain currency pairs experience huge price fluctuations for no apparent reason? Or why you sometimes see price gaps when looking at a particular pair? It's because of low liquidity in the market which can lead to a sharp price movement up or down.

Types of liquidity:

1. Major - major liquidity is buy & sell stops that form at the highs and lows of each session, day, week, and monthly timeframe charts. Use the weekly, monthly, quarterly, and yearly charts to build a HTF bias and look at the daily for where you think the largest pool of liquidity is.

2. Medium - medium liquidity is buy & sell stops that form at the highs and lows on the 15m, 1h charts. These two timeframes are also the best in my opinion to look at when it comes to market structure for day traders.

3. Minor - minor liquidity is buy & sell stops that form at the highs and lows on 1m-5m charts. The 1m-5m LTF often has stop hunts after medium or major liquidity is swept raided. Once liquidity is taken, you're then looking for the next market structure shift in the opposite direction.

4. Equal Lows/Highs EQL and EQH.

5. Swing Points - significant swing high or low.

6. Range (the market moves sideways) – above highs and below lows in a range.

7. Trendline - liquidity behind the trendline: All liquidity accumulates on highs and lows and that liquidity is not going to be taken immediately. It remains so that after taking a large position, the price moves freely and renews the key high of the structure. All liquidity at the bottom acts as a magnet for price In the future, the trader can see the formation of equal EQLs.

Taking stops on EQL and EQH is carried out with strong news. Speculators before the news release often place limit orders for the break of equal highs/lows. But this is an extremely aggressive type of trading, which usually results in the loss of a trading account.

Why is Market Liquidity so Important?

In a liquid market, you can open and close positions like lightning, with minimal hassle. It's like having a squad of eager traders ready to take the other side of your trade. And you know what that means? Less risk, my friend!

When there's high liquidity, you don't have to worry about slashing the price of your asset to attract buyers or paying a premium to secure what you want. It's a smooth sailing experience, where sellers easily find buyers and vice versa.

But that's not all. Liquidity plays a big role in determining the spread offered by leveraged trading providers. See, high liquidity means there's a boatload of orders flooding the underlying market. And that's good news because it brings the highest buying price and the lowest selling price closer together. We're talking about a tighter bid-ask spread.

Now, here's the real deal. Since we base our prices on the underlying market, a narrower bid-ask spread there translates into lower spreads offered on our platform. It's a win-win situation! But hold up, if a market is illiquid, brace yourself for a wider spread. It's like the difference between a narrow street and a wide highway.

So, remember this: market liquidity is crucial for quick trade execution, reduced risk, and tighter bid-ask spreads. It's the secret sauce that attracts speculators and investors to the market. Liquidity is the name of the game, my trading amigo!

Buyside and Sellside Liquidity

*Buy and Sell Side Liquidity (BSL/SSL) are areas of price in which buy stops and or sell stops are mostly residing. If you can understand the higher time frame perspectives and see where the "money" is, then you have a bias once you see price moving off known areas of support or resistance. Price will seek the liquidity to either reverse or continue in within its expansion move.

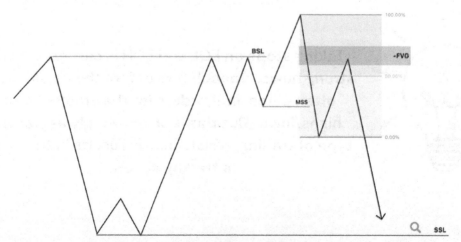

History of BSL/SSL Trading Strategy

In fact, liquidity in the form of BSL/SSL does not happen suddenly. This happens because liquidity is a follow-up action at lower TFs for entry, after market makers have placed orders at significant levels on higher TFs.

BSL/SSL trading is part of a market maker's strategy in order to buy at a low price and sell when the price becomes expensive. BSL/SSL price action generally occurs at the round number level, which is a liquidity area that provides huge profits.

In order for the price to quickly return to the order block at a significant level. Market makers then perform one of the "bubble bursting" tricks. In general, this trick often leads retail traders to make the wrong decisions.

If we see price as reversing at the buy or sell side of liquidity, then we trade the developed price action, if we see price continue to move through the buy or sell side liquidity.

Retail traders rely on brokers to execute our trades, and let me tell you, our privileges are quite limited. That's why it's crucial for us to trade smartly and efficiently by understanding the power of market makers.

On the other hand, we have the banks, the big players in the game. They operate as wholesalers with massive transaction volumes, allowing them to create significant supply and demand. They hold the power to move the market according to their well-crafted trading plans.

Now, let's talk about the retail trader. Unfortunately, many retail traders, especially beginners, tend to trade based on emotions. It's a rollercoaster ride! Sometimes we're too slow to make decisions, and other times we're too hasty. Our decision-making process is often driven by indicator signals and fragile emotions. It's a tough spot to be in.

To make matters worse, retail traders tend to strictly react to support and resistance (S/R) areas, following the prevailing S/R strategy. And guess what? Market makers exploit this tendency to distort retail trader's perception and hunt for their stop losses. It's a game they play, and we need to be aware of it.

Now, here's an interesting tidbit: wholesalers, just like any other savvy business folks, love high liquidity locations. They have tricks up their sleeves to maximize their profits. One of their strategies is to smooth out their pre-determined trading plan. And guess what helps them achieve this? You got it, liquidity!

Support and resistance (S/R) levels act as entry points for traders like us. These levels witness a flurry of buy and sell transactions. So, what do market makers do? They make these S/R levels easily visible to us traders, and once we're lured in, they liquidate their positions at those levels. Sneaky, huh?

Liquidity is a vital aspect of trading. It holds great significance for a couple of reasons:

Firstly, the trick to making substantial profits lies in entering the market at favorable locations and liquidating our positions at the right time. Liquidity plays a key role in achieving this.

Secondly, liquidity can provide us with clear insights into the direction of future price movements. Market makers manipulate liquidity to create rejection patterns and reversals. It's all part of the game.

So, remember, understanding the dynamics between retail and wholesaler perspectives, the influence of emotions, and the role of liquidity is crucial for navigating the forex market like a pro.

Bull and Bear Liquidity Traps

Now, let's look at the most common type of trap: bull and bear liquidity traps. They are identified very simply - in the market on the higher timeframes, as a clear change in the structural or turning point of supply or demand. According to the classics, if there is a bullish structure, that the next high and low is higher than the previous one, it is this idea that allows a large player to lure traders into buying and then will reverse the price after collecting liquidity. The same is true for the bearish structure. We do NOT buy at the break of the old HIGH and we do NOT sell at the break of the old LOW!

Reminder: Daily Chart - locate liquidity and imbalances. Hourly Chart - observe price seeking liquidity or imbalances.

In other words, liquidity is an established level in the market where stops and orders are resting, leaving these areas exposed for smart money to hunt these areas

29

taking stop losses and triggering new buy and sell orders into the market.

The more liquidity accumulates above a significant price level, the more likely that liquidity will be taken. Where price consistently bounces from the level of support or the level of resistance several times, there is a huge number of stops of some players and orders in the opposite direction of other players. It is important to focus on finding such places, as you can find great entries after liquidity is collected. The more bounces, the better.

[The more liquidity accumulates above a significant price level, the more likely that liquidity will be collected]

Draw on Liquidity (DOL)

How to identify the draw on liquidity?

As a day trader, the DOL can be PWH/PWL (Previous Week High/Low) , PDH/L (Previous Day High/Low) , or session High/Low from Asia, London, or New York paired with EQH/EQL (Equal Highs/Lows) with a Low Resistance Liquidity Run (LRLR) condition. EQH/EQL (Equal Highs/Lows) are large pools of liquidity so institutions will always draw towards those levels to take out retail.

How do I find the next Draw On Liquidity?

First thing, price is always either rebalancing or taking liquidity.

Next, price is going from P/D array to P/D array. Hence, you must annotate your P/D zones to know if price rebalanced or will rebalance, you must also annotate your liquidities and P/D arrays.

To find the next Draw On Liquidity, you can follow a displacement, use the reaction on a P/D array.

Internal range liquidity: Understanding internal range liquidity is important for identifying short-term lows or highs within a price leg. This information can help you make more informed decisions about entering or exiting trades. By paying attention to the opening prices of candles and how they are violated, you can determine the change in the state of delivery. This change can indicate shifts in the market's sentiment and offer opportunities for trading.

Here are some ways to find internal liquidity:

- **Fair value gaps:** These are gaps between the fair value of an asset and its current price. Traders can look for fair value gaps to determine where the market is likely to draw to or reach for.

- **Order blocks:** These are areas where large orders were executed, creating a block of orders. Traders can look for order blocks to determine where the market is likely to draw to or reach for.

- **Volume imbalance:** is a term used in trading to describe a range between where one candle's body and another candle's body doesn't touch but there are wicks that overlap in between. It can be a difference between a lower close with a higher opening or a volume imbalance between a higher close and a lower opening. Volume imbalances can be traded through multiple times, but if you know your bias and where it's likely to draw to at a later time, you can come right back up and go back to respecting the very specific levels, which is the low, the consequent encroachment midpoint, and the high of the volume imbalance.

- **Gaps in price:** These are areas where the price of an asset has a sudden jump or drop, creating a gap in the price chart. Traders can look for gaps in price to determine where the market is likely to draw to or reach for.

External and Internal Range Liquidity

Always remember price is doing only 2 things: Rebalance FVG and Seek Liquidity.

External Range Liquidity, also known as ERL (External Range Liquidity), can act as a draw on liquidity based on order flow. This means if we have external range liquidity on the previous low and the institutional order flow is bearish, price will be attracted or pulled towards our external range. While Internal Range Liquidity is the liquidity inside the defined range (External Range Liquidity). This could be in form of any institutional reference that we can use as entry such as FVG.

When external range liquidity is taken, a FVG becomes the next draw on liquidity. And when a FVG is stacked, an old low or an old high - External Range Liquidity - becomes the next draw.

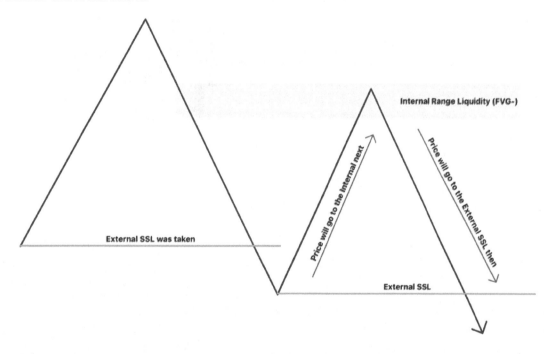

So, we have External Range Liquidity in the diagram above, which is an old low in this case. We then move up. After that, going down, down, down, taking out the low. So, that is External Range Liquidity.

Now, price only does two things: it goes to old highs and old lows or seeks to reprice into imbalances.

In this range, there was a FVG or an imbalance up higher; price took out External Range Liquidity then. So, what is the next thing price will do?

Price will draw to internal next, which is a FVG. Think about it, when you see an old high or an old low get raided, you want to either look for an imbalance inside that range to get repriced into. And then once that gets hit, we can move for the next one, which is external again.

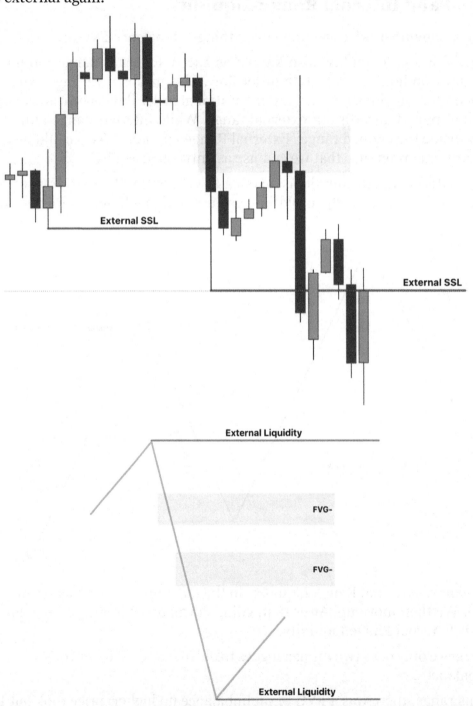

To put it simple, **EXTERNAL means outside of something, on the exterior. INTERNAL means inside of something; within the body. LIQUIDITY refers order above highs and lows.**

We must understand price only moves in two direction: from external to internal or internal to external.

The flow of the market place is that internal range liquidity being tagged will be the catalyst for price draw to external range liquidity. And external range liquidity being taken is the catalyst for price to draw to internal range liquidity.

Using this understanding on the monthly, weekly, daily & 4 hour is the key you've all been looking for when it comes to daily bias.

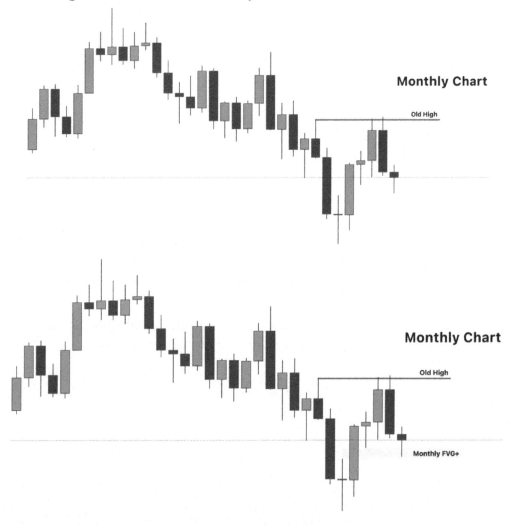

Let's take a look on Monthly chart above. We have run on old high. Now without going further, what where does your eye draw into?

You should be looking at an internal range liquidity in the form of a FVG. So, after external gets raided, where do we want to reach into? We can see the imbalance down, which is a FVG, right? If you look at this area after we got this external range liquidity raided, you're on the right path.

And we can see this monthly internal range liquidity in the form of a FVG get stacked. Now, what happens afterwards?

Let's look at this from a daily perspective.

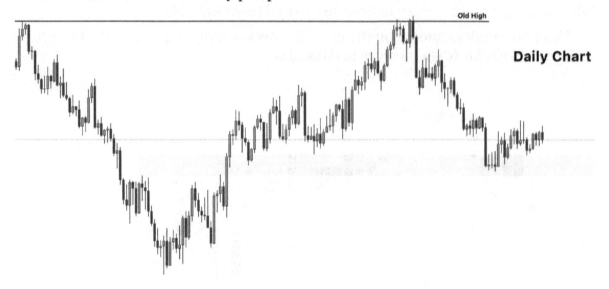

We take out a monthly external range liquidity. Now, we can use daily structure to frame our setups. What are we going to be waiting for after this monthly external range? We see that liquidity has been taken. We're going to look for a monthly internal range to be the draw on liquidity. This is our monthly FVG.

Now we need to wait for a little bit of confirmation, as always. So, we wait for a break of structure that happens after we raid the monthly external.

We have break of structure, return back into premium, and it continues down into that Monthly FVG.

Let's take a look another example.

External BSL has been raided and we draw back into internal.

Weekly Chart

Old High

Weekly FVG+

Internal has been tagged. Where are we going to go? We're going to go to external. It's simple as that.

So, weekly external range liquidity has been liquidated after going into internal. And looking at the daily charts now, we can see how we can frame our bias on the daily.

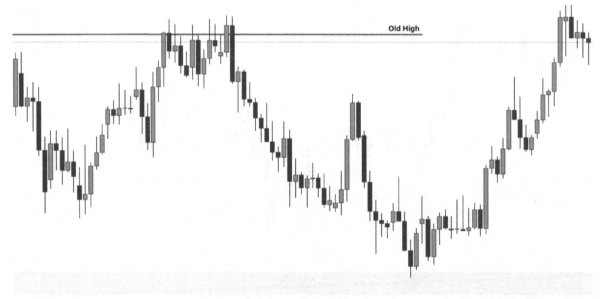

Old High

[Daily Chart]

We hit the weekly internal range liquidity – Weekly FVG. So, we went from external back to internal.

Now, we've hit that internal range liquidity going into a market maker buy model, right? We have sellside of the curve. Then we're going into buyside of the curve because we hit a higher time frame discount array, right? It's a FVG.

So, we're going to eye up the liquidity, which is also a break of structure after we hit that higher time frame array.

[Daily Chart]

Now when the market displaces above ERL, we have internal range liquidity formed, right? So again, we go from external to internal.

And after we hit that internal, where do we want to go? External again. And that remember, internal range liquidity will be that FVG we're looking for to mitigate with and continue up.

We take out this external range liquidity again, where are we going to go? Do we see any FVG? Yes, we have one a FVG.

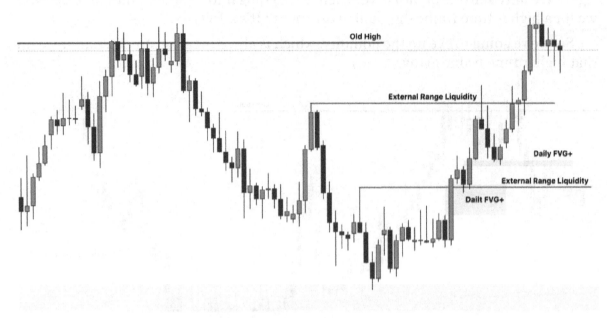

[Daily Chart]

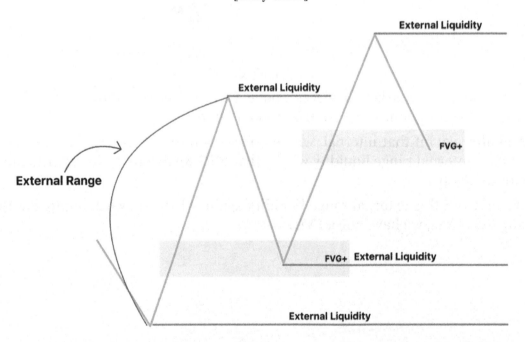

Let's look at the diagram above, we have our external range (I pointed with purple arrow) from the low to the high. What is going to happen after?

Ok, let's imagine that there was a liquidity sweep just before an external BSL. That is External Liquidity Sweep.

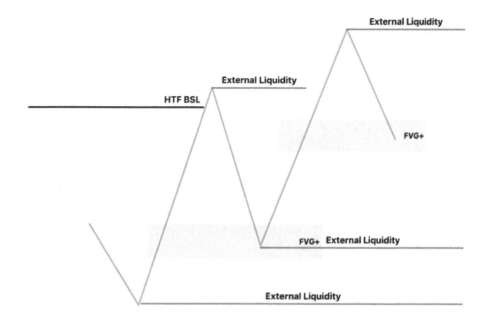

Price then will go to an internal range liquidity which is FVG. After that, we expect it should bounce from FVG to the External Range Liquidity.

After External Range Liquidity what is going to happen? Right, we are going to test another Internal Range Liquidity. In the diagram above, it is FVG but it can be OB or Internal SSL.

Now I have a question for you, how do you think where will we go next based on the diagram below?

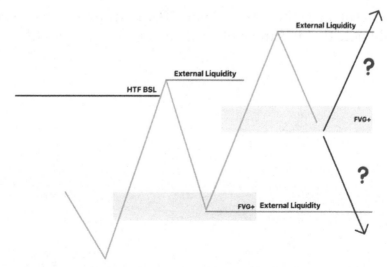

What do we see? We see price going up and coming down, and as we said before there was an external liquidity sweep. So, you will answer it will go up, right? But what if I add this?

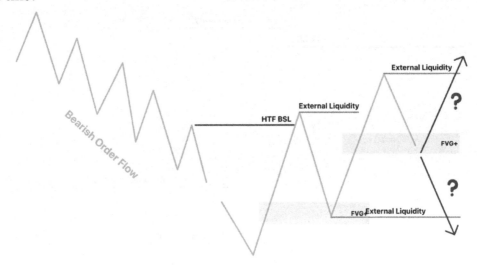

To answer where price will go next, we should consider HTF Order Flow. It is what was happening before. If you zoom out and you see that price was coming down, then we can expect a break of structure to the downside.

So, most likely the price will continue to the downside but if we are coming from down and price was going up, up, up, up, and this is part of the move to the upside, then we are expecting price to come to the FVG and then give us a break of structure on the upside.

What is another thing to determine if we're going up or down? It's a displacement. So, when price reaches FVG, I would like to see a displacement either to the upside or the downside and from there, I'll determine if I'm going up or down.

If I see a displacement to the upside from FVG, I mean there was a reaction from FVG, then I would note that it is most likely going to the external BSL.

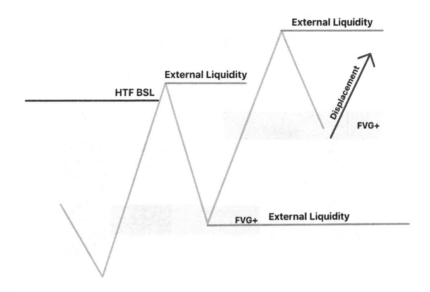

However, if price displaces below the FVG and doesn't respect it at all, then we're looking to go down and External SSL.

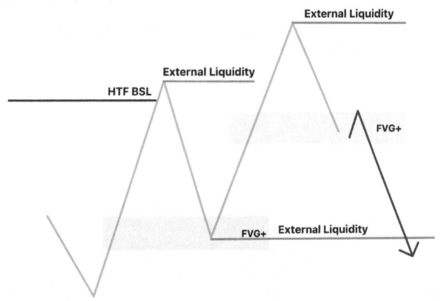

One more thing that can help to determine this is also the weakness or the strength of the candle. If you get a kind of an engulfing candle, you will know that most likely we're going up but if you see some weakness and there is no retracement, there is no hint of reversal, then most likely we're going down for the external SSL.

Engulfing Patterns

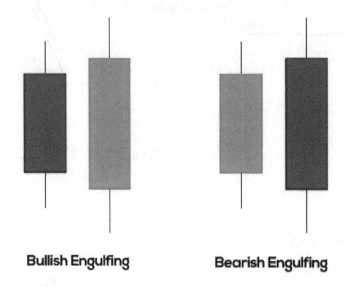

Bullish Engulfing   **Bearish Engulfing**

So, orderflow, displacement, weakness, and strength of candles, this is what can help you to determine if we're going up or down.

Inside bar

As the name implies, an inside bar forms inside of a large candle called a mother bar. It's a pattern that forms after a large move in the market and represents a period of consolidation.

Notice how the second candle in the image below is completely contained by the previous candle. In this case, the bullish candle (mother bar) represents a broader downtrend, while the bearish candle (inside bar) represents consolidation after the large decline.

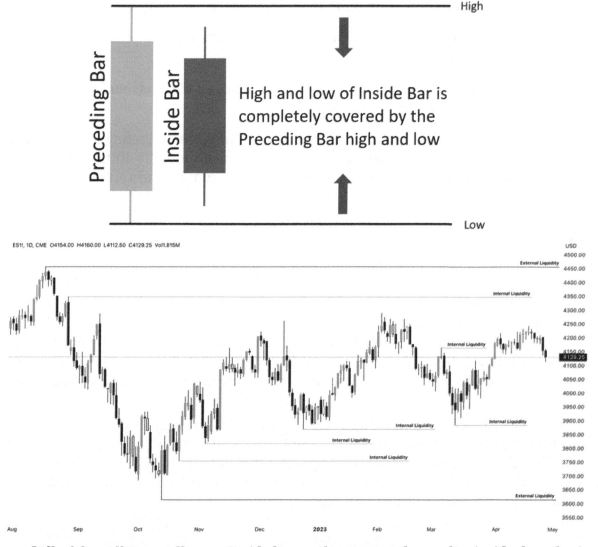

[All of the yellow candles are inside bars so because we know that inside days don't happen often on $ES we can expect the previous day's high or low to get taken out for our Draw on Liquidity as day trader.]

High and Low Resistance Liquidity

HRLR = High Resistance Liquidity Run.

- We want to see these form on the side of our structure:

- A low that ran a previous low and rejected is a High Resistance Low.

- A high that ran a previous high and rejected is a High Resistance High.

LRLR = Low Resistance Liquidity Run.

- We want to see these form on the opposite side of our structure:

- A bearish failure swing is a high that fails to take out the previous high - we want to see this form where we are bullish.

- A bullish failure swing is a low that fails to take out the previous low - we want to see this form where we are bearish.

Low Resistance Liquidity Run: This refers to liquidity that is resting with minimal resistance, making it easy to be swept. Low Resistance Liquidity Runs (LRLR) are the most ideal trading conditions in the market. You should always aim to target low resistance liquidity.

Targeting low resistance liquidity offers a significantly higher probability of success. It represents the easiest area to engage. These trades will feel straightforward, quick, and effortless, almost like "a knife cutting through butter." Price movement requires minimal effort to access this liquidity. ICT consistently encourages traders to go after the "low-hanging fruit."

Low-Hanging Fruit refers to easily achievable objectives in trading. ICT aims for five handles or 10 handles (ES/SP500) below your entry can be considered low hanging fruit objectives. These objectives help build confidence and consistency in trading, as they are easier to achieve and can result in positive results when done repeatedly.

High Resistance Liquidity Run: This pertains to liquidity that is resting with substantial resistance before it can be swept. HRLR, on the other hand, present the opposite scenario. Price will encounter greater difficulty in expanding and accessing this liquidity. It will demand maximum effort from the price to reach this liquidity, often resulting in longer trade durations.

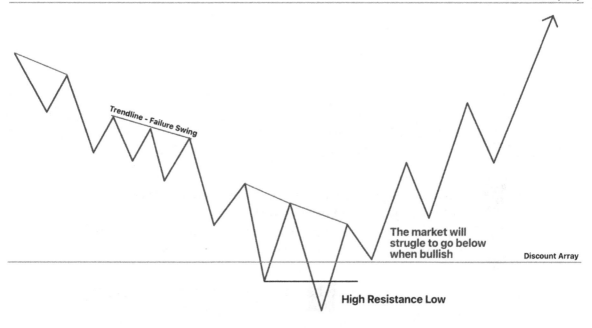

Draw on Liquidity

Trendline - Failure Swing

The market will
strugle to go below
when bullish

Discount Array

High Resistance Low

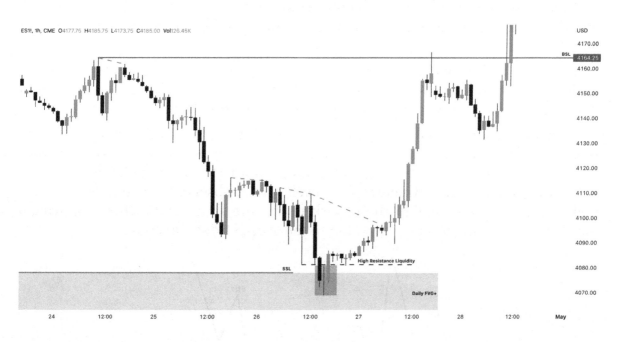

ES1!, 1h, CME O4177.75 H4185.75 L4173.75 C4185.00 Vol126.45K

USD

BSL 4164.25

High Resistance Liquidity

SSL

Daily FVG+

Chapter 4

Market Structure Shifts

Market Structure Shift (MSS) - is a shift in direction of price delivery. When price is going in a direction and shifts to the exactly opposite. It occurs when price takes out previous short-term lows or highs within a trend. Identifying these shifts allows for an understanding on which side of tvhe market to be trading with.

 **A market structure shift refers to a noticeable change in the pattern or behavior of price movements within a single trading day. It often leads to an intraday draw, which means that price is drawn towards specific levels or areas of interest.**

MSS must be energetic and leave behind displacement to ensure that market is looking to reverse.

Remember that structure means nothing without narrative. Lose sight of the draw on price, HTF structure, and resting liquidity and you are vulnerable to being faked out.

As the ICT disciples are well aware, the foundational concept of trend analysis posits that in an uptrend, price action forms higher highs and higher lows, while in a downtrend, price action manifests as lower highs and lower lows.

A market structure shift is depicted as a significant level on the chart where the prior trend is invalidated. When the market is in an uptrend, the market structure shift level is typically identified as a point where a lower low is formed. Conversely, in a downtrend, the market structure shift level is often observed at a juncture where a higher high emerges. Notably, these market structure shifts tend to arise following a displacement, signaling a potential shift in the overall trend direction.

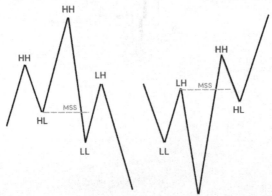

The Bearish Market Structure Shift

The market will see Price deliver a rally above an Old High or Highs, then quickly shift lower. Significance is placed on the term "quick" and with Displacement Lower - not a small candle move lower or a wick only, after a candle close.

The Bullish Market Structure Shift

The market will see Price deliver a decline below an Old Low or Lows, then quickly shift higher. Significance is placed on the term "quick" and with Displacement Higher - not a small candle move higher or a wick only, after a candle close.

Points of Interest (POI) where Market Structure Shifts Occur

Areas of Support and Resistance: Market Structure Shifts often occur when price breaks through key levels of support or resistance (e.g. session high or low).

It is important to note that Market Structure Shifts should not be forced or anticipated without valid signals. Traders should wait for price action to validate their analysis before considering a Market Structure Shift.

High-frequency trading algorithms often utilize Market Structure information on shorter timeframes, such as 5, 4, 3, 2, or 1-minute charts. These algorithms seek to capitalize on short-term price movements and may contribute to increased volatility during potential Market Structure Shifts.

> Significant Market Structure Shifts often coincide with price taking out liquidity in the market. This means that when price surpasses key support or resistance levels, it can lead to a notable change in market dynamics, attracting more participation from traders and algorithms.

Important Time Frame and Session for Liquidity:

Highs and lows of the Asian Killzone (8:00 PM to 12:00 AM): This period is relevant for identifying liquidity pools and potential support/resistance levels established during the Asian trading session.

Highs and lows of the London Killzone (2:00 AM to 5:00 AM): This timeframe is important for determining liquidity pools and key levels of support/resistance created during the London trading session.

Highs and lows of the NY Session (7:00 AM to 10:00 AM): This session is significant for identifying liquidity pools and crucial levels of support/resistance that emerge during the New York trading session.

Chapter 5

How London Session Highs and Lows Can Provide Valuable Insights

1. **Market Sweeping:** London session highs and lows often act as important levels that the market may "sweep" above or below. This means that the market is likely to briefly move beyond these levels before reversing its direction.

2. **Key Support and Resistance:** London session highs and lows can also serve as key support and resistance levels. When the market approaches these levels, it is likely to encounter increased buying or selling pressure, leading to potential price reversals. We can use these levels to identify areas where the market is more likely to change direction and plan their trades accordingly.

3. **Intraday Trading Opportunities:** By monitoring the formation of intraday highs and lows before the equities market opens, traders can identify potential trading opportunities. These levels can act as significant price levels that may influence market behavior during the trading day. We can use these levels to plan their trades and take advantage of potential breakouts or reversals.

Identifying and Interpreting London Session Highs and Lows

To identify and interpret London session highs and lows, traders can follow these steps:

1. **Determine London Session Time:** The London session starts at 2 o'clock in the morning and ends at 5 o'clock in the morning New York local time. It is important to note that these times may vary depending on your time zone.

2. **Identify Highs and Lows:** During the London session, identify the highest and lowest price points reached by the market. These levels will serve as the London session highs and lows.

3. **Monitor Market Behavior:** Pay close attention to how the market reacts when it approaches these levels. Look for signs of price reversals or significant market moves. These observations can provide valuable insights into market sentiment and potential trading opportunities.

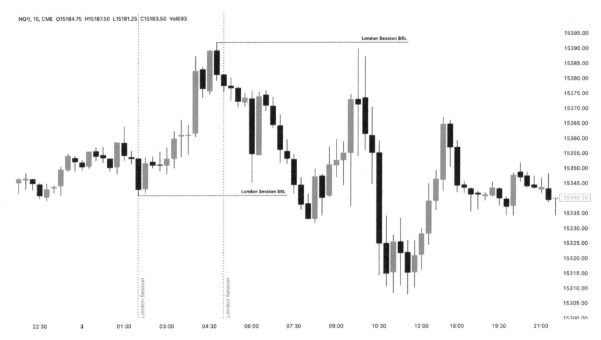

Entering and Exiting Trades Based on Conditions

When it comes to entering and exiting trades, it is important to have a clear set of guidelines to follow.

Identifying key highs and lows: One important aspect to consider is the identification of key highs and lows during different trading sessions. For example, during the London session, which typically occurs between 2:00 AM and 5:00 AM New York time, it is important to identify the session highs and lows. These levels often act as points of interest for the market and can indicate potential breakout or reversal opportunities.

Hours of operation: Another factor to consider is the hours of operation for trading. Typically, trading hours are between 8:30 AM and 11:00 AM, but they can be extended to include the New York lunch hour. However, it is generally advisable to avoid taking trades after noon local time in New York, as this period can be problematic. Instead, it is recommended to wait until 1:30 PM to 4:00 PM to take advantage of the afternoon trend.

Chapter 6

Intraday Order Flow & Understanding The Daily Range

Contract Delivery Month:

March – H

June – M

September – U

December - Z

Example: ESU2023 (TradingView) – September 2023

Amount per Tick:

ES/MES: 12.50 [0.25] or $50 per one point – ES / 1.25 or $5 per one point – MES.

NQ/MNQ: 5.0 [0.25] or $20 per one point – NQ / 0.50 or $2 per one point – MNQ.

YM / MYM: 5.0 [1.00] or $5 per one point – YM / $0.50 per one point - MYM

***On the week prior to expiration, monitor what Volume suggests. This can be viewed on Barchart.com. You want to select the Contract with largest Volume.

ICT recommends also monitor Open Interest.

Contract Name	Last	Change	High	Low	Volume	Time	Links
S&P 500 E-Mini (Sep '23)	4,478.00	-12.25	4,489.50	4,466.00	745,847	11:42 CT	
Nasdaq 100 E-Mini (Sep '23)	15,366.50	-109.25	15,480.75	15,322.25	167,913	11:42 CT	
Dow Futures Mini (Sep '23)	34,761	+79	34,780	34,556	47,138	11:42 CT	
S&P 500 VIX (Sep '23)	14.4500	-0.1344	14.8200	14.4000	41,832	11:42 CT	
10-Year T-Note (Dec '23)	109-250	unch	109-285	109-220	644,195	11:42 CT	
Crude Oil WTI (Oct '23)	89.10	+1.81	89.29	87.22	226,303	11:42 CT	
Natural Gas (Oct '23)	2.741	+0.133	2.782	2.604	139,162	11:42 CT	
Gold (Dec '23)	1,935.5	-11.7	1,947.5	1,929.9	138,108	11:42 CT	
Silver (Dec '23)	23.385	+0.002	23.480	23.110	35,784	11:42 CT	
Corn (Dec '23)	476-4	-9-2	486-6	473-4	133,941	11:42 CT	
Wheat (Dec '23)	586-0	+1-4	586-6	570-0	46,894	11:42 CT	
Soybean (Nov '23)	1349-6	-19-2	1372-2	1340-6	146,612	11:42 CT	
Sugar #11 (Mar '24)	27.22	+0.56	27.47	26.36	95,882	11:42 CT	
Coffee (Dec '23)	152.25	-0.60	153.00	150.45	14,926	11:42 CT	

The importance of 15-minute Time Frame

The 15-minute time frame is important in our trading strategy. Why? During this period, we focus on identifying key highs and lows, imbalances, fair value gaps, and order blocks. We pay particular attention to the London or New York kill zones, where we expect algorithms to seek liquidity by either buying or selling.

In our trading routine, we start in the morning between 8:30 AM and 12:00 PM. We aim to position ourselves in a trade before 11:00 AM, which allows us to ride the market movement during the NY Lunch and Afternoon Session if key liquidity has not been reached.

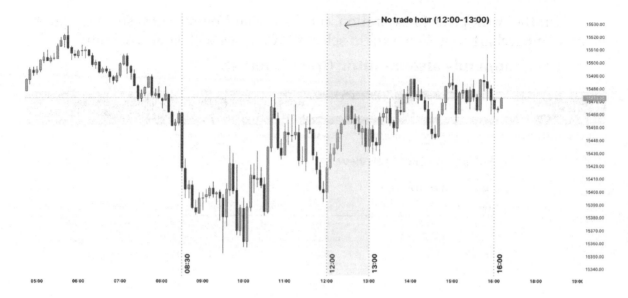

Before 8:30 AM, we look for potential price levels that could act as significant highs or lows. This helps us identify areas where stop hunts might occur.

Once we have analyzed the 15-minute chart and identified relevant market conditions, we switch to the 5-minute chart for precise entry points. This allows us to make well-timed trades based on the information gathered.

Overview of Intraday Order Flow and its Significance in Trading

Intraday order flow refers to the buying and selling activity that occurs within a single trading day. It provides valuable insights into market dynamics and can help us make informed decisions. Here are some key points to consider:

- Intraday order flow reflects the interaction between buyers and sellers in the market. By analyzing the volume and price movements, we can identify trends, reversals, and potential entry or exit points.

- It is important to pay attention to the timing of order flow. For example, there is often a surge in activity towards the end of the trading day, known as the 'afternoon acceleration.' This can be attributed to market on close orders and algorithmic trading strategies.

- By studying lower time frame charts, we can observe repeating patterns in intraday order flow. This can help us anticipate price movements and take advantage of trading opportunities.

- Intraday order flow can be influenced by various factors, such as economic news releases, market sentiment, and institutional trading activity. We should stay updated on these factors to better understand and interpret order flow data.

Understanding the Concept of Daily Range and its Importance

The daily range refers to the difference between the highest and lowest prices reached by a security or market within a single trading day. It provides valuable information about price volatility and potential trading opportunities. Here are some key points to understand about the daily range:

- The daily range helps us gauge the level of market activity and volatility. A wider range indicates greater price fluctuations, while a narrower range suggests a more stable or consolidated market.

- We can use the daily range to set profit targets and stop-loss levels. For example, if the daily range is large, a trader may set a wider profit target to capture potential gains. Conversely, in a narrow range, a trader may set a tighter profit target to manage risk.

- The daily range can also provide insights into market trends and momentum. We can analyze the relationship between the daily range and the direction of price movement to identify potential trend reversals or continuations.

Chapter 7

Three Drives Pattern

The Three Drives Pattern is a forex/futures trading pattern developed by Inner Circle Trader (ICT). The pattern is based on the idea that price tends to move in a series of three drives, with each drive consisting of a higher high and a higher low (or a lower low and lower high in a downtrend). This can be seen on any timeframe and is a sign that the market is pressing up and running out of liquidity. It is not necessary for the third high to take out the old high, as the market is already pressing into running out of liquidity.

The Three Drives Pattern will Help you Understand Stop Hunts.

The Three Drives Pattern consists of three main components:

1. The first drive: This is the initial move in the direction of the trend to the HTF PD Array. In an uptrend, this drive is characterized by a higher high and a higher low. In a downtrend, this drive is characterized by a lower low and a lower high.

2. The second drive: This is the second push to the HTF PD Array that characterized by a higher high and higher low in the uptrend. In a downtrend, this is a second drive is characterized by a lower low and a lower high.

3. The third drive: This is the final move in the direction of the HTF PD Array. In an uptrend, this drive is characterized by a higher high and a higher low, which should exceed the high of the first drive. In a downtrend, this drive is characterized by a lower low and a lower high, which should exceed the low of the first drive.

If we see 3 Drives towards Liquidity Pool, we do not need to see that Liquidity Pool hunted with the 3rd drive. The market is already running out Short-term Liquidity every time it drives into a new Short-term High.

This is how Smart Money established a new position.

You want to see an Displacement afterwards. This is what you are looking for and why you are in-front of the chart. The Displacement should be so obvious similar to how an Elephant would jump into a Children's pool and cause a scene.

When this occurs, you are ready to look for the Fair Value Gap.

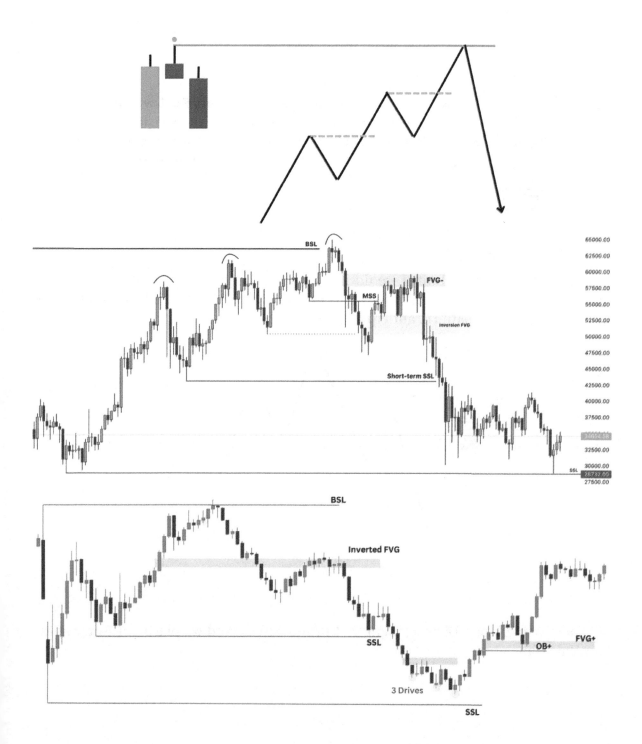

If it does not reach the liquidity zone or POI and reverts strongly, it is an even more powerful signal, since it confirms that there were no orders on the other side of these points, and that the institutional ones have already positioned.

IF we see 3 Drives towards Liquidity Pool, we do not need to see that Liquidity Pool hunted with the 3rd drive. The market is already running out Short-term Liquidity every time it drives into a new Short-term High.

Look for 3 "impulses" + reversal.

Anticipate the Stop Hunt if we do not see the 3 Drives Pattern. Study how price reacts when it takes out a recent Short-term highs. If the price is not pressing higher similar to a 3 Drives pattern, anticipate a Stop Hunt.

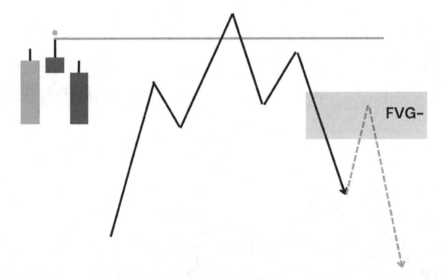

Then we look for a Displacement that prints a FVG. And we place our Entry at the Fair Vale Gap.

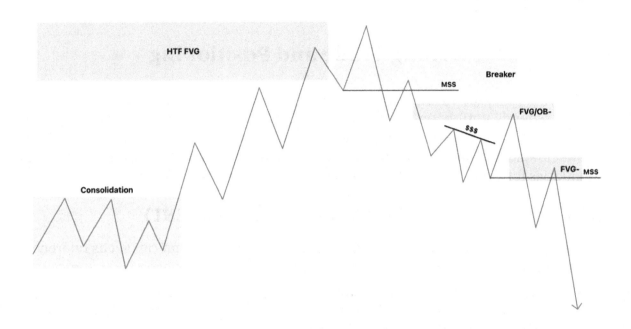

Chapter 8

Morning Trade and Positioning

As I have already mentioned, the morning trade session typically starts at 8:30 am and extends until noon. During this time, there is usually a lot of volatility and excitement in the market, making it an opportune time for traders. It is important to understand the specific time frame of the morning trade session as it sets the boundaries for when you should be actively trading and observing the market.

Why You Should Use 8:30 & Midnight Open (EST)

The 8:30 open and midnight open are specific time points that can act as reference levels for identifying trading opportunities based on the daily range.

- On a sell day, traders aim to catch the Judas swing that occurs above the 8:30 open and midnight open. This indicates a potential reversal in price movement from the high of the day back towards the low.

- On a buy day, traders look for the Judas swing that occurs below the 8:30 open and midnight open. This can lead to a potential reversal in price movement from the low of the day back towards the high.

These reference levels, along with the daily range, can be considered as points of interest or targets for traders to make informed trading decisions.

Lower Time Frame Setups Around the 8:30 and Midnight Open

To further refine the buy strategy, we can look for lower time frame setups within the 8:30 open and midnight open prices. Lower time frames, such as 15-minute or 30-minute charts, provide more detailed information about price movements within these specific periods.

We can look for PD arrays that indicate a swing or range within the market, particularly below the 8:30 open and midnight open prices. This can provide additional confirmation for a potential buy opportunity, as it suggests that the price has reached a lower point within the trading day.

In addition to being potential entry points, the 8:30 open and midnight open can also be considered points of interest or targets for buy days.

We can set their targets to reach or surpass these levels, indicating a potential upward movement in the price.

Identifying a premium in the 8:30 open and midnight open for sell opportunities

When trading on sell days, it is important to identify areas of premium that can indicate potential sell opportunities. Two key areas to consider are the 8:30 open and the midnight open.

- The 8:30 open refers to the opening price of the market at 8:30 AM. If the price of the asset is above the 8:30 open, it is considered a premium. This indicates that there may be selling opportunities as the price is higher than the opening price.

- The midnight open refers to the opening price of the market at midnight. Similar to the 8:30 open, if the price of the asset is above the midnight open, it is considered a premium. This can also indicate potential sell opportunities.

Within the 8:30 open and midnight open, it is important to look for lower time frame setups. Lower time frames, such as 15-minute or 30-minute charts, can provide more detailed information about price movements within these key areas.

In addition to lower time frame setups, we should also analyze potential PD arrays above the 8:30 open and midnight open. A PD array refers to a range of prices where the market consolidates or distributes before making a significant move.

The 8:30 open and midnight open can also serve as points of interest or targets for sell positions. These price levels can act as psychological levels where traders anticipate a reaction from the market.

For example, if the price of an asset reaches the 8:30 open or the midnight open during a sell day, traders may consider taking profits or closing their sell positions. These price levels can also be used as reference points for setting stop-loss orders to manage risk.

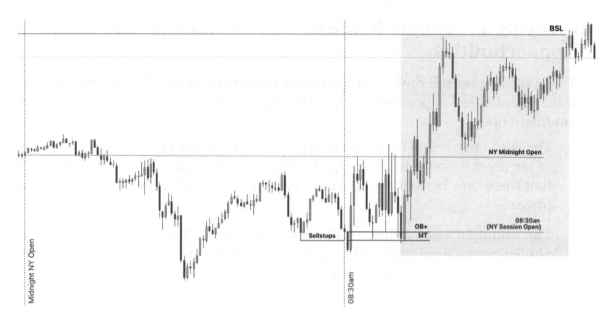

Incorporating the Power of 3

Use the midnight opening (NMO) – 00:00am NY Time. We want to see the price trades toward the MNO Price to act as Manipulation between 8:30am to 9:45am EST.

It can act as a Judas Swing, and it is countering where the price will want to go.

During the last portion of the day if you are bearish, you can use the opening price at 1:30pm NY Time the same way the Midnight/8:30 open is used.

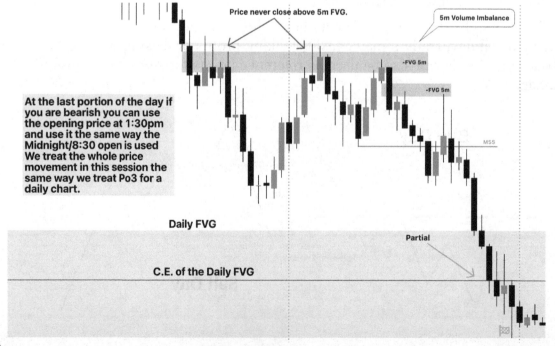

Strategies for Maximizing Profits During the NY AM Session

One strategy is to closely monitor market profiles and daily ranges. By analyzing these patterns and understanding if the daily candle is more likely to expand higher or lower, you can make informed trading decisions.

Another strategy is to pay attention to intraday order flow and the daily range. By setting up your daily range and intraday layouts, you can identify potential trading opportunities and determine the direction in which the market is likely to move.

Remember, the morning trade session is characterized by its volatility. This means there may be opportunities for quick profits, but it also comes with increased risk. It is important to have a clear trading plan, manage your risk effectively, and stick to your strategy.

The Step-by-Step Guide for Morning Trades

Here's a simplified version of the steps in your trading strategy:

1. Before 8:30am, we identify a liquidity pool in the market.

2. Now our 15 minute chart is ready, and we can drop to 5 minute for entries.

3. We look for a displacement in price movement that occurs below the liquidity pool.

4. We use the concept of a fair value gap (FVG) to determine our entry point.

Afternoon Session and Swing Highs/Lows

Swing highs and swing lows are important technical indicators that help us identify potential reversals or continuations in market trends. During the afternoon session, we are particularly interested in identifying swing highs and swing lows that occur after 1:30 PM. These levels are significant because they often serve as turning points or areas of consolidation before the market makes its next move.

To identify swing highs and swing lows, follow these steps:

1. Begin by analyzing your charts, starting from the morning session, and moving into the afternoon session.

2. Look for significant price peaks that form after 1:30 PM. These are swing highs and indicate potential resistance levels.

3. Similarly, identify notable price troughs that occur after 1:30 PM. These are swing lows and suggest possible support levels.

4. Pay attention to the formation of swing highs and swing lows. Ideally, each candle should have a higher low to the left and a higher low to the right. This pattern indicates accumulation and a potential upward trend.

Strategies for Capitalizing on Market Movements during the Afternoon Session

Once you have identified swing highs and swing lows during the afternoon session, it's time to develop strategies for capitalizing on market movements. Here are a few approaches you can consider:

1. Continuation Trades: If the morning session showed a bullish move and the afternoon session continues in the same direction, consider taking a continuation trade. Look for opportunities to enter the market based on the logic used in the morning session. This strategy aims to ride the momentum of the market and profit from further upward movement.

2. Reversal Trades: In some cases, the morning session may exhibit a bullish move but reverse in the afternoon. This presents an opportunity for reversal trades. If you notice a shift in market sentiment or a significant change in price action, consider taking a trade in the opposite direction. This strategy allows you to capitalize on potential trend reversals and profit from market corrections.

3. Measured Moves: Another strategy to consider is measuring the morning move and anticipating a potential duplicate move in the afternoon. For example, if the morning move was 70 points (NQ), there is a possibility that the afternoon session could see an additional 70-point move in the same direction.

Remember, the afternoon session often experiences accelerated market movements, especially around 20 minutes to four and 10 minutes before four o'clock. These movements are driven by market on close orders and can create significant opportunities for traders.

What your Daily Bias and do you expect Range Expansion?
If your Daily Bias is Bullish, and you expect Range Expansion to the upside...
Trade with that expectation in the Afternoon Session and base it off the framework given in the Morning Session.

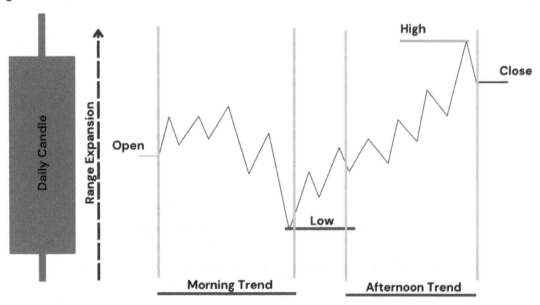

Market Profile

THERE ARE 3 TEMPLATES:

Template 1: morning trend, afternoon reversal.

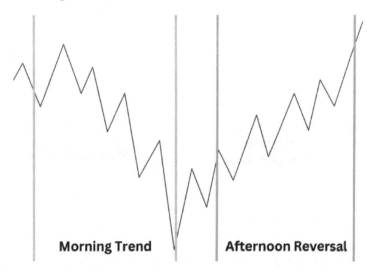

Template 2: morning trend, afternoon continuation for a 1:1 measured move

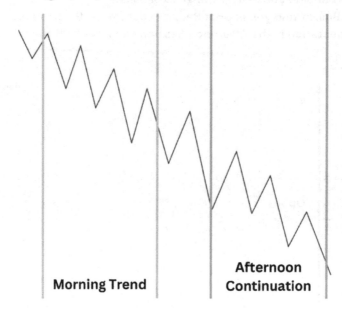

Morning Trend

Afternoon Continuation

Template 3: morning consolidation, afternoon trend

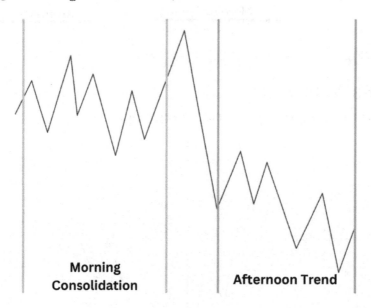

Morning Consolidation

Afternoon Trend

Chapter 9

Market Efficiency Paradigm & Institutional Order Flow

Market efficiency refers to the degree to which prices in the financial markets reflect all available information. In an efficient market, prices quickly adjust to new information, making it difficult for traders to consistently outperform the market.

Inefficient markets, on the other hand, present opportunities for traders to exploit price discrepancies and make profitable trades. However, it is important to note that market inefficiencies can be short-lived as market participants quickly react to new information, leading to price adjustments.

How we internalize price delivery:

1. Do not trade patterns for pattern's sake.

2. Do not trade indicator readings or momentum.

3. We look to enter Longs when Retail Sells.

4. We look to enter Shorts when Retail Buys.

5. We anticipate Price seeking opposite liquidity.

6. Time of Day is vital when engaging with Price.

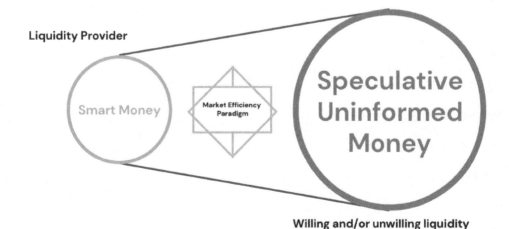

This model acts as a bridge between the trader, the markets, and the efficiency paradigm.

This model aims to trade the market when the algorithm will seek to rebalance a BISI/SIBI. We will suggest that the market is in a retracement phase. This pattern will be traded in high volatility conditions. This is an internal range liquidity model.

The Market Efficiency Paradigm is a way of looking at financial markets for what they really are.

To understand this paradigm, we need to break it down into three components:

1. **Smart Money:** This component is about understanding how and why smart money is fundamentally different from dumb money.

2. **Market Efficiency Paradigm:** This component is about understanding how the Interbank Price Delivery Algorithm provides data for the market.

3. **Speculative Uninformed Money:** This component is about understanding the reverse psychology of speculative uninformed money and how it can be used to gain an edge in the interbank market.

Concept :

- Time
- BISI/SIBI
- Consequent Encroachment
- News embargo
- Change in order flow
- PD Arrays
- Narrative
- Draw on liquidity

Importance of Not Blindly Following Trading Patterns or Indicators

Many retail traders fall into the trap of blindly following trading patterns or indicators without considering the underlying market dynamics. While technical analysis can be a useful tool for identifying potential trading opportunities, it is important to remember that it is just one piece of the puzzle.

Smart money traders, such as institutional investors, do not solely rely on trading patterns or indicators. Instead, they focus on analyzing market liquidity and the underlying narrative in the marketplace. By understanding the broader market context, smart money traders can make more informed trading decisions and potentially capitalize on market inefficiencies.

BUYSIDE ORIENTED MARKET:

1. We will wait for a big bearish displacement after a news embargo.

2. Don't trade the first 10 minutes of the news: If the news is at 10 a.m., then we will look for a setup from 10:10 a.m. to 12:00.

3. We will wait & observe order flow:

   a. We will wait for Bearish PD arrays to fail.

   b. We want to see Bullish displacement.

   c. We want to see a change in order flow.

4. Down close candles act as support.

5. Up close candles invalidated.

6. Premium arrays invalidated.

7. Discount arrays respected.

8. We will anticipates a buy at discount arrays: FVG / Inversion FVG, Order block, Breaker.

9. We will put a maximum of 5 points stop loss. We will aim for 10 points for ES (SP500).

SELLSIDE ORIENTED MARKET:

1. We will wait for a big bullish displacement after a news embargo.

2. Don't trade the first 10 minutes of the news: If the news is at 10 a.m., then we will look for a setup from 10:10 a.m. to 12:00.

3. We will wait & observe order flow:

    a. We will wait for Bullish PD arrays to fail.

    b. We want to see Bearish displacement.

    c. We want to see a change in order flow.

4. Up close candles act as support.

5. Down close candles invalidated.

6. Discount arrays invalidated.

7. Premium arrays respected.

8. We will anticipates a sell at premium arrays: FVG / Inversion FVG, Order block, Breaker.

9. We will put a maximum of 5 points stop loss. We will aim for 10 points for ES (SP500).

When to trade it ?

1. We will use economic calendar to frame our trades.

2. The news we are interested in are the NFP, CPI, FOMC, PPI, FED talks.

3. Trending days.

What is the market mechanics behind it?

After a large market displacement, retailers tend to follow the market. Instead, we will take the opposite approach. It is likely that a countermove will occur, known as a retracement, before the market continues in its initial direction.

This is where we plan to enter our trade, aiming to catch the retracement. Typically, the market will retrace at least 50% of the initial move. Also, remember that a news embargo can be used like a Judas swing sometimes. I personally aim to gain a maximum of 10 points (ES/SP500), but a 50% BISI/SIBI can be the final objective.

Who Makes up Speculative Uninformed Money?

Speculative Uninformed Money consists of several different types of market participants, including retail traders, new hedge funds, and large fund traders. Let's take a closer look at each of these groups:

1. **New Pool of Retail Traders:** There are many different statistics available that pertain to retail trading in the financial markets i.e. the high failure rates, the short career duration, lack of education, and emotional/overleveraged trades. New traders entering the forex market have increased significantly in recent years due to the growing popularity of online trading platforms and the increasing accessibility of forex trading to retail traders.

2. **New Hedge Funds:** According to some studies, the average lifespan of a hedge fund is around 5 to 7 years. However, there are also many hedge funds that have been in operation for much longer and have established themselves as major players in the financial industry. One of the most famous hedge fund failures is Long-Term Capital Management (LTCM). LTCM was founded in 1994 and was once considered one of the most successful hedge funds in the world. However, in 1998, the fund suffered significant losses due to a series of trades that went wrong and eventually had to be bailed out by a consortium of major banks.

3. **Large Fund Traders:** Large fund traders may also be classified as Speculative Uninformed Money, despite having more resources and experience compared to retail traders. However, they still follow retail methods, such as relying on indicators, instead of a deep understanding of Smart Money. The main difference between large fund traders and retail traders is their risk management, which helps ensure their longevity in the financial markets.

Enhance Your Trading Performance with a Price Action Trade Journal

Keeping a trade journal is a crucial aspect of successful trading, and it can help you gain a deeper understanding of Price Action.

This journal should consist of the following elements:

a. Displacement of Price from a specific level

b. Clean Highs and Lows neutralized

c. Swing Highs and Lows in between A and B

By adopting a Long-term, Intermediate-term, and Short-term Perspective, you can better navigate through price movements and have a clear idea of what to look for on each time frame.

For example, in day trading, the Long-term Perspective could be a Weekly Chart or Daily Chart, the Intermediate-term Perspective could be a 4 Hour Chart or 1 Hour

Chart, and the Short-term Perspective could be a 15 Minute Chart or 5 Minute Chart.

Journaling the Daily Range

Journaling the Daily Range should consist of the following elements:

a. Displacement of the Daily Range from a specific level

b. Clean Highs or Lows neutralized for the Daily Range

c. Price reaction at Swing Lows and Highs between A and B

Journaling the Weekly Range

Journaling the Weekly Range should consist of the following elements:

a. Displacement of the Weekly Range from a specific level

b. Clean Highs and Lows neutralized for the Weekly Range

c. Price reaction at Swing Highs and Lows in between A and B

Consider the following questions for the Weekly Range:

• What day did the Weekly High or Low form?

• What Killzone did the Weekly High or Low form?

By journaling your trades on a daily basis, you are training your mind.

Just like how we exercise and train our muscles for size and strength, we can apply similar principles to our minds to expand our knowledge and understanding of IPDA.

Use this journaling framework as a guide to enhance your trading performance and take your interbank trading to the next level.

Institutional Order Flow & Secrets of Efficient Price Delivery

Institutional Order Flow (IOF) is the analysis of how large institutions and banks trade in the market on a daily, weekly, and monthly basis. It involves reading the tape and internalizing how price is being delivered in real-time, whether it's in a buy program or a sell program. IOF is used to locate price levels that align with institutional order flow, which is key to identifying high probability setups. It can also involve partial entry into a fair value gap that is expected to remain open. Understanding IOF on higher time frames can help frame out low-risk, high-probability setups.

What the macro does here is: run Buyside then attack Sellside. It could also have done the other way, so first run on Sellside then Buyside.

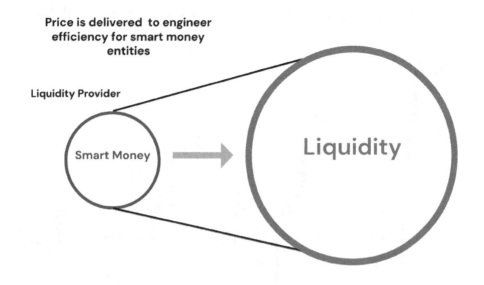

Price is delivered to engineer efficiency for smart money entities

Liquidity Provider

Smart Money

Liquidity

We can see sell off here.
All down close candles.

OB

OB

More likely liquidity stops is
here, right?

All up close candles.

[Monthly Chart]

After the market took Sellside liquidity, what will it do next? Look for liquidity at the top.

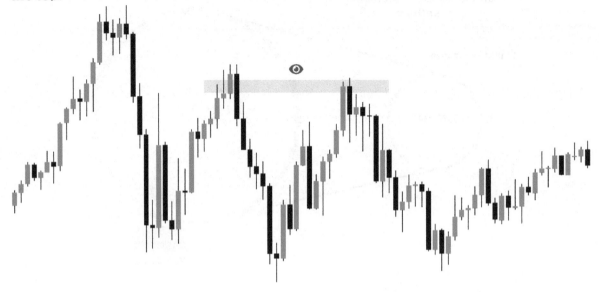

Let's pay attention to the middle of the last up candle. We see how the body of candles respects them. It may be that the price will go up slightly above the wicks.

When the price goes up to this liquidity area, it will now seek liquidity on the opposite side that has remained below the low.

Liquidity.
Pay attention to the bodies of the candles.

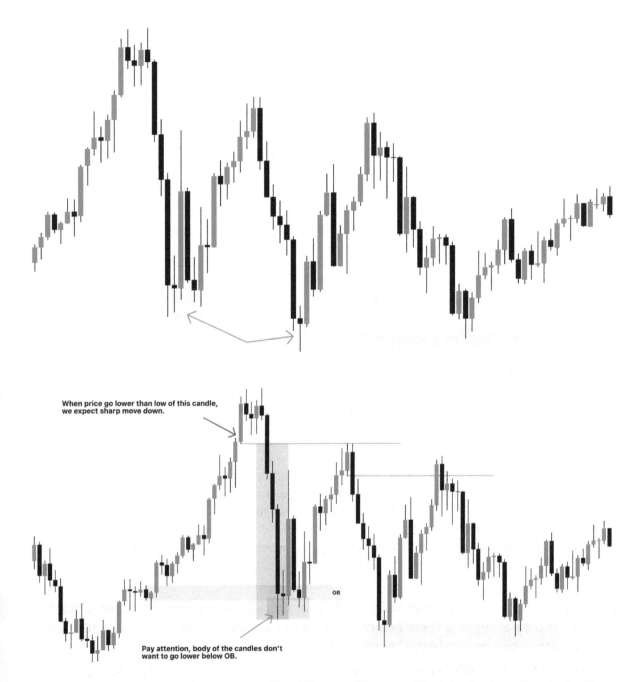

When price go lower than low of this candle, we expect sharp move down.

Pay attention, body of the candles don't want to go lower below OB.

OB

Internal versus external range liquidity and how to define the interbank dealing range (IDR):

As I have already mentioned in the previous chapters, you want to look to where the most recent dealing range has traded. Did it take out BSL? Or SSL? I like 15m TF. If you use an hourly chart, you'll come up with a different dealing range. You trade the TF that you're looking at.

The interbank dealing range:

- It is a range, so you can identify discount and premium and EQ. As price goes above the EQ, so technically is in premium, it doesn't mean that ICT automatically takes a trade, we can anticipate some measure of decline though but overbought conditions can stay in premium and the market can go higher. Keep that in mind.

- It means that there will be a lot of interest in seeing price return back inside that range to a particular price level.

- Your focus should be where price is drawing to. If the Draw On Liquidity is bearish price will draw below the interbank dealing range low. When bullish price will draw towards dealing range high.

Po3 means we open (accumulation), make high of the week (manipulation) and from there trade lower (distribution).

What is the Dealing Range?

A dealing range is a price range where both buy and sell sides have been taken out. It is a useful concept because it allows traders to anticipate the market's movement back to a discount and eventually to its sell side. Traders can look for areas within the range to do analysis and anticipate a run back up into a premium.

A dealing range is the range that is formed after liquidity has been swept on both sides. i.e: We're ranging, then we sweep the top of the range, then the bottom of it, now we have formed a dealing range.
Dealing Ranges are so powerful because they are only formed after price sweeps both sides of liquidity and they can provide an amazing bias when used on the higher timeframes.

This concept is based on the idea that large market players leave footprints on the charts, and by analyzing their behavior, traders can gain valuable insights into their trading strategies and potential market movements.

To identify the dealing range, we need to identify key support and resistance levels. This allows them to visualize the range where the price is likely to trade within a certain period. The range can be narrow or wide, depending on the market conditions and TF.

One key characteristic of the dealing range is that it tends to be a consolidation period, where price moves sideways without making significant progress in either direction. This can be seen as a pause or a balance between the buyers and sellers in the market. During this time, traders may use various technical indicators to identify potential breakouts or reversals from the range.

ICT emphasizes that traders need to be patient and wait for the price to either break out of the range or bounce back from the support and resistance levels. He also advises traders to be aware of the market context and the fundamental factors that can impact the price movement.

Dealing ranges show up in many forms, and every time it's different, but, generally, after we have swept liquidity on both sides, you start looking for a bottom to form, and once you see a clear reversal, you can start maintaining a bullish bias up until the equilibrium of the dealing range.

Dealing Ranges show up on all timeframes, you can look for a dealing range within a dealing range within a dealing range, and just like that you can form a bias and base a trade on that.

Premium / Discount Arrays

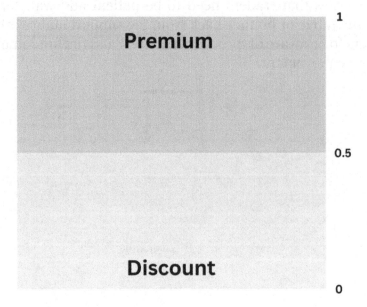

How to identify discount? First, look for a bullish displacement in price. Once that occur in price, you want to see price forming a swing high. Now you can draw your Fibonacci tool from swing high to swing low. Wait for price return back to discount and look for longs there.

How to identify premium? Look for a bearish displacement in price. Then, you want to see price form a swing high. Draw your Fibonacci tool from swing low to swing high. Wait for price to return back to premium and look for shorts there.

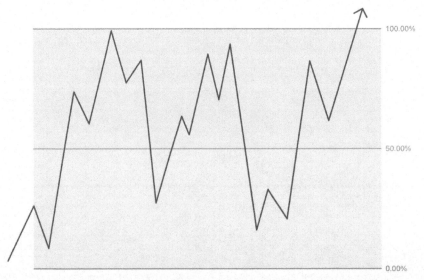

Old High/Low
Rejection Block
Bearish Order Block
FVG
Liquidity Void
Bearish Breaker
Mitigation Block

Bearish Premium Array

Equilibrium

Mitigation Block
Bullish Breaker
Liquidity Void
FVG
Bullish Order Block
Rejection Block
Old Low/High

Bullish Discount Array

Old High

An Old High refers to a previous high point in the price that can act as areas of resistance or potential targets for liquidity runs, as buy stops may be resting above these levels.

When the market reaches an Old High, it may encounter resistance in the form of Old Lows and Old Highs, making it difficult for the price to continue rising. However, not every Old High should be considered a selling point, as the market may trade through it and continue to rise.

Old Low

An Old Low refers to a previous low point in the price that can act as areas of support or potential targets for liquidity runs, as sell stops may be resting below these levels.

When the market reaches an Old Low, it may encounter resistance in the form of Old Lows and Old Highs, making it difficult for the price to continue dropping. However, not every Old Low should be considered a buying point, as the market may trade through it and continue lower.

Bearish Rejection Block (-RB)

A Bearish Rejection Block occurs in major to intermediate term downtrends when a price high has formed with long wicks on the high or highs of the candlestick(s).

Price reaches up above the body of the candle or candles to run the buyside liquidity out before the price declines. This pattern shows underlying distribution and can be used to identify potential resistance levels.

Bullish Rejection Block (+RB)

A Bullish Rejection Block occurs in major to intermediate term uptrends and is formed when a price low has a long wick or multiple wicks. The low or lows of the candlestick(s) reach down below the body of the candle to run the sellside liquidity out before the price rallies higher.

To frame the Bullish Rejection Block, identify the lowest wick low and the lowest open or the lowest close that makes the swing low on the timeframe you're looking for the pattern. When price trades back down into the high of the block, you can be a buyer just below it or wait for the price to trade through it and then be a buyer on a stop just above that particular level.

Bearish Order Block (-OB)

A Bearish Order Block is a concept in trading where a series of up candles or price bars occur right before a significant downward move in the market. It is considered a potential area of resistance and can be used as a selling opportunity.

To identify a Bearish Order Block, look for the last consecutive up candles before a down move, as these candles represent the potential Bearish Order Block.

Bullish Order Block (+OB)

A Bullish Order Block is the lowest candle or price bar with a down close that has the most range between open to close and is near a support level. It is validated when the high of the lowest down candle or price bar is traded through by a later formed candle or price bar. When price trades higher away from the Bullish Order Block and then returns to the Bullish Order Block candle or price bar high, this is considered bullish and can be used for a bullish entry.

Fair Value Gap

A Fair Value Gap (FVG) is a concept in trading that refers to a range in price delivery where one side of the market liquidity is offered and typically confirmed with a liquidity void on lower time frame charts in the same range of price. It can occur when price gaps create a vacuum of trading, resulting in an actual price gap.

In the context of Inner Circle Trader's teachings, FVGs are used to identify areas where price is expected to eventually trade back up into the gapped area, filling in the gap and finding fair value.

Bearish Liquidity Void

A Bearish Liquidity Void refers to a situation where there is a lack of buyside liquidity in the market, causing the price to move aggressively lower. In such cases, the market is expected to eventually move back up with a high probability, filling the Liquidity Void and trading over the same price levels that were previously void of buyside liquidity.

This means that the price is likely to revisit the range where the void occurred, balancing out the price action with bullish price movement.

Bullish Liquidity Void

A Bullish Liquidity Void refers to a situation where there is a lack of sellside liquidity in the market, causing the price to move aggressively higher. In such cases, the market is expected to eventually move back down with a high probability, filling the Liquidity Void and trading over the same price levels that were previously void of sellside liquidity.

This means that the price is likely to revisit the range where the void occurred, balancing out the price action with bearish price movement.

Bearish Breaker Block (-BB)

A Bearish Breaker Block is a bearish range or down close candle in the most recent swing low prior to an Old High being violated. It occurs when the market trades higher, takes out an Old High, and then breaks below the low that made the new high. The Buyers who bought this Low and later see the same swing low violated will look to mitigate the loss. When the price returns back to the swing low, it is considered a bearish trade setup worth considering.

Bullish Breaker Block (+BB)

A Bullish Breaker Block is a bullish range or up close candle in the most recent swing high prior to an Old Low being violated. It occurs when the market trades lower, takes out an Old Low, and then breaks above the high that made the new low. The sellers who sold this High and later see the same swing high violated will look to mitigate the loss. When the price returns back to the swing high, it is considered a bullish trade setup worth considering.

Bearish Mitigation Block (-MB)

A Bearish Mitigation Block is a bearish range or down close candle in the most recent Swing Low that fails to take out a Swing High. The Buyers that bought this Low and later see this same swing low violated will look to mitigate the loss. When Price returns back to the Swing Low, this is a Bearish Trade Setup worth considering.

Bullish Mitigation Block (+MB)

A Bullish Mitigation Block is a bullish range or up close candle in the most recent Swing High that fails to take out a Swing Low. The Sellers that sold this High and later see this same swing high violated will look to mitigate the loss. When Price returns back to the Swing High, this is a Bullish Trade Setup worth considering.

 **A long wick in the context of PD arrays refers to candles with wicks at short-term highs or lows. These wicks indicate gaps in the market, and the bodies of the candles are important for understanding the market narrative. Liquidity often rests just above the bodies of candles with wicks above them and below the bodies of candles with wicks below them. These wicks are used to identify potential premium and discount PD arrays in various timeframes, such as monthly, weekly, daily, and four-hour charts.**

- Inexperienced traders may place their stop-loss orders too shallow, risking premature stop-outs, or too high, resulting in significant losses.

- This conundrum arises due to a lack of knowledge and experience in determining optimal stop-loss levels.

Chapter 10

Fair Value Gap

Fair Value Gap - is a range in Price Delivery where one side of the Market Liquidity is offered and typically confirmed with a Liquidity Void on the Lower Time Frame Charts in the same range of Price. Price can actually "gap" to create a literal vacuum of Trading thus posting an actual Price Gap. It occurs when price leaves a specific level where there's less trading activity seen and only has a one-directional price movement.

FVGs are an entry point, a target, and a means to measure shift in sentiment as Price shifts from buy to sell program or shift from sell to buy programs.

Liquidity Void - is a range in price where one side of the market liquidity is shown in wide or long one-sided ranges or candles. It occurs when the market aggressively moves away from a consolidation, creating a void of buy-side liquidity. This means that very little buying took place during the price movement. The nature of a liquidity void is that, with a high probability, the price will eventually move back up and trade over the same price levels that were previously void of liquidity.

 The idea behind FVGs is that the market will eventually come back to these inefficiencies in the market before continuing in the same direction as the initial impulsive move. FVGs are important since traders can achieve an edge in the market. Price action traders can also use these imbalances as entry or exit points in the market.

Fair Value Gaps are created within a three-candle sequence and are commonly visualized on the chart as a large candle whose neighboring candles' upper and lower wicks do not fully overlap the large candle. The reason why a trader might be interested in where these FVGs occur is simply that the imbalance created by them can become a magnet for price in the future.

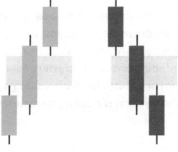

The illustration below does not depict a Fair Value Gap, as the previous candle's high level has counterbalanced the low level of the third candle. This price action is considered to be balanced.

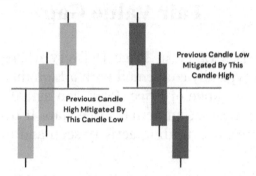

Previous Candle High Mitigated By This Candle Low

Previous Candle Low Mitigated By This Candle High

*FVG (Fair Value Gaps) is a candle in which there is an impulse, where an insufficiently large volume is traded with a lack of liquidity. This caused a sharp momentum without consolidations.

An impulse movement can be triggered by large orders of one big player. The market maker seized all the liquidity, causing it to be scarce for most other players. Since a certain number of orders within the imbalance of a major player remains unfilled, the market returns and closes this zone.

Fair Value Gaps (FVGs) can be found on all timeframes and there are numerous trading strategies that can be implemented using them. In this example, we will focus on utilizing FVGs for trend continuation after a significant impulsive move. As previously mentioned, we can anticipate the price to return to these FVGs before continuing in the same direction as the impulse move. Traders can take advantage of this by waiting for the price to reach the FVG area of interest and then entering a trade, targeting trend continuation.

Displacement is a location in price where someone with a lot of money comes into the marketplace with a strong conviction to move price higher or lower very quickly. Displacement is characterized by strong and quick price movement that leave behind Fair Value Gaps.

In trading, when price goes above an old high and then trades down below it, you want to see an obvious displacement, not just a small, lethargic move. This displacement helps traders identify potential market structure shifts and fair value gaps, which can be used to make informed trading decisions.

Again, a displacement candle is a candle that breaks through a previous high or low. When there is displacement over structure, it means that the price has broken through a key level of support or resistance. Conversely, a lack of displacement occurs when the price fails to break through a previous high or low. Identifying displacement is important because it can signal a trend reversal or continuation.

To identify displacement, look for aggressive moves and closes below a low or above a high. In a bullish trend, look for lows taken without displacement as potential long entries. In a bearish trend, look for failures to displace over highs as potential short entries.

For example, if the price breaks below a low but immediately moves back into the range, it is not a displacement candle. On the other hand, if there are large aggressive candles down, that is displacement over structure.

Let's consider short trade: to use displacement for short entries, traders should look for a short-term low and wait for an aggressive break below it. This break should be accompanied by large and aggressive candles that close below the structure. This indicates that the market is likely to continue moving lower.

However, it's important to wait for displacement before entering a trade. If there is no displacement and the market immediately moves back into the range, it's best to wait for a clearer signal.

Lack of displacement can also be a signal for long entries, as it indicates that the market is likely to continue moving higher.

Examples of short entries using displacement include waiting for a break below a previous high or a short-term low. Traders should also look for fair value gaps and breakers as potential short entry points. It's important to wait for displacement over structure to confirm the short entry signal.

The key takeaway is that displacement can be a useful signal for short entries, but it's important to wait for confirmation before entering a trade.

Lack of Displacement

Lack of displacement is when there is no large aggressive candle with a close inside a high or low. It is important to identify lack of displacement in trading because it can give you entries to get long or short. Here are some tips to identify lack of displacement:

- When trying to get into a trend on the buy side of the curve, look for lows taken without displacement. These can give you entries to get long.

- When on the sell side of the curve, look for failure to displace over highs. These can be your short entries.

- If you fail to displace lower in a bullish trend or want price to go in one direction, look at those as your long entries.

It's important to remember that lack of displacement can be just as important as displacement in trading.

1. Look for lows taken without displacement when trying to get into a trend on a buy side of the curve. This can give you entries to get long.

2. When you're on the sell side of the curve, look for a failure to displace over highs. This can be your short entry.

3. Back test these strategies on your charts to see how they work in different market conditions.

Here are some examples of long entries using lack of displacement:

If price take a low and notice that there are no large aggressive candles down and price moves back into the range immediately, this can be a good entry to get long.

If price fail to displace lower when a bullish trend or wants to keep going higher, look at those for long entries.

It's important to wait for lack of displacement before entering a trade. This can help you avoid false breakouts and ensure that you're entering the market at the right time. Remember to always back test your strategies and look for patterns in your charts before making any trades.

The Bearish ICT FVG:

- The Institutional Order Flow pattern is based on the 3-candle formation.

- The Optimal formation of the Bearish FVG will be found after a run into BSL.

- Typically found just above a single price high or multiple price highs in a relative basis (double top).

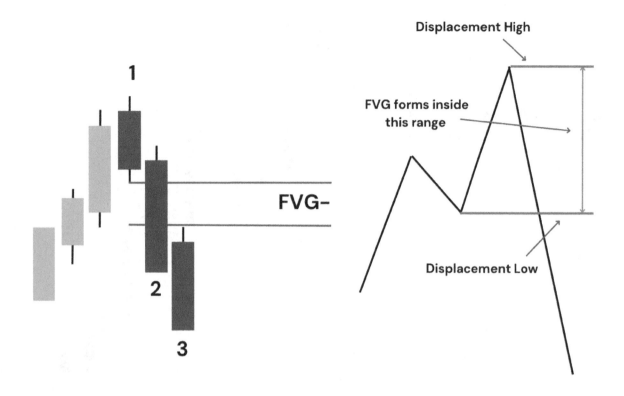

Understanding the Three-Candle Formation

1. Candle 1: This candle represents the high of the fair value gap. It is important to note that the low of this candle will be the starting point for the fair value gap.

2. Candle 2: This candle is where the fair value gap is formed. It is the candle that separates the high and low of the fair value gap. Traders should pay attention to the price action within this candle.

3. Candle 3: This candle represents the low of the fair value gap. It is important to note that the high of this candle will be the ending point for the fair value gap.

The Bearish Market Structure: The Market will see Price Deliver a rally above the Old High/Highs, then quickly shift lower.

The Bullish ICT FVG:

- The Institutional Order Flow pattern is based on the 3-candle formation.

- The Optimal formation of the Bullish FVG will be found after a run into SSL.

- Typically found just below a single price low or multiple price lows in a relative basis (double bottom).

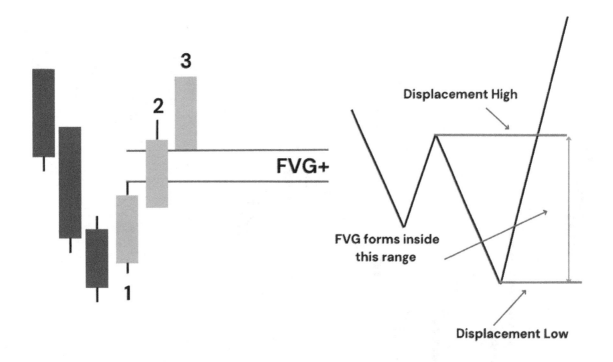

1. Candle 1: This candle represents the low of the fair value gap. It is important to note that the low of this candle will be the starting point for the fair value gap.

2. Candle 2: This candle is where the fair value gap is formed. It is the candle that separates the low and high of the fair value gap. Traders should pay attention to the price action within this candle.

3. Candle 3: This candle represents the high of the fair value gap. It is important to note that the low of this candle will be the ending point for the fair value gap.

The Market will see Price Deliver a rally below the Old Low/Lows, then quickly shift higher.

The Bullish Market Structure: The Market will see Price Deliver a decline below the Old Low/Lows, then quickly shift higher.

At 8:30 AM we are looking for a stop run to occur.

Before 8:30 AM look for a potential liquidity pool for price to raid.

We are looking at 8:30 AM due to the News Embargo Lifts.

Equity market opens at 9:30 AM. This creates surge in volatility.

Many times surge in volatility creates a Judas Swing.

1. When you are bullish and MNO price is lower than NYO price -> use NYO. When you are bullish and we are trading below MNO and NYO is still below MNO, then we are in a heavy discounted area.

2. When you are bearish and MNO price is higher than NYO price -> use NYO. When you are bearish and we are trading above MNO and NYO is still above MNO – heavy premium area.

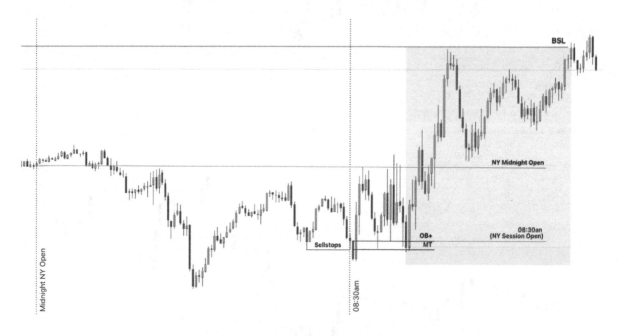

IF A STOP RUN OCCURS, THIS SETS UP A POTENTIAL TRADE.

WE ARE WAITING FOR A MS SHIFT, THEN A FVG FOR ENTRY.

WE ARE LOOKING FOR 5,4,3,2,1 MINUTE TIME FRAMES, FOLLOWING A TOP-DOWN APPROACH.

IF YOU DO NOT GET YOUR ANTICIPATED STOP RUN, YOU DO NOT HAVE A TRADE.

Chapter 11

ICT Killzones and Sessions

SESSION	TIME (EST)
IPDA Reset	00:00
London Open Kill Zone	02:00 – 05:00
NY AM Session	07:00 – 10:00
US High Impact Data	08:30
London Close	10:00 – 12:00
NY Lunch	12:00 – 13:00
NY PM Session	14:00 – 16:00
CBDR	14:00 – 20:00
Asian Killzone	20:00 – 00:00

THE IMPORTANCE OF TIME

"Algorithmic theory is based on time and price, price levels are useless until Time is considered, Time is of no use unless Price is at a key PD array. Blending the two yield astonishing results and precision." – ICT.

First, you need to know what a killzone is. To understand everything, you need to know that, even if forex is open 24h a day, people around the world do not trade as much, the three most important locations are London, New York, and Asia, considering the jet lag between them, they don' t trade at the same time, we call the moment when they individually trade "sessions". Killzones are based on that, they are the times when sessions overlap, and when there is the most volume.

There are 5 killzone:

1. London open, from 02:00 to 05:00am

2. New-York open, from 07:00 to 10:00am

3. London close, from 10:00am to 12:00pm

4. Central Bank Dealers Range, from 14:00 to 20:00

5. Asia, from 20:00 to 00:00 NY Local time.

Asia Killzone

The Asian Range determines the directional bias or likely direction for the majority of the London & NY sessions. Where the money is positioned in Asian dictates the profit release on the trading day. Typically, Asian session trades counter the NY session direction in a corrective bounce. The Asian Trading Session extends beyond the Midnight hour in NY Time.

Currency pairs **AUD, NZD** and **JPY** are best suited for this time of day. USD pairs or crosses are not active at this time of day.

AUDJPY Model:

If we are bullish, we want to see a 15m swing low get run between 8pm – 12am EST for Turtle Soup Long.

If we are bearish, we want to see a 15m swing high get run between 8pm – 12am EST for Turtle Soup Short.

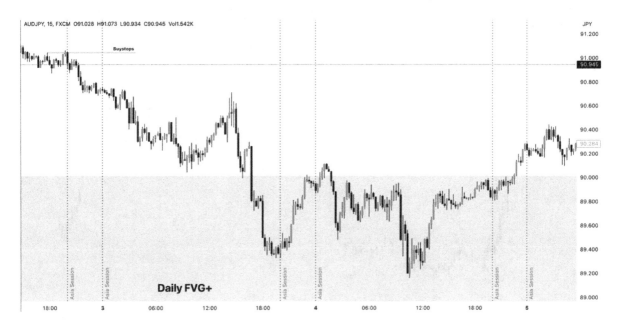

AUDJPY, 15, FXCM O91.028 H91.073 L90.934 C90.945 Vol1.542K

Buystops

Daily FVG+

AUDJPY, 3, FXCM O91.006 H91.006 L90.934 C90.945 Vol3

Buystops (15m)

-FVG 3m

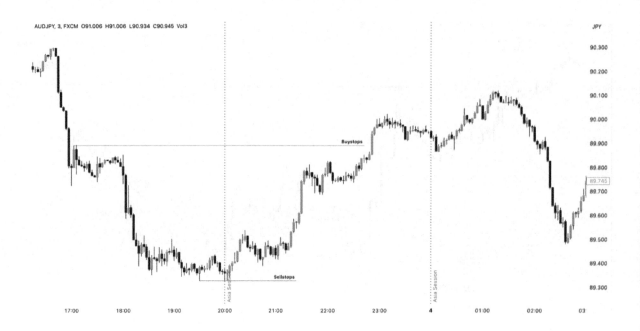

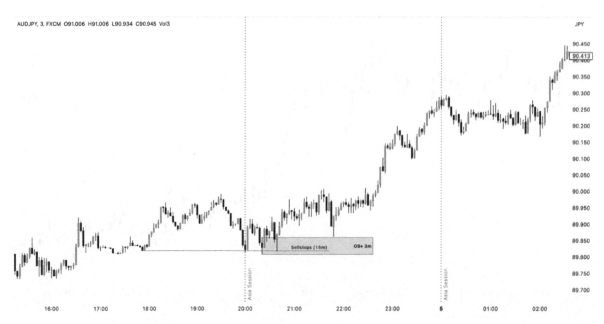

Most of the time Asia Killzone usually consolidation. Consolidation contains many clues as to how the daily range will develop throughout the remainder of the trading.

The open of the day and the Asian range can help determine the further movement of the asset's price during the day.

During **a downtrend**, it is best to consider short positions in the premium zone above the NY Midnight opening price and / or at the upper border of the Asian session.

When the high of the Asian session is updated and a test of the point of interest (POI) of the higher timeframe (HTF) occurs, this often indicates a continuation of the bearish trend.

On an uptrend, it is best to consider long positions in the discount zone below the NY Midnight opening price and / or at the lower border of the Asian session. When the low of the Asian session is updated and a test of the point of interest (POI) of the higher time frame (HTF) occurs, this often indicates a continuation of the bullish trend.

At the start of the Asian session, short-term changes in market sentiment occur, and less experienced traders may enter positions against the general price direction, carried away by the momentum.

Usually, we extend Asia Session Trendline to the 11am.

The height of the range = Highest High and Lowest Low between the 8pm to Midnight hour. The width of the range is the duration of 8pm to Midnight NY Time.

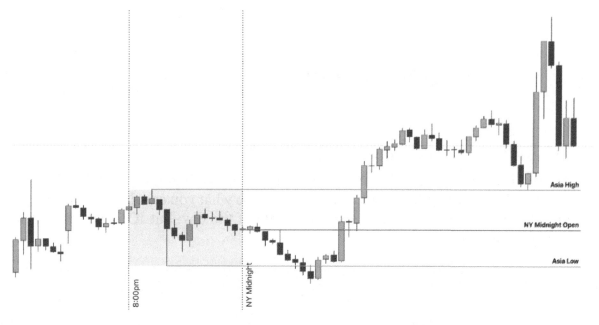

Implementing the Asian range

The Asian range can be very indicative of the future intraday price movement. When we have directional bias Asia is your context to frame the market's likely intentions. Often consolidation before intraday price swing. In itself the range is nothing magical but if you have a storyline on what you expect price to do it is unbelievably helpful. ICT learned about this from Chris Lori.

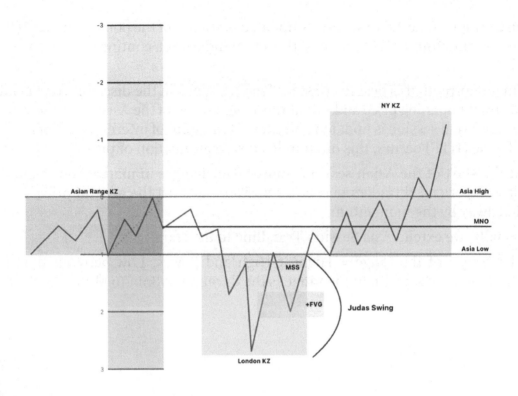

Characteristics Asian range:

Time: ICT says 20:00-00:00 NY Time.

How to draw the range? ICT draws the range from the highest high till the lowest low during that time window. There's a lot of voodoo what you can do with this range, it can take you to the highest and the lowest pip of the day, but ICT teaches that in private mentorship.

If we have a very narrow range, that sets up a huge opportunity of the algo going into a trending model. The manipulation will either be to the upside, taking the buy orders (bearish daily expansion) or the downside, taking the sell orders before expanding up (bullish daily close).

Utilization in bullish conditions:

Extend the Asian range high and low into the future. **When price retraces to Asian range high, we can anticipate institutional buying.**

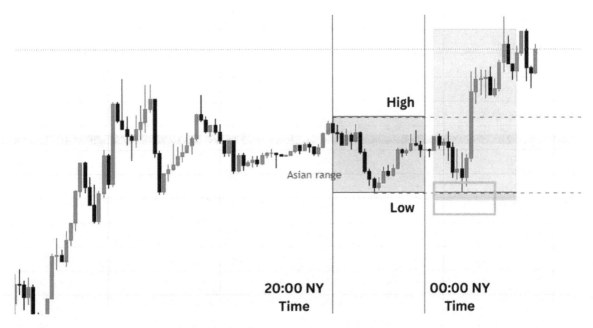

Utilization in bearish conditions:

Extend the Asian range high and low into the future. **When price retraces to Asian range low, we can anticipate institutional selling.**

The reason why I would rather play the Asia Range than the continuation is also the fact, that you rarely often see Asia having more than 15 points (ES/SP500) and having a slight trend, but still taking out both ends of the range before any further direction.

The plan: You wait for one side to get taken out within the range of 1-2 Standard Deviations, then look for reversals (ideally back inside the Asia Range) and enter after a break in structure targeting the opposite side.

Depending on your Daily Bias you can often leave a runner:

For example, you take out say 80% at the opposite side of the range, put your Stop Loss at your entry and leave a runner targeting 1-2 Standard Deviations away.

London Killzone

The Key Times to monitor is 2am to 5am NY Time.

Why do people love the London session? Asia tends to accumulate liquidity within or around its range, the further away the more volatility in the market increases. When trading opens in Frankfurt or London, a huge volume of orders enters the market. This creates ideal trading conditions, especially for those looking to capitalize on large intraday moves.

The London Trading Session extends beyond the 5am to 7am in NY Time. The London Session typically creates the Low of the day when the market is primarily Bullish and the High of the day when Bearish.

When the Market is poised to trade Higher on the Daily timeframe, we can focus on the London Session to post the Low of the Trading Day. If the Daily is posed to trade Lower – we can focus on the London Session to post the High of the Trading Day. Measure the London session range to right before the NY open the extreme high and low. If were bearish then that range is going to help find the next trading day retracement up. During the protractionary state, that move up is going to be a retracement into that London session range from London going into the beginning of NY, so 2am to 7am.

BUY: Raid Stops then shoot for Support. Goal is to dial in on the Low of the day to go long from.

First objective after London Open is to raid Asian High stops.

After stops are taken out, price moves lower testing key support levels & OTE. From London Open to Close, the Daily Range is put in and you should not use tight trailing stops. Buy below opening price and below Asian Session Swing Low.

Sell: Goal is to dial in on the High of the day to go short from. First objective after London Open is to raid Asian Low stops.

After stops are taken out, price moves higher testing key resistance levels & OTE. From London Open to Close, the Daily Range is put in and you should not use tight trailing stops. Sell above opening price and above Asian Session Swing High.

Turtle soup is the initial fake out outside Asian range before the real Judas swing to the key support/resistance level. After turtle soup the Judas swing will begin and break Asian Session High/Low to the key support/resistance, on the move to key support/resistance anticipate price to retest the broken Asian range but sometimes there might be a minor to no pullback to the Asian range (refer to the ICT Buy and Sell Model).

Key support/resistance can be Higher Time frame Support/Resistance, Higher Time Frame Order Block, Previous Day High/Low, Previous Week High/Low, Week Open, New Day Open, Previous Day New York High/Low.

WHEN TO AVOID LONDON OPEN

Some of obvious Reasons:

- Interest rate announcement

- Key Speeches

- Holiday trading

- Global and Economic events

- Weekly Range objective achieved

Occasionally: If the Asian session range is over 15-20 points (ES/SP500), wait for New York trade to be safe.

New York Killzone

The key times are 7am to 10am EST.

High or Low of the day can be formed in New York open too. New York session is the easiest one to trade as London session high/low already in place. Consider HTF Premise.

The majority of time, this session will trade in sync with Higher Time Frame direction. Consider London and Asian session highs and lows (price might bounce off these levels). Most of the time price will trade to the direction of the move that was established in London session. Expect a pullback to the high or low that was formed is London, most of the time price will retest these levels as they may act as liquidity pool.

The NY Session typically has two potential scenarios – continuation of London's Move or a complete reversal on the daily direction.

If the low of the day is formed in the London session, the uptrend continues in New York and the trading range is exited at the next bearish point of interest (POI) or upper liquidity zone (sell stops). To enter a short position, anticipate the high of the daily range.

If the high of the day is formed in the London session, then the downtrend in New York continues and the trading range is exited to the next bullish point of interest (POI) or to the lower liquidity zone (buy stops). To enter a long position, consider the low of the daily range.

If in **the Asian and London sessions** the price was in a narrow range and accumulated liquidity on top of a downtrend or from below on an uptrend, then there will probably be a liquidity withdrawal from this range in the New York session. This can lead to a high of the day on a downtrend or a low of the day on an uptrend, and then move in the opposite direction.

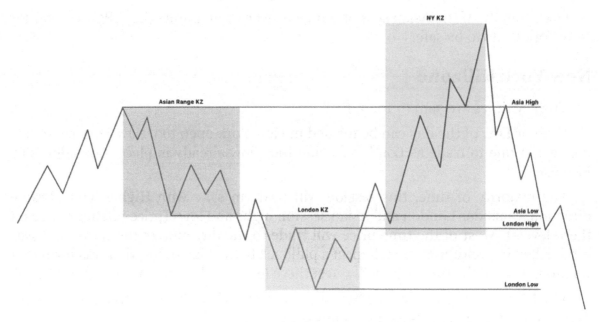

If a day's low was formed at the London session, we can expect the beginning of an upward move in New York, as well as the formation of a significant low, from where further price movement will begin.

If the high of the day was formed at the London session, then at the New York session we can expect the beginning of a downward move, as well as an exit from the daily range and the opportunity to open a short position using a bearish OB.

Continuation:

Continuation of the movement is easier to trade. For this, you need to be sure in the direction of the day. If the market is Bullish - we will see Low formed in London. If the market is Bearish - we will see High formed in London. It is worth waiting for a pullback during the NY session and getting confirmation to enter positions in the direction of London.

Based on the analysis of ES charts, NY often returns to the most obvious zone, it is best to look for a FVG, BB, or OB on the 5/15m chart.

New York Session Reversal

Knowing the Higher Timeframe PD Arrays and the IPDA Data Ranges the market is presently respecting - scenarios can be outlined in our analysis. If there is a HTF Discount Array that is below the market price but has yet to be met - the day it trades down into it during London's move and crosses over to New York Open - this is classic New York Session Reversal conditions.

Unless the NY session opens up at a premium array or discount array on the HTF, NY will always be expected to be a continuation of London. That changes if London trades down lower and then crosses into New York Open and New York trades into a HTF discount array.

If we're trading at a level that we expect to be bearish and it does this during NY, expect a reversal.

The characteristics are simple, but you need to study it over and over again. Have the HTF PD arrays on your chart, and then you won't be blindsided and you'll see it coming.

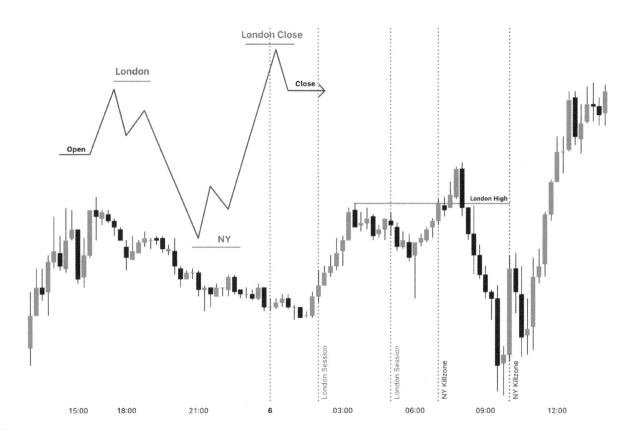

London Close Killzone

As a rule, at the close of the London session, a corrective movement can be observed after the price has reached its targets in New York.

In the case of a downtrend, when the price is in a bullish point of interest (POI) or a significant pool of liquidity has been withdrawn, you should look for a false breakout on the 5-minute timeframe to open a long position.

If there is an uptrend, then when the price is in the bearish point of interest (POI) or when a significant liquidity pool is removed, it is necessary to look for a false breakout on the 5-minute timeframe to enter a short position.

London Close can be used for intraday reversals on Large Range Days for scalps. The large range day that exceeds its 5 ADR tends to retrace about 20% of its total daily range at 10:00 am to Noon NY time.

Importance Characteristics of London Close Killzone

It is important to understand that London Close Killzone can continue to move in NY and even London during NY lunch hours.

What was the main movement of the Day or the Week may change during the

London Close. That is, this period of time can show a reversal in the market.

In longer term conditions, the London Close can bring a Market Reversal that can lead to a series of days of one-sided direction. This is best determined with the use of the Weekly Templates and study of the current Market Structure.

Everything mentioned in New York reversals, the same applies to London close. The London close can be a sweep of the New York session reversal 1 last time and then it really takes off.

If you expect a NYO reversal but then London close takes out NYO and is still in the HTF PD array then you can still get in.

Chapter 12

Daily Bias & Consolidation Hurdles

WHAT IS THE NARRATIVE?
Have we taken out Liquidity? Then it is likely to retrace inside the Range.
Have we rebalanced an FVG? Then it is likely to expand towards Liquidity.

It took out Weekly SSL. Then we can anticipate possible retracement into the range or a reversal

Weekly SSL

To understand daily bias and consolidation hurdles, traders often turn to the daily chart. The daily chart provides a broader perspective of price movements and helps identify key levels and trends.

When analyzing the daily chart, we pay close attention to the number of up days or green candles from a high to a low. This information helps determine the strength of the sell scenario. Same for buy scenario. If there are multiple up days during a bearish bias, it may indicate that the sell scenario is not as strong as initially anticipated.

It is important for us to understand that we don't have to be right all the time. Embracing imperfection and accepting that trading involves uncertainty is crucial for long-term success. We should focus on developing a solid trading plan based on our analysis and manage our risk accordingly.

WHAT IS THE PRESENT DEALING RANGE?

Are we at Premium zone? When we are at premium zone or the algorithm takes buy side liquidity, we anticipate price will go down.

Are we at Discount zone? Similarly when we at discount zone or the algorithm takes sell side liquidity, we anticipate higher prices.

Are we at Equilibrium zone? This is when it is most difficulty to predict the next moves.

What is the Draw on Liquidity?

Is price going to draw towards a. Discount FVG or Old Low?

Is price going to draw towards a Premium FVG or Old High?

Until the price reaches the Draw on Liquidity, you will have to stick towards the idea of it trading towards it.

You don't want to flip flop back and forth between your Draw on Liquidity idea.

INTERMARKET ANALYSIS (SMT):

In Intermarket analysis we use SMT divergence.

SMT Divergence serves as a confirmation tool for identifying Accumulation/ Distribution phases in trading. It is not typically used as an entry pattern on its own. By observing SMT Divergence, traders can gain insights into potential Stop Hunts in the market and make more informed decisions.

WHICH PAIR TO CHOOSE FOR TRADING?

As traders, we need activity in the markets, volatility is what makes trading easier. The news plays a significant role in contributing to market activity, so we typically start the trading day by checking the economic calendar.

◄ This Week: Jul 23 - Jul 29 ►					► Up Next	Q Search Events			▼
Date	8:38pm	Currency	Impact		Detail	Actual	Forecast	Previous	Graph
Sun Jul 23	All Day	EUR	▦	Spanish Parliamentary Election	🗐				
Mon Jul 24	3:15am)))	EUR	▦	French Flash Manufacturing PMI	🗐	44.5	46.1	46.0◄	▥
	)))	EUR	▦	French Flash Services PMI	🗐	47.4	48.5	48.0	▥
	3:30am)))	EUR	▦	German Flash Manufacturing PMI	🗐	38.8	40.9	40.6◄	▥
	)))	EUR	▦	German Flash Services PMI	🗐	52.0	53.2	54.1	▥
	4:00am)))	EUR	▦	Flash Manufacturing PMI	🗐	42.7	43.5	43.4◄	▥
	)))	EUR	▦	Flash Services PMI	🗐	51.1	51.7	52.0◄	▥
	4:30am)))	GBP	▦	Flash Manufacturing PMI	🗐	45.0	46.1	46.5◄	▥
	)))	GBP	▦	Flash Services PMI	🗐	51.5	53.1	53.7	▥
	9:45am)))	USD	▦	Flash Manufacturing PMI	🗐	49.0	46.1	46.3	▥
	)))	USD	▦	Flash Services PMI	🗐	52.4	54.0	54.4◄	▥

However, it's essential to note that if there's a scheduled news release on the GBP (British Pound), it doesn't automatically imply that GBPUSD will be more preferable than EURUSD, for example. Market dynamics are influenced by various factors, and it's crucial to consider technical analysis, market sentiment, and so on before making a trading decision.

The logic is that pairs that are closely correlated with each other are likely to move in a symmetrical manner.

However, during the formation of SMT divergences, one of the pairs will display strength or weakness, signaling an approaching high volatility for that particular pair.

For instance, if GBPUSD reaches a new high, while EURUSD fails to do so (showing weakness), it suggests a potential trading opportunity. In this scenario, one may consider opening short positions on EURUSD.

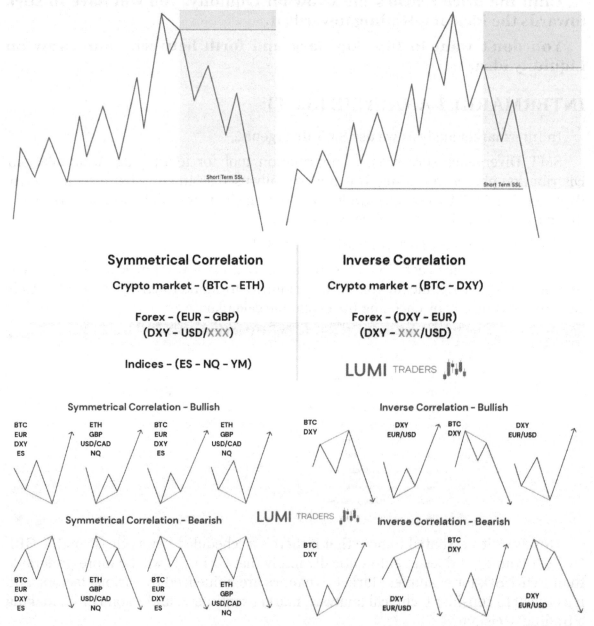

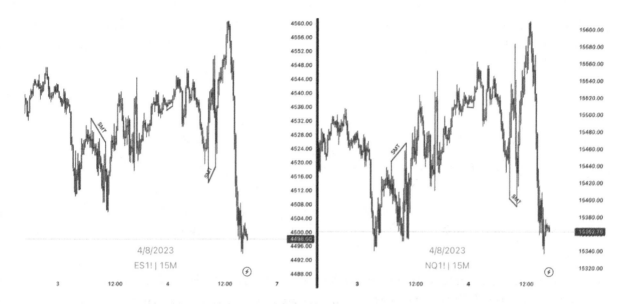

Premium: If BTCUSD or ETHUSD in premium fails to make a new higher high it presents a divergence in price.

Discount: If BTCUSD or ETHUSD in discount fails to make a new lower low it presents a divergence in price.

SMT Divergence is a crack in correlation between two closely correlated pairs like EUR/USD & GBP/USD. If the Fiber is making a lower low, while the Cable is making a higher low, this is bullish for the pairs. If the Fiber is making a higher high, while the Cable is making a lower high, this is bearish for the pairs. The same applies if you switch the pairs.

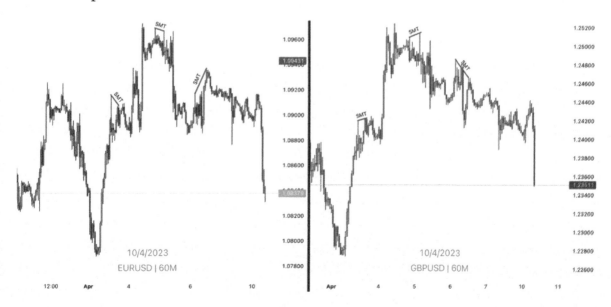

You are not looking for SMT divergence to take a trade, you use it only around predetermined levels with trade idea in mind. Then once pattern unfolds that is the green light to get into the trade.

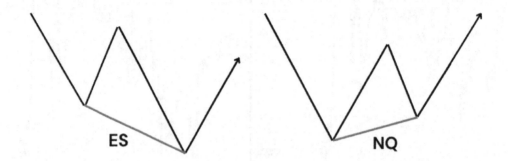

In this scenario we were looking for a long setup. ES made a new LL and NQ made a HL. This indicates more strength on NQ hence why we want to long NQ instead of ES

114

However, it is important to note that SMT Divergence should be used in conjunction with a clear understanding of the market's direction. Utilizing SMT as a confirmation tool follows the principle of analyzing time and price theory to enhance trading accuracy and effectiveness.

> **SMT Divergence is used as a Confirmation for Accumulation/Distribution.**
> **SMT Divergence is NOT used an Entry Pattern.**
> **SMT Divergence is the key to identifying and trusting Stop Hunts.**
> **You have to need to know where the market is heading, then use SMT for confirmation following that bias.**
>
> **SMT MUST OCCUR FOLLOWING TIME & PRICE THEORY.**

Trading on Smaller Time Frames and Looking for Liquidity Pools

ICT mentions using a one/two-minute chart for his analysis. This shorter time frame allows for a more detailed view of price action and can help traders make more precise trading decisions. However, it is important to note that trading on smaller time frames also comes with its own set of challenges, such as increased volatility and noise. Therefore, it is important to have a solid understanding of technical analysis and market dynamics to effectively trade on smaller time frames.

One concept that traders should be aware of when trading on smaller time frames is the concept of liquidity pools. A liquidity pool refers to an area on the chart where there is a concentration of buy or sell orders. These areas often act as magnets for price and can provide profitable trading opportunities.

A liquidity pool refers to areas in the market where there is a high probability of resting buy and sell orders. These pools are often targeted by traders to take advantage of price movements. Liquidity pools can be found on various timeframes, such as 5-minute, 15-minute, and hourly charts. Traders often look for these pools to identify potential trade opportunities and manage their positions accordingly, such as taking profits or adjusting stop-loss orders.

Validation: When the low is violated, or price moves below the recent low - the Sell Stops become Market Orders to Sell at Market. This injects Sell Side Liquidity into the Market - typically paired with Smart Money Buyers. Or when the high is violated, or price moves above the recent High – the Buy Stops into the Market – typically paired with Smart Money Sellers.

Entry Techniques: When underlying asset is Bullish: before price trades under the recent low - place a Buy Limit Order just below or at the recent Low. You are buying the sell stops like a interbank trader, or any other "Smart Money" entity would.

When underlying asset is Bearish: before price trades above the recent high - place a sell limit order just above or at the recent high. You are Selling the buy stops like a interbank trader, or any other "Smart Money" entity would.

Reinforcing liquidity pools refers to the concept of identifying areas in the market where there is a concentration of orders, which can be used to define risk in trading. As a trader, you want to trade in low resistance conditions, meaning there should be minimal resistance in the path of profitability.

It is important to understand that every time when the market makes a new range, mark the high and the new low and you'll be trading in the range, so if you trade at a bearish order block that is going to be a return to internal range liquidity but you're going to be looking for external range liquidity to exit on. ICT's entries are mostly entries on internal liquidity and exits on external liquidity. Once you understand where the HTF wants to go you can frame your setups to lower timeframe.

We can run external range liquidity on the daily, but on the monthly it can still be internal. When we understand where the weekly and monthly are willing to trade to, on the daily it creates a recipe for low resistance liquidity runs. This means when we expect a high to be taken because of the monthly and weekly bias, then these highs are a low resistance liquidity run. Because price has an agenda. So, with this idea we can classify whether it's a high resistance or low resistance liquidity run.

If we know that the higher time frame is bullish, our mind switches to: "well, where are the sell stops, they are aiming for?" Because if it wants to go higher and it drops, we look for external range liquidity. And as soon as we trade below that level and it gives a quick reaction and sees institutional sponsorship, look for a bullish OB.

Key times to trade: Mark the highs and lows for

- 2am-5am - London session

- 7am-10am – New York session

- 8pm-12am - Asia session

Best time to trade this model is from 8:30am to 11:00am EST. Wait for 1:30pm if you're going to trade the PM session.

At 8:30am EST look for old highs or old low to be swept, then wait for the model.

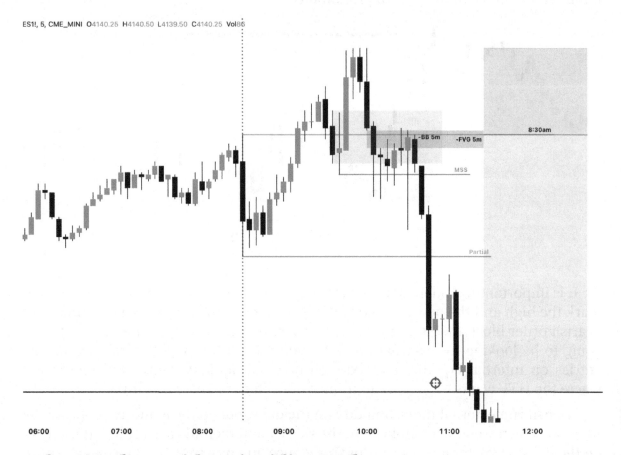

False Breakout with a Liquidity Pool

Definition: Under the low, which is below the current move of the market price, there are usually stop losses of traders with long positions. Or sell limit orders by traders who want to breakout a short position. Above the high, which is above the current move of the market price, there are usually stop losses of traders with short positions. Or buy limit orders by traders who want to breakout a long position.

Confirmation: When the low is broken, the price moves below the recent low - sell stops become market sell orders in the market. This brings Sell Side Liquidity into the market - usually paired with smart money buyers.

When the high is broken, the price moves above the recent high - buy stops become market buy orders on the market. This brings Buy Side Liquidity into the market - usually paired with smart money sellers.

Entry Methods: When the underlying asset is bullish: before the price trades below the recent low, place a buy limit order just below or at the level of the recent low. You buy sell stops just like a bank trader or any other smart money entity would.

When the underlying asset is bearish: before the price trades above the recent high, place a sell limit order just above or at the level of the recent high. You sell buy stops just like a bank trader or any other smart money entity would.

A false breakout refers to a situation where the market appears to break above an old high, but it's actually a false break, and smart money traders sell into it, expecting the market to reverse.

This is often done in the form of a run on liquidity or a liquidity pool. To trade this setup, you need to identify the low and place a buy limit order just below or at the recent low, essentially buying the sell stops like a interbank trader or smart money entity would. Defining the risk with this setup requires you to see the low and determine how far it could reasonably trade below it. It's essential to look for clear signs in the chart, such as a fair value gap, a shift in market structure, and a liquidity pool, to avoid gambling and ensure you're trading with a proper strategy.

Profit Taken With Buy Stops Raided

Old Low
Liquidity Pool

Price Trades Under Old Low
Sell Stop Raid

Accumulation of SSL for long positions and distribution of long positions to BSL.

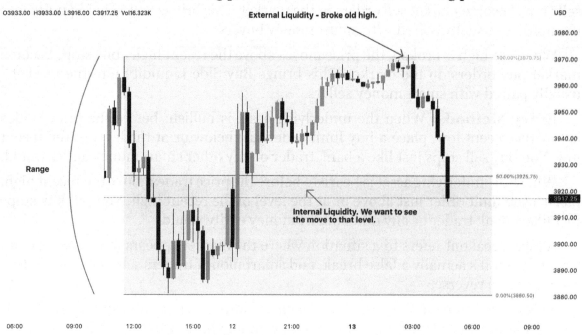

O3933.00 H3933.00 L3916.00 C3917.25 Vol16.323K

USD

External Liquidity - Broke old high.

100.00% (3970.75)

Range

50.00% (3925.75)

3917.25

Internal Liquidity. We want to see the move to that level.

0.00% (3880.50)

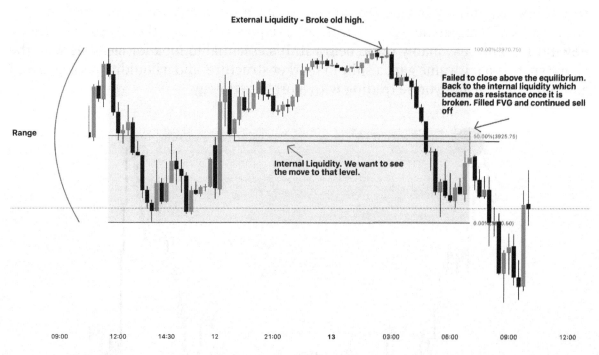

External Liquidity - Broke old high.

100.00% (3970.75)

Failed to close above the equilibrium. Back to the internal liquidity which became as resistance once it is broken. Filled FVG and continued sell off

Range

50.00% (3925.75)

Internal Liquidity. We want to see the move to that level.

0.00% (3880.50)

Each time the market forms a new range, mark a high and a new low and you will be trading in a range, so if you trade bearish Order Block (OB), it will be a return to the internal range liquidity but you will be looking for external range liquidity to exit. ICT entries are mainly internal liquidity entries and external liquidity exits. Once you understand where the price wants to move on the HTF, you can plan your setups on the LTF. It can take external range liquidity on a daily basis, but on a monthly basis it can remain internal.

When we understand where the weekly and monthly prices are willing to trade, a recipe is created on the daily charts to take low resistance liquidity. Thus, when we expect a high to be made due to the monthly and weekly bias, then these highs represent low resistance liquidity withdrawals.

So, with this idea, we can classify whether this is a high or low resistance liquidity withdrawal:

You want to buy with internal range liquidity or bullish OB inside the previous range and try to take profits at or above the old external high.

Trading Off Liquidity Levels

To properly illustrate a level of liquidity where an opportunity to buy or sell may be present, simply draw a horizontal line from the latest wick or swing high/low and extend it all the way until it intersects with price again.

In this ES hourly chart I present below, I randomly selected over a month worth of trading the ES, with a blue line drawn if the liquidity level led to a break of the market structure (via higher highs or lower lows) or a red line if the retest of the liquidity level occurs amid a failure of a break in market structure.

I assume an entry strategy based on trading off liquidity levels for a 2:1 risk to reward with a stop half the size of the previous swing low/high (making it more difficult to reach the stop before an opportunity to move to break even), a move to break even at 1:1 (it comes down to one's own discretion), and with the pre-condition of a previous breakout of the market structure by printing higher highs or lower lows in the hourly chart.

Trades as Liquidity Level that fail without a previous BOS
Trades as Liquidity Level that fail with a previous BOS
Trades as Liquidity Level that succeed without a previous BOS
Trades as Liquidity Level that succeed with a previous BOS

By the end of the exercise, it should be abundantly clear how engaging in buy/sell trades with the pre-condition of a breakout of a market structure carries much greater chances of success (blue lines) as opposed to entering against the dominant market structure (red line). If you had only traded at the liquidity levels in blue, as I initially suggested to maximize one's odds of success, it would have led to potentially 6 winners for 2:1 risk to reward and 1 loser.

Combine this with additional confluences such as trading with the dominant market cycle in HTF, aligning with fundamentals, a mechanical risk management, awareness of news events, and this might well be a strategy that may suit your style. It's now your time to find out, through your own backtesting, whether or not this is a methodology worth exploring further to make it your own.

To conclude, when we talk about high levels of liquidity, we're talking about a situation where trading activity is off the charts. It's like a bustling marketplace where everyone and their cousin is buying and selling. This happens when there's a massive demand for an asset, and at the same time, a lot of folks ready to supply it. With so many players in the game, finding a buyer or seller is a piece of cake.

So, remember this: high liquidity equals a wild trading frenzy with lots of buyers and sellers, while low liquidity means things are slow and sluggish with a limited number of players.

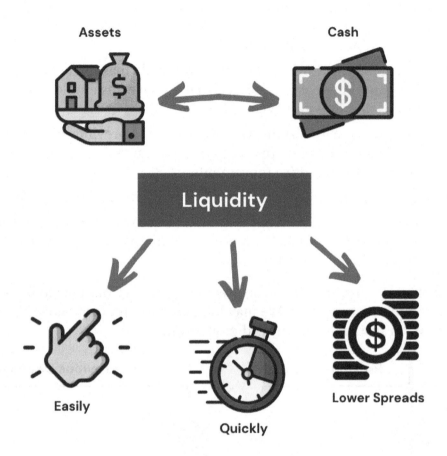

Daily Bias

Determining the daily bias in trading is not about establishing a preconceived bias before the market commences trading, as this approach can often prove to be inaccurate.

Instead, it relies on experience and adherence to specific rules.

For instance, adopting a bullish stance does not equate to purchasing assets every day, nor does embracing a bearish outlook necessitate daily selling. Traders must exercise patience, waiting for distinct conditions to align with their expectations. This involves seeking discounted arrays for bullish trades and premium arrays for bearish trades, all within designated timeframes.

Furthermore, the economic calendar can be effectively employed alongside the daily chart to foresee potential manipulation linked to high-impact news catalysts.

Ultimately, determining the daily bias demands the amalgamation of diverse insights acquired through mentorship and hands-on experience.

One of the key factors in determining daily bias is the previous day's high and low. These levels act as reference points that help traders gauge the strength of the current trend and anticipate potential price movements.

Here, I will demonstrate how to determine the daily bias using both the Previous Day's High (PDH) and Previous Day's Low (PDL), as well as employing the Previous Week's High (PWH) and Previous Week's Low (PWL).

One of the key factors in determining daily bias is the previous day's high and low. These levels act as reference points that help traders gauge the strength of the current trend and anticipate potential price movements.

Previous day highs and lows can also serve as liquidity pools for reversals.

- If the price reaches the previous day's high but fails to break above it, this can indicate a reversal. We may look for entry points to go short as the price is unable to sustain its upward momentum.

- Similarly, if the price reaches the previous day's low but fails to break below it, this can indicate a reversal. We may look for entry points to go long as the price is unable to sustain its downward momentum.

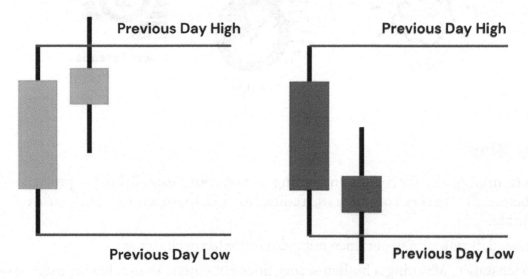

Reversals can be framed off Previous Day High and Previous Day Low when there is a failure to displace.

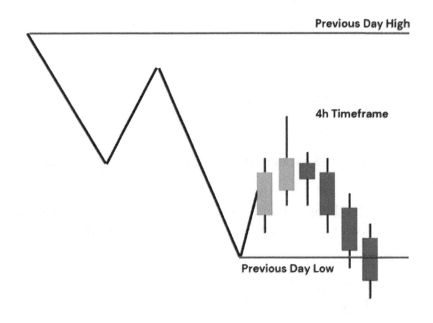

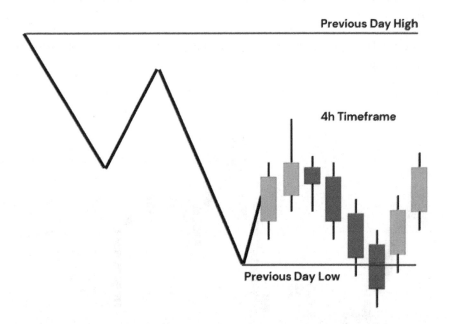

In the example above, Previous Day Low used as a draw on liquidity and being used to frame a reversal.

Let's begin by analyzing some examples to see how previous day high and low can act as liquidity pools for reversals:

1. Example 1:

- We start with an uptrend, where price is trending upwards.

- The previous day high becomes our draw on liquidity, indicating that price is likely to reach for this level.

- If price fails to close above the previous day high, it suggests a potential reversal.

- In this case, we would expect price to reach for the previous day low as the next draw on liquidity.

- By analyzing the displacement and closure of price in relation to the previous day high and low, we can frame a narrative for a potential reversal.

2. Example 2:

- In a downtrend, the previous day low becomes our draw on liquidity, indicating that price is likely to reach for this level.

- If price fails to close below the previous day low, it suggests a potential reversal.

- We can also use swing points in the market as additional liquidity pools for reversals.

- By observing the displacement and closure of price, we can identify potential reversal points.

125

Previous Week High and Low

Previous Week High and Low are liquidity levels that can be used as a draw on liquidity (DOL) or frame a reversal or continuation.

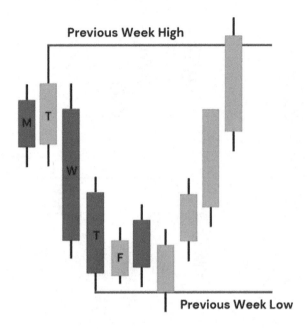

NQ1!, 1D, CME O15198.50 H15218.25 L15063.25 C15187.00 Vol609.953K

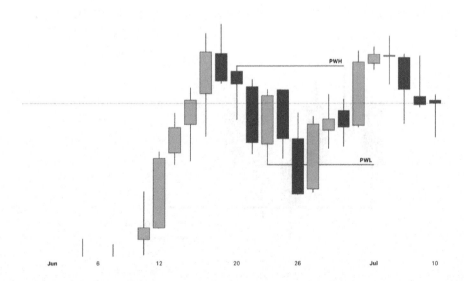

Swing Point

Swing points in the market can be used as a DOL or be used to frame a reversal.

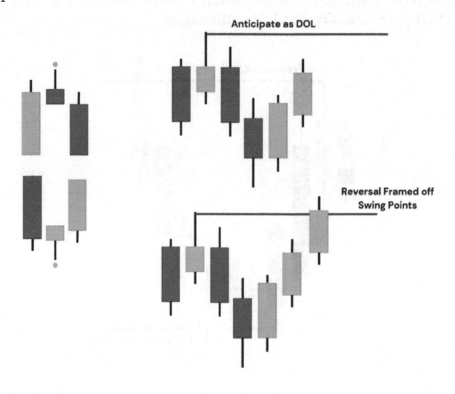

[credit to @TTrades_edu]

Failure to displace over old highs and lows can be used to frame a reversal.

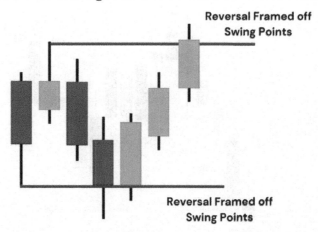

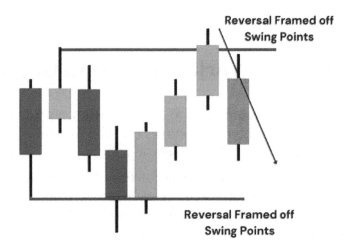

Reversal Framed off Swing Points

Reversal Framed off Swing Points

When price respects a PD array or fails to displace over a swing high or low, the next candle can be anticipated.

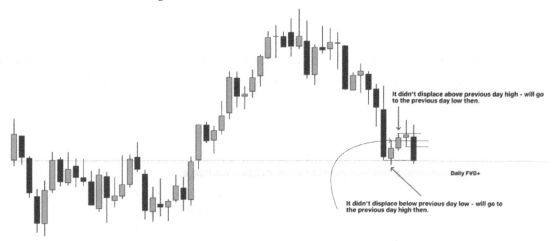

It didn't displace above previous day high - will go to the previous day low then.

Daily FVG+

It didn't displace below previous day low - will go to the previous day high then.

Chapter 13

Power Of 3 & New York PM Session Opportunities

Power 3, also known as accumulation, manipulation, and distribution, is a key concept in trading. It refers to the three phases that the market goes through before a significant price move. Let's break down each phase:

1. Accumulation: This is the first phase of Power 3, where market participants accumulate positions in anticipation of a future price increase. During this phase, prices may consolidate or trade in a range as traders position themselves for the next move.

2. Manipulation: The second phase of Power 3 involves market manipulation. In this phase, traders with large positions use various techniques to influence the price in their favor. This manipulation can create false moves or fake runs, such as the Judas swing.

3. Distribution: The final phase of Power 3 is distribution, where market participants who accumulated positions in the first phase start to distribute or sell their holdings.

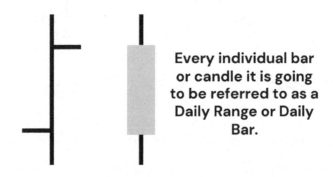

Every individual bar or candle it is going to be referred to as a Daily Range or Daily Bar.

The Power of Three, as described by Inner Circle Trader (ICT), is a trading concept that encompasses three essential phases in the financial markets: accumulation, manipulation, and distribution.

Power Of 3 are candle/bar formation stages that are relevant for all timeframes, especially used with daily and weekly trading ranges, where the opening price is considered to be the beginning of the period.

For intraday trading, it is enough for us to use the weekly and daily power of three, but you should also pay attention to the monthly candlestick, since points of interest on higher timeframes increase the chances of success.

WEEKLY POWER OF THREE

The logic of the weekly PO3 is useful for building a trading bias (Bias), that is, choosing a direction.

Bullish Bias: Expect a move below the opening at the beginning of the week, which would be a weekly manipulation (Judas Swing).

The week low is usually formed between Monday and Wednesday, most often on Tuesday or Wednesday.

If the price returns back below the opening level after it left it, then; reversal scenario is possible.

Tuesday Low of the Week

Bearish Bias

Expect a move above the open at the beginning of the week, which would be a weekly manipulation (Judas Swing).

The weekly high is usually formed between Monday and Wednesday, most often on Tuesday or Wednesday.

If the price returns back above the opening level after it left it, then a reversal scenario is possible.

Wednesday High of the Week

DAILY POWER OF THREE

The opening level is used to determine the profitable zone for opening long and short positions.

Manipulation (Judas Swing) - wait for the liquidity capture to complete before

131

making a decision.

Expansion is a movement from which we try to benefit.

Distribution is an area in which we take profits.

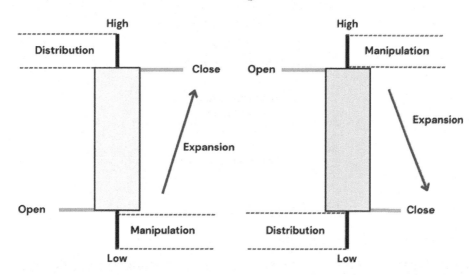

In Accumulation phase, we see consolidation where lot of liquidity is generated and then we see a fake rally to clear all the liquidity and market shifts the structure and moves. In order to understand that you need to have directional bias. For example, "I'm Bullish & I'm waiting for market to go little bit lower and retrace into higher timeframe price delivery array after clearing liquidity pool(s) and shifts structure on timeframe that you're looking at according to your own trading style (day trader, short term trader or scalper).

Accumulation refers to the initial phase of market activity, where large institutional players, known as "smart money," strategically accumulate positions. During this phase, price action tends to be range-bound, with low volatility and relatively small price movements. Smart money takes advantage of this period to build substantial positions at favorable prices, often by absorbing selling pressure from retail traders.

After accumulating their desired positions, smart money moves into the Manipulation phase. Here, they create deceptive market moves to lure in retail traders and investors. This phase involves a variety of techniques, such as false breakouts, stop runs, and fakeouts, designed to trap traders on the wrong side of the market. These manipulative tactics induce panic or excitement among retail participants, leading them to make emotional trading decisions.

Once smart money has executed their desired trades and manipulated the market, the distribution phase begins. During this stage, smart money starts to unwind their positions and distribute them to retail traders and investors who are typically late to recognize the change in market dynamics. The price action may exhibit signs of exhaustion or reversal, as smart money takes profits and begins to exit their positions.

The Interbank Price Delivery Algorithm moves from consolidation periods to expansion periods and in-between these two periods Manipulation will happen to take out retail buy or sell stops before the real expansion move.

Daily Range Structure:

Price Equilibrium
Manipulation
Expansion
Reversal
Retracement
Consolidation

Price Equilibrium - Asian range.

Manipulation - this will always happen through some kind of news event, news driver. During manipulation or right before it. This is Judas Swing.

Expansion - In other words, this is when a high or low is formed. It will drop before 5:00 AM NY or goes up before that time (depending on the daily direction of the price, we will use the buy day perspective). This means that the Asian range has a slight consolidation and then after midnight NY there is a drop in price - a manipulation that makes a false move to the low.

Expansion

Expansion is when price moves quickly from a level of Equilibrium.
This shows a willingness from the Market Makers to reprice to the next objective.
If markets start from a Consolidation, a Displacement will be used to break out of the Consolidation.
Price will then print an Order Block whilst breaking out of the Consolidation.
The Order Block will be found near or at the Equilibrium of the Consolidation.

LUMI TRADERS

Expansion

Then the market moves to **Reversal**. A classic scenario for a London opening. When the market goes down, taking stops and then it expands again - **Expansion**. Until what time? - **Until 5am NY**.

Reversal

Reference Point in Institutional Order Flow: Liquidity Pool

Reversal is when Price completely reverses its current trend established.
Reversals occur at Liquidity Pools.
Bullish Liquidity Pools are found under old lows.
Bearish Liquidity Pools are found above old highs.

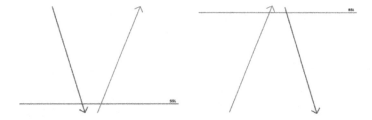

Between 5:00 AM and 8:00 AM EST, during this time frame, the market will return to **Consolidation**.

Consolidation

Reference Point in Institutional Order Flow: Equilibrium

Consolidations occur when the price is constricted by a trading range and has no willingness to break out yet.
Consolidations show us that the Market Makers are building liquidity above and below the market.
We can anticipate Expansions to occur after Consolidation.
Be patient and look for a Displacement away from the Equilibrium price point of the Consolidation.

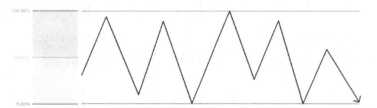

Then there will be a **Retracement** pullback, between 8:00am and 8:30am EST.

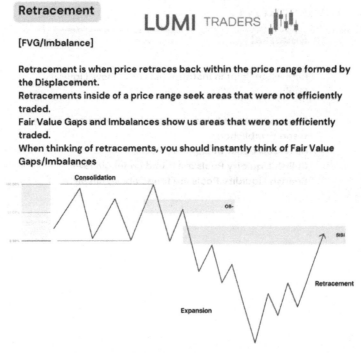

Then there will be either a **Reversal** in the NY session, or an **Expansion move**. The range will widen over the rest of the day, going up to 10:00am or 11:00am EST then the **Reversal** is back (that's the London close).

The market will enter **Consolidation**, ending at the end of the day around 16:00 EST.

We can see the interbank price delivery algorithm on a daily basis by studying these events and viewing them on charts. And we will know what is most likely to happen.

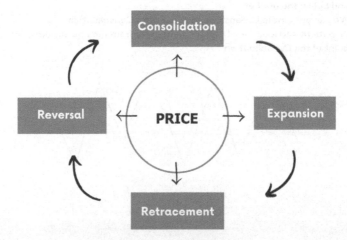

So, we must understand that everything starts with Consolidation.
*Nothing can happen without consolidation. It occurs when the market is calm. This is important because when orders pile up in the market, MMs allow orders to build above and below the range.

The next stage is always **Expansion**. This is not a pullback and not a reversal. That is, after consolidation there is always an impulse movement.

We determine what kind of movement it is and in what direction it is. Once we have an Expansion, we have a choice:

- there may be a **Retracement** pullback (we can return to the order block it just left and then make another move up or down, depending on the direction in which it moves).

- or maybe a **Reversal**.

Once it reversed, there might be another **Expansion move**. It will then return to Consolidation.

***Again, **Consolidation** cannot be followed by **Retracement** or **Reversal**.

Consolidation is always followed by **Expansion**. After **Expansion** comes either **Retracement** or **Reversal**.

***The market **does NOT** do **Consolidation -> Expansion -> Consolidation**.

It does: **Consolidation -> Expansion -> Retracement** (before order block and resumption of movement) OR **Consolidation -> Expansion -> Reversal.**

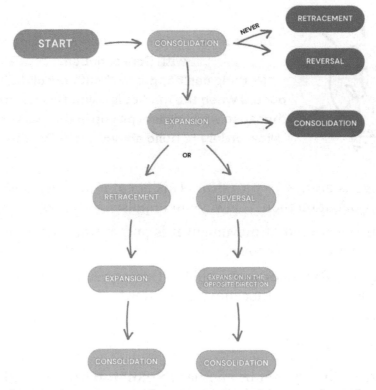

There are only certain processes that must occur in a certain order.

General structure:

Consolidation - Asian session -> **Expansion** -> **Reversal** - in the London session by making the high or low of the day -> **Expansion** -> Small **Consolidation** - New York -> **Retracement** - between 8 - 8:30 am -> **Expansion** -> **Reversal** -> and again **Consolidation**

The same happens with the weekly range:

1. Opening Sunday - Consolidation

2. Monday - Expansion move

3. Monday/Tuesday - Reversal

4. Other expansion move

5. Midweek - Consolidation

6. Reversal or Retracement

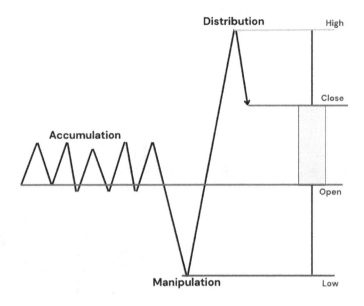

If bullish then you're looking for manipulation to happen under the midnight opening price. When manipulation occurs, this is where smart money is accumulating long positions.

To confirm the manipulation move you need to see a market structure shift & price needs to get back and stay above or below the midnight opening price depending on if it's bullish or bearish.

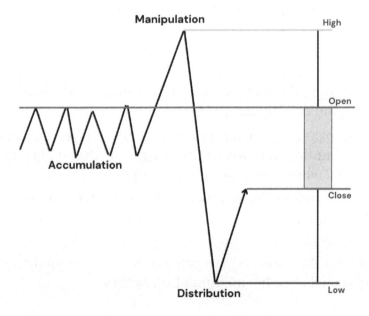

If bearish you're looking for manipulation to happen above the midnight opening price. When manipulation occurs, this is where smart money is accumulating short positions.

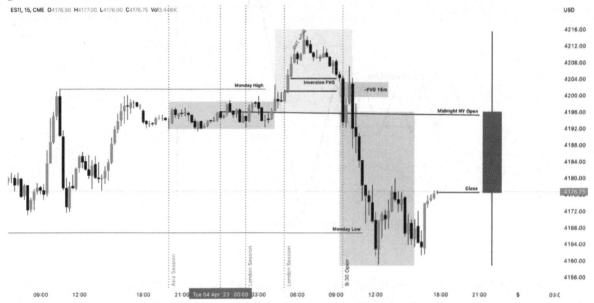

Once price is back below or above the midnight opening price you can expect distribution/expansion move to the next draw on liquidity.

We also can see it as a consolidation being the Accumulation, and then Manipulation of the lows, and then Distribution phase when we go back above the range. Why? The reason for the Accumulation phase is for the market makers to enter as many orders as they would like.

Then comes the Manipulation phase, here the market makers are going to enter the last bit of their order before taking the price to their target, they will stop all the retail traders out, flooding the market with market orders, which the market makers will buy out entirely, and directly take us to the opposite direction.

How to apply? For example, when a daily candle open, if you expect it to be bullish, then we should start hunting liquidity to the down side after daily open, and you can consider price oversold while it is under the daily open.

Then, you will start to look for points of interest (POI) and your entry model to enter a long and look for targets above the daily open.

Or you can just look for a consolidation, and then look for POI & targets below & above the consolidation to decide where price is destined to go, then based on that, look for your entry model once the manipulation occurs.

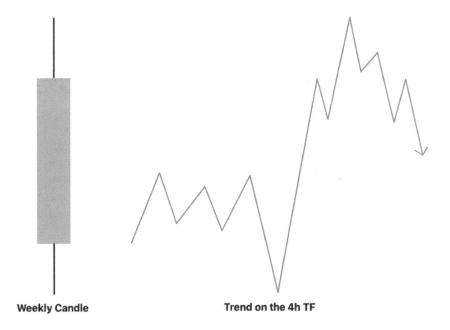

Weekly Candle   **Trend on the 4h TF**

On the diagram you see a weekly full-bodied candle. On a lower timeframe, this will be a side trend (price moves in the range).

We will consider this example through the prism of a weekly candle, so it will be easiest to understand the logic of this concept. Until distribution begins, the price accumulates, that is, big capital collects its position. This is usually shown on the chart as a sideways move, it can also look like a descending or ascending channel. A position can accumulate for both longs and shorts.

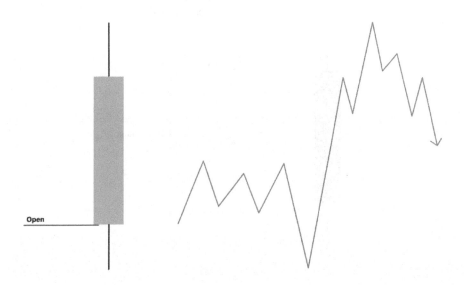

Open

The bottom line is where a week opens, the price starts trading near the opening for several days, after which it moves in the opposite direction to mislead traders, and the final stage will be distribution.

* Looking only at the weekly candle, you will be able to predict the future direction of the price, at least for next week.

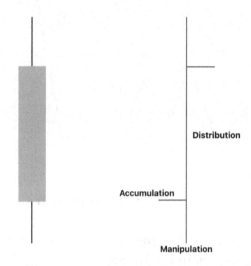

When the weekly candle opens, we want to see consolidation. After that, manipulation, and distribution. In the first days of the opening of the candle, all trading occurs near the opening of the candle. Further, manipulation takes place, on the weekly timeframe it will look like a wick. The final phase is the expansion and closing of the candle.

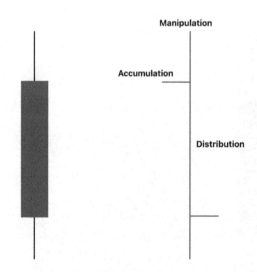

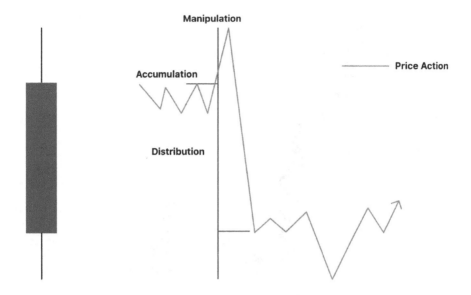

The bearish example works in exactly the same way, but in a mirror image. We will also have Accumulation near the opening of this candle. Then the rise, which is actually Manipulation to get traders to trade in the wrong direction. And the last step is distribution. Which we can understand as the distribution of a large player of his/her position to ordinary retail traders.

So, on the weekly chart above, we have SSL. Also, the previous 2 weeks have equal lows - that's the target. Let's see what happened next.

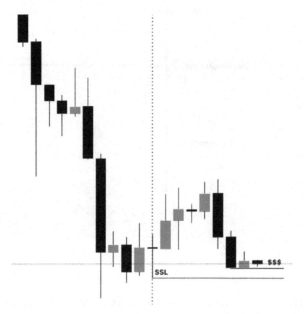

New week opens – price started consolidating. After that, it tested EQL and took SSL.

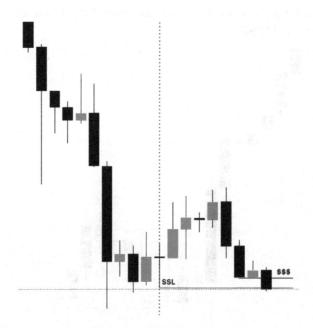

After the liquidity pool was taken, the price began to go up. This works on absolutely all TFs. See for yourself on the chart.

AND NOW THE SAME SITUATION, BUT ON THE LTF:

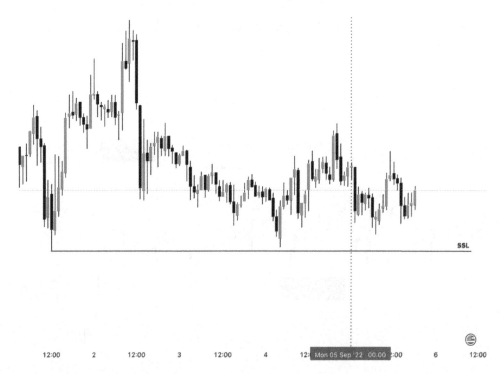

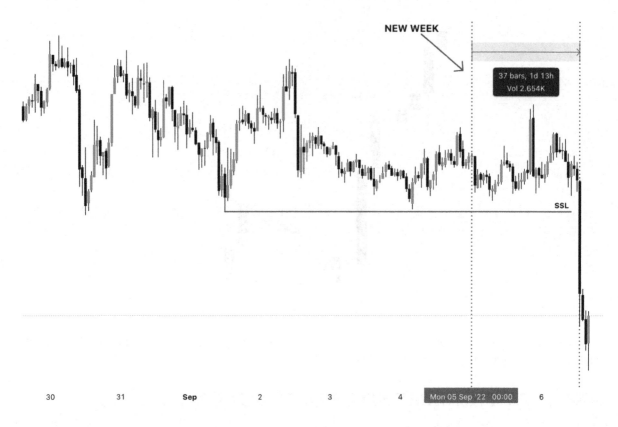

But here it is important that the accumulation began last week, this can be seen on the 1hr timeframe.

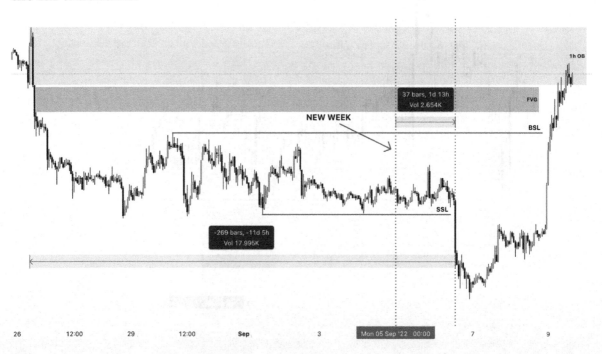

After the manipulation, an aggressive move occurs. This is done so that no one can enter and buy long on highs, and a major player at this time is selling the position. After that, greedy traders who experience FOMO remain in the red again.

Opening Price

"Initial Value Price – Prior to Imbalance"

Opening price is the initial value price – prior to any imbalance.

Closing Price

"Ending Value Price – Prior to Imbalance"

Range Expansion

"Dynamic Price Imbalance"

The portion that makes range between the open and close is referred to as range expansion and this is a dynamic price imbalance.

Accumulation
"Long Position Built Up"

Opening price just above it or below it when we're bullish, that's where longs are accumulated. Who's accumulating those long positions? Smart money.

Manipulation
"Engineering Short Liquidity"

When we're bullish and we're anticipating a bullish range expansion to the upside or higher close, we would be hunting a manipulation cycle immediately after the open price. Immediately below the opening price on the daily range when it's bullish, this initial drop down is very significant because it's going to engineer willing parties to sell short. That selling short will flood the market with the counterparties to smart money wanting to buy it at a deep discount.

Manipulation
"Neutralizing Long Liquidity"

That means there are individuals who have probably already entered long positions either at or just recently near the opening price. When the price drops below the opening price, it can upset their long positions. In other words, it appears to hit their stop-loss levels not to facilitate a new lower entry but to force them out of their initially well-placed positions.

We are observing two conditions occurring simultaneously: First, when the market opens at a price below the prior session's closing, some bullish traders are getting stopped out, even though their positions could have been profitable if the market rallied. Second, this situation is inducing a short-term shift in sentiment, turning some traders bearish, as they see the market breaking below short-term lows.

This sequence of events not only clears out long positions from traders using stop-loss orders, but it also tricks some short-sellers into entering their positions at unfavorable moments, during an overall bullish market.

Manipulation
"Sell Stops Paired With Buy Interest"

Finally, as we interpret this, the manipulation is we're looking how the market makers pair orders by pairing these sell stops with smart money buying interest, we can see the manipulation cycle as it really is a run below the opening to accumulate long positions before the big up move.

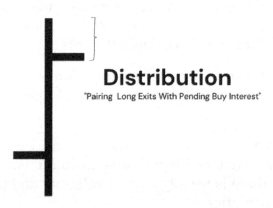

Distribution
"Pairing Long Exits With Pending Buy Interest"

The distribution cycle involves smart money strategically pairing their long exits by selling to those who show pending buy interest. The pending buy interest usually manifests as traders looking to buy above a previous high, anticipating a breakout. These breakout enthusiasts perceive buying above a previous high as a display of strength, and they are keen on entering such positions.

At the same time, smart money aims to sell their long positions to these breakout artists who are willing to buy above the old high, or to those individuals attempting to sell short intraday but have a buy stop placed above the intraday high. Smart money's intention is to run the price through that intraday high, triggering those buy stops, and then selling their positions to them.

As the trading day progresses, if we witness a substantial retracement lower before the market closes, it suggests an area of distribution. This implies that the smart money is actively selling off their positions to the breakout traders and those with buy stops above the intraday high, thereby effectively distributing their holdings to other market participants.

Note, for equities (not Forex) typically when a big run up or down happens we often see a consolidation shortly after. When price takes out liquidity, it likes to take off, it did its job by taking people out of the market and it doesn't want to give retail another chance to get back in, so the entries will be subtle and sneaky.

The typical weekly market maker cycle looks like this:

1. The week starts with a trap move on Sunday night or early Monday morning.

2. The follows an 'accumulation phase' and the setting up of an initial high and an initial low in the Asia Session, during which price is usually held a narrow range.

3. The accumulation phase is followed by Judas Swing, an engineered false breakout against the real intention of the market maker to 'support or resistance levels' to harvest the retail traders' entry and stop loss orders there. The market maker considers these levels as 'liquidity pools'.

4. Next the market maker initiates the actual planned market move. This results in the formation if a trend that can be slow and steady, or it could be swift and furious.

London and New York Sessions: The London and New York trading sessions are considered the most active and liquid sessions in the Forex and Futures market. During these sessions, there is usually a lot of volatility and price movement, which can create trading opportunities.

Asian Session: The Asian session is generally less active than the London and New

149

York sessions, and price movements can be relatively muted. However, there may still be trading opportunities during this session, particularly for traders who focus on trading the major currency pairs.

End of Day Trading: ICT also recommends paying attention to end-of-day trading, which is the last hour of the New York trading session. During this time, there may be significant price movements as traders close out positions before the end of the day. This can create trading opportunities for traders who are looking to enter or exit positions.

> **Avoid Trading During Major News Releases: ICT advises traders to avoid trading during major news releases, such as central bank announcements or other economic data releases. These events can create unpredictable price movements and can be difficult to trade.**

Market Open: ICT suggests paying attention to the first 1-2 hours of each trading session, as this can often set the tone for the rest of the session. Traders should look for significant price movements and market reactions during this time, as these can provide valuable information for making trading decisions.

Overlapping Sessions: There are periods during the day when two trading sessions are open at the same time. For example, the overlap between the London and New York sessions is usually a time of high trading activity and can provide good trading opportunities. Traders should pay attention to the behavior of the market during these periods and look for trading opportunities based on the price action.

Quiet Periods: There may be times during the day when the market is relatively quiet, with little price movement or volatility. For example, the period between the close of the New York session and the open of the Asian session is often a quiet period. During these times, traders may want to avoid taking new positions and instead focus on managing existing positions.

End of Week Trading: ICT also suggests paying attention to end-of-week trading, as this can be a time when traders close out positions ahead of the weekend. Traders should be aware of potential liquidity issues and increased volatility during this time, as well as the potential for "weekend gaps" when the market reopens on Sunday.

Weekly Bias - Excellence In Short Term Trading

Mark the weekly opening price in your chart and extend it all the way to Friday. Leave it on your chart.

- We are looking for a power of three formation on the weekly range, so Accumulation (A), Manipulation (M) and Distribution (D).

- Look at the monthly and the weekly charts to see what you expect; are we going to move higher or lower?

- Weekly high/low is between Sunday and Wednesday (often before NY open - before 7 AM). On Tuesday ICT is really active looking at London open, because you want to buy or sell close to the weekly low/high.

Weekly smart money view for Bullish conditions:

Weekly low forms between Sunday and Wednesday. Odds increase between Tuesday and Wednesday. Focus on Tuesday Low until Wednesday NY. If it doesn't happen on Tuesday, anticipate it to happen on Wednesday.

If Wednesday puts in the low and we go lower, stand sideways on the day. Stop and submit to the fact you are wrong. It will happen, it happened to me.

Example (1h timeframe; we can see the entire weekly range).

Purple horizontal line = Sunday opening.

- We're bullish, so we wait for a drop down from the weekly opening price (which is the Judas Swing). If we rise from the opening, we're not interested. ICT doesn't trust the high set on Monday, he likes to see the Monday's range first to give him insights. If the week makes its low on Monday, he's missing that because he likes to sit on the sidelines. He looks for lower low on Tuesday or Wednesday at some key level.

- If we trade above the opening price on Tuesday/Wednesday, he permits Wednesday/Thursday a retracement back to weekly opening price as support before expanding higher.

- If we trade above the opening price on Wednesday, it should not come down to opening price. The algo wants to expend away after Wednesday, because it only has NY opening till Friday close. If it does, expect consolidation for the rest of the week or reversal.

Weekly smart money view for Bearish conditions:

- Weekly high forms between Sunday and Wednesday (often before NY open - before 7 AM). Odds increase between Tuesday and Wednesday. Focus on Tuesday London Open till Wednesday NY. If it doesn't happen on Tuesday, anticipate it to happen on Wednesday.

- Example (1h timeframe so we can see the entire weekly range). Purple horizontal line = Sunday opening. On Tuesday you see equal highs of Friday and Monday to be taken.

Note that when price expands away from weekly opening price, it doesn't come back.

Introduction to the Concept of Equilibrium and Discounts/ Premium in the Market

Another important concept related to Power of 3 is the idea of equilibrium and discounts/premium in the market. Let's explore this concept:

1. Equilibrium: In trading, equilibrium refers to a balanced state where supply and demand are relatively equal. It represents a fair value for an asset based on market dynamics. Understanding the concept of equilibrium can help traders assess whether an asset is overvalued or undervalued.

2. Discounts: When an asset is trading below its fair value or equilibrium, it is said to be trading at a discount. This presents an opportunity for traders to enter buys in the market at a favorable price. Identifying discount can help traders find potential buying opportunities.

3. Premium: When an asset is trading above its fair value or equilibrium, it is said to be trading at a premium. This presents an opportunity for traders to enter sells in the market at a favorable price. Identifying premium can help traders find potential selling opportunities.

"Judas Swing" is a term used in trading to describe a deceptive price move intended to shake out retail traders before the market turns in the desired direction. This manipulation tactic is commonly employed by larger players like institutions and banks to trigger stop-loss orders and accumulate positions at more favorable prices.

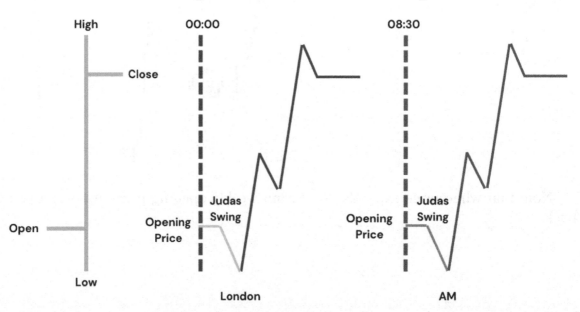

When Judas Swing Forms – Essentially is a stop raid that many times trades into:

1. Key Support and Resistance Level

2. Previous High or Low

3. Counter-Swing to Form OTE

4. Raid the Previous Week High or Low

5. Raid the Previous Session High or Low

6. Raiding Intrasession of High and Low.

1) If trading London Open, look for Asian stops to be raided.

2) If trading NY Session, identify 15 mins order flow, then you need to identify BSL/SSL before 9:30am indices.

Trading window period is from 9:30-10:00am NY time.

When significant market-moving news is released at 8:30am, it often means that there won't be a Judas Swing at 9:30am.

London Judas Swing

Look for an Asian range in a tight consolidation.

Look for an initial run-up/run-down that trips traders in. At this point, buy/sell stops are hit, and traders are now long/short on a breakout. Wait for the market to trade down/up below/above the Asian range low/high to take the stops. Anticipate a sweep of about 5-10points (ES) / 20-25points (NQ) or 10–20 pips.

The move below/above the opening price is the ICT Judas Swing. This is a bullish/bearish Judas Swing and creates the low/high of the day inside the London session.

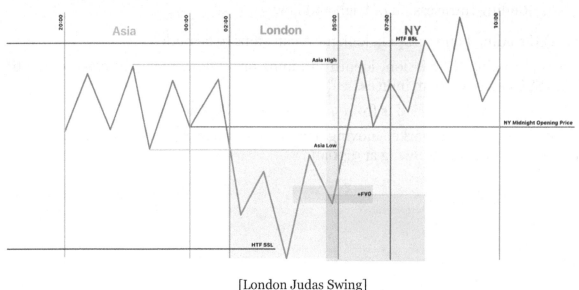

[London Judas Swing]

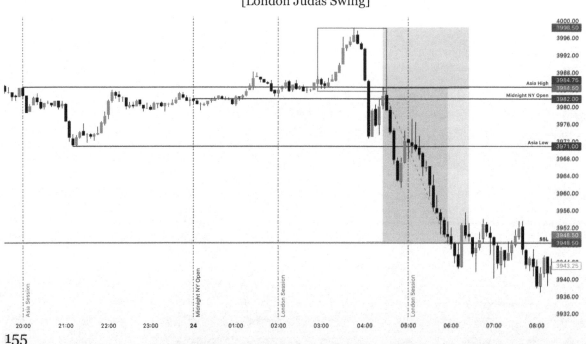

During the New York Session, there are two possible scenarios for a Judas Swing that we anticipate.

The first scenario occurs at 9:30am. In this case, we are looking for short-term SSL/BSL to be taken out, followed by an immediate reversal. As I mentioned earlier, the Judas Swing involves a fake move, so after it takes out the liquidity level, we want to see a reversal right from that point.

The second scenario applies only when we have news at 10:00am. When news is scheduled for 10:00am, we do not expect to see a Judas Swing at 9:30am. Instead, we wait between 10:00am and 10:10am for the liquidity level to be taken out, giving us the Judas Swing, followed by an immediate reversal. Typically, our target is the opposite liquidity level.

It's important to note that these scenarios are based on the concept of the Judas Swing as discussed by the Inner Circle Trader or other traders who utilize this strategy. As with any trading approach, it's crucial to conduct thorough analysis, manage risks effectively, and adapt the strategy to suit your individual trading style and goals.

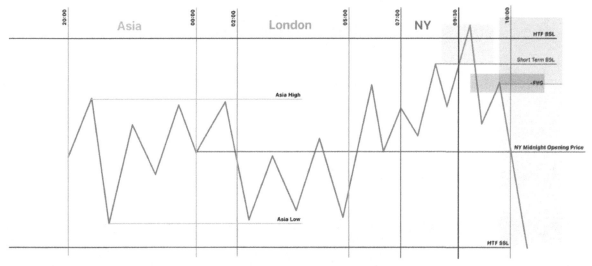

[New York Judas Swing]

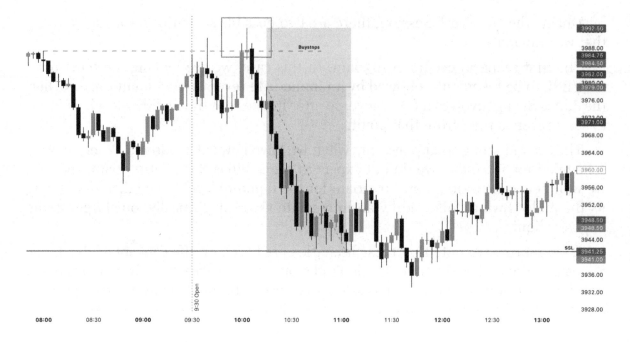

[New York Judas Swing]

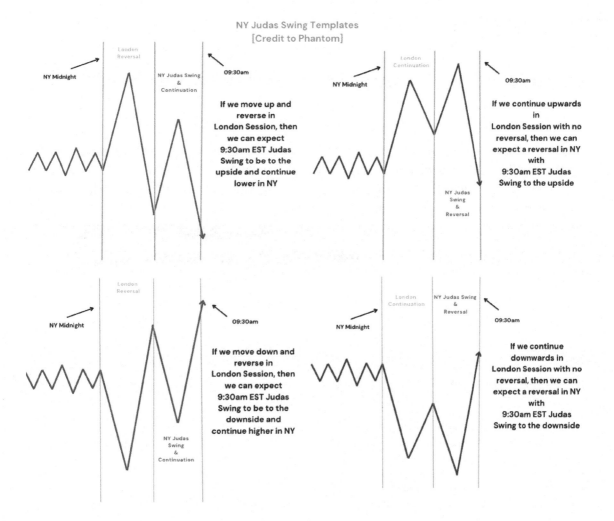

NY Judas Swing Templates
[Credit to Phantom]

If we move up and reverse in London Session, then we can expect 9:30am EST Judas Swing to be to the upside and continue lower in NY

If we continue upwards in London Session with no reversal, then we can expect a reversal in NY with 9:30am EST Judas Swing to the upside

If we move down and reverse in London Session, then we can expect 9:30am EST Judas Swing to be to the downside and continue higher in NY

If we continue downwards in London Session with no reversal, then we can expect a reversal in NY with 9:30am EST Judas Swing to the downside

Chapter 14

Implementing Economic Calendar Events With The Open

The economic calendar is an important tool for traders and speculators in the financial markets. It provides a schedule of important economic events, such as interest rate decisions, GDP releases, employment reports, and other key data points that can significantly impact market movements.

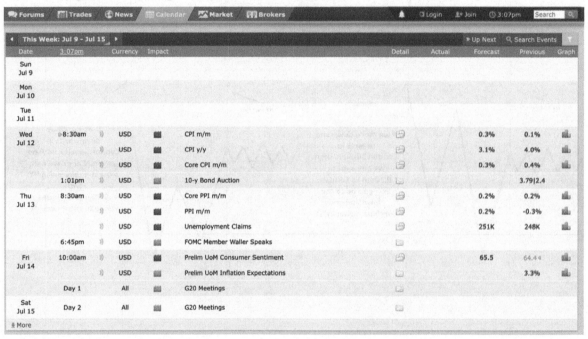

Understanding Potential Volatility and Unexpected Events

One of the primary reasons for studying the economic calendar is to anticipate and manage potential volatility in the markets. Economic events can have a profound impact on market sentiment and can cause significant price fluctuations. For example, an unexpected interest rate hike by the Central Bank can lead to a sharp sell-off in the stock market, while positive economic data can boost investor confidence and drive prices higher.

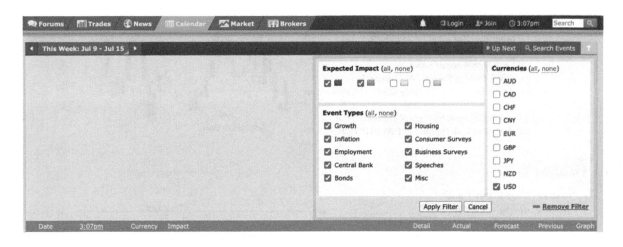

Red = High Impact Expected

Orange = Medium Impact Expected

Yellow = Low Impact Expected

The focus should be on High Impact and Medium Impact News Events. Low Impact Events are less significant.

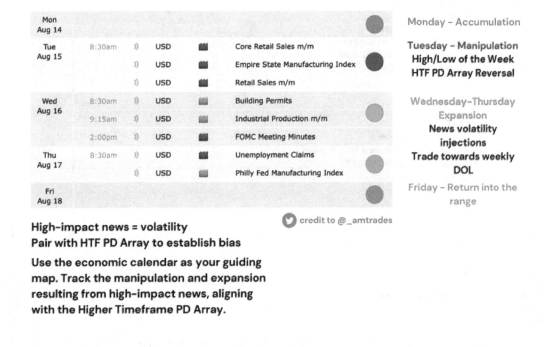

credit to @_amtrades

High-impact news = volatility
Pair with HTF PD Array to establish bias

Use the economic calendar as your guiding map. Track the manipulation and expansion resulting from high-impact news, aligning with the Higher Timeframe PD Array.

MONDAY

- Monday – Not Ideal to Day Trade
- Weekly Open
- Lack high-impact news
- Small Trading Range – Accumulation
- Judas Swing from Weekly Open – Manipulation

If Bearish Bias look for Raid of PWH/HTF POI
If Bullish Bias look for Raid of PWL/HTF POI

Accumulation

TUESDAY

- Tuesday – Good to Day Trade
- Typically Low/High of the Week
- Judas Swing / Raid of Monday HL / FVG Fill – Manipulation
- London Open/Close/Fix Pivotal
- Monitor for SMR/MMxM
- High Probability Price returns to Monday London Close/Fix

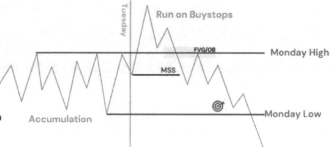

WEDNESDAY

- Wednesday – Good to Day Trade – Expansion
- If above Weekly Open & Previous Weeks Range Equilibrium, look for Longs
- If below WO & PW EQ look for Shorts
- Monitor for move into Premium/Discount of Previous Days Range & Internal BSL/SSL Raid
- Continuation of Trend – Distribution

THURSDAY

- Thursday – Good to Day Trade
- Continuation of Trend – Distribution
- Look to Take Profit by 10:00 EST or once DOL is taken
- Trend Reversal at London Close/Fix 11:00 EST
- Typically Low/High of the Week

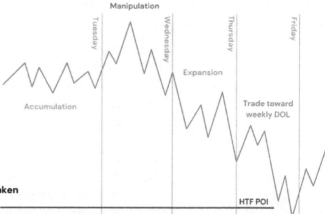

FRIDAY

- Friday – Not Ideal to Day Trade
- Return into the Range
- Small Trading Range
- Reversal to complete Weekly AMD Profile
- Profit Taking – Distribution
- Weekly Close

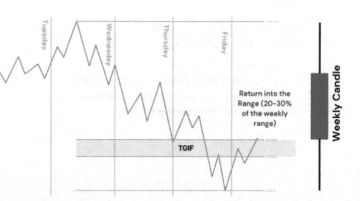

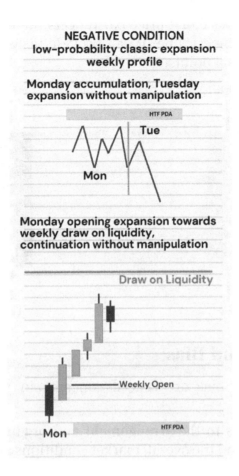

NEGATIVE CONDITION
low-probability classic expansion
weekly profile

Monday accumulation, Tuesday
expansion without manipulation

HTF PDA

Tue

Mon

Monday opening expansion towards
weekly draw on liquidity,
continuation without manipulation

Draw on Liquidity

Weekly Open

Mon   HTF PDA

If MON – WED high-impact news unable to manipulate external range, anticipate potential consolidation reversal profile.

Analyzing the open, high, low, and close

To effectively apply the Power Three Formation, it is important to understand the significance of the open, high, low, and close of price bars. Here's a breakdown of what each of these elements represents:

- Open: The opening price of a price bar represents the starting point of a trading session or time frame. It provides valuable information about market sentiment at the beginning of a period.

- High: The high of a price bar indicates the highest price reached during the trading session or time frame. It can signify market strength or resistance levels.

- Low: The low of a price bar represents the lowest price reached during the trading session or time frame. It can indicate market weakness or support levels.

- Close: The closing price of a price bar reflects the final price at the end of the trading session or time frame. It can provide insights into market sentiment and potential reversal points.

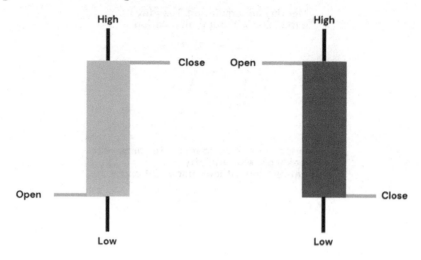

Market Structure and Bias

Market structure and bias are crucial concepts in making informed trading decisions.

Market structure refers to the arrangement and organization of price data on a chart. It helps us understand the overall market conditions and the behavior of market participants.

One important aspect of market structure is swing highs and swing lows. A swing high is formed when there is a high with a lower high to the right and left of it, while a swing low is formed when there is a low with a higher low to the right and left of it. These swing highs and swing lows provide valuable information about potential market reversals and trend changes.

Market bias refers to the directional inclination of the market. By determining the bias, we can anticipate whether the market is more likely to move higher or lower.

To determine the bias, we can analyze the relationship between the opening price and the daily range. If the daily range is more likely to expand higher than the opening price, the bias is bullish. Conversely, if the daily range is more likely to expand lower than the opening price, the bias is bearish.

1) Based on what the market has previously done, determine the current Framework:

1. Did the Market take out any Significant Liquidity Pools?

2. Did the Market hit a Significant FVG?

3. Did the Market create a Market Structure Break with an Displacement?

This is because Price is Fractal. What can be seen on a Monthly Chart, can be seen on a Daily Chart. What can be seen on a Daily Chart, can be seen on a 5 Minute Chart.

2) Based on the current Framework, determine the next Draw on the Liquidity?

1. Do we have clean lows or highs?

2. Do we have any FVG's that need to be rebalanced?

Avoid the temptation of picking bottoms and tops. It's a situation that will cause more losses than necessary.

Retail methods and teachings will give you false confidence that you are able to do it.

If you are wrong by following trend, the market will give you a chance to get in on the opposite side.

3) Based on the current Dealing Range, determine whether the Market in a Premium or Discount?

Dealing range is the new trading range formed after buyside and sale side is taken.

PD array is the distinction between Premium to Discount inside that dealing range including the array list inside the two ranges.

Old High/Low Rejection Block Bearish Order Block FVG Liquidity Void Bearish Breaker Mitigation Block	**Bearish Premium Array**
	Equilibrium
Mitigation Block Bullish Breaker Liquidity Void FVG Bullish Order Block Rejection Block Old Low/High	**Bullish Discount Array**

1. A price run which takes liquidity on both sides of a previous range.

2. A framework which forms ICT's PD array matrix. IE: the top/bottom of a dealing range becomes an "old high/low", then RB, then OB, then FVG, etc.

When the very first candles ever printed on a new asset class, the only thing which existed was a series of price runs forming a range and defined by a swing high and a swing low. Once the range high and low are taken. The move which ran them out becomes the first dealing range.

When your new day/session opens. The first range is the opening range. When both sides of an opening range have been taken, that run is considered a dealing range.

Bearish Market Structure and Bias:

Daily Chart Mindset: Every UP Candle (or multiple) should be considered a SELLING OPPORTUNITY. You are waiting for price to get a key POI or above an opening piece or take BSL on a LTF. You are then targeting Old Lows on the Daily Chart or Previous Day's Lows.

Swing Points for Daily Bias and PO3

Stage 1

1. You need a Swing High with a Bearish Context.
2. Study what occurred on the 3rd Candle Intraday.
3. If the 3rd Candle Intra-day indicates a REVERSAL, expect the 4th Candle to be an Expansion lower.

Stage 2

After a Swing High has been confirmed with a 4th candle close, Price will most likely build another short-term premium before it has another expansion lower.
This is when you wait for Price to trade back into a Premium market relative to it's range. Expect this to occur when Price hits a counter-trend level. Price will either pause and consolidate, or retrace back into a Premium.

Bullish Market Structure and Bias:

Daily Chart Mindset: Every DOWN Candle (or multiple) should be considered a BUYING OPPORTUNITY. You are waiting for price to get a key POI or below an opening piece or take SSL on a LTF. You are then targeting Old Highs on the Daily Chart or Previous Day's Highs.

Close Proximity Entries [CPE]

Power of 3 consists of 3 Stages: Accumulation, Manipulation and Distribution.

<u>Bearish Example</u>

Accumulation Phase: When price is trading at and above the Opening Price, Smart Money is accumulating a net short book.

Above the Opening Price or at "Close Proximity Entries" is where Smart Money is looking to go short.

Manipulation Phase: The False Price Move caused at Market Openings or prior to news releases is a form of Manipulation.

The False Price Move is intended to lead Retail Traders on the wrong side of the Market. ICT calls this a Judas Swing.

Distribution Phase: Distribution is where opposite side of the Candle forms into the closing of the Candle (where the expansion occurs).

This is where Smart Money distributes their accumulation of Shorts.

We can expect the Distribution Cycle to take place around 3:30 - 3:45 PM NY Time.

You do NOT need to predict where the Low will form or where the candle will close to be PROFITABLE.

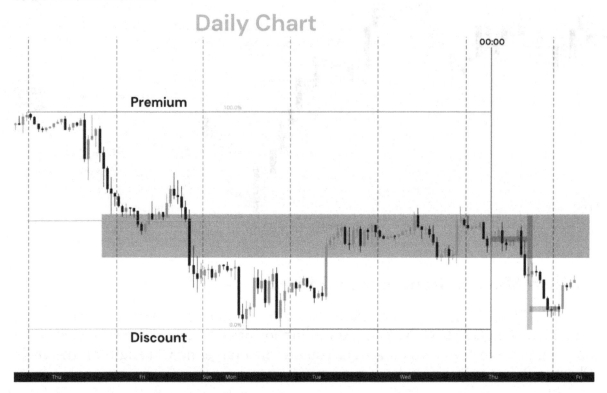

The Opening Range defines how much movement below the Opening you will allow for High Probability Short scenarios.

The opening range is a concept used to identify the high and low price levels during a specific time frame. In the context of index futures, the opening range is a 60-minute period from 9:30 a.m. to 10:30 a.m. New York time, with the first 30 minutes being particularly important. The opening range can help traders identify support and resistance levels that other traders might not be aware of.

This is called "Close Proximity Entries" [CPE]. This is ideal if you missed an entry above the Opening or if you want to **Pyramid a setup**.

To pyramid a setup, you would start by putting your biggest position on first. Then, reduce the size of your next entry and continue to reduce the size for each subsequent entry. This approach allows you to add to your position while minimizing the risk of a compounded loss if the market moves against you.

***Above the Opening Price or at "Close Proximity Entries" is where Smart Money is looking to go short. Another way I can explain: [Opening price] + [Range from Open to HOD], we want to see 1:1 deviation below. In this "CPE" Areas every potential short in a daily range is found. This is where FVGs, Imbalances, Raids occur.

Opening Range:

Step One: Open + HOD = Opening Range Projection

Step Two: Opening Range Projection - Opening Price = Opening Range

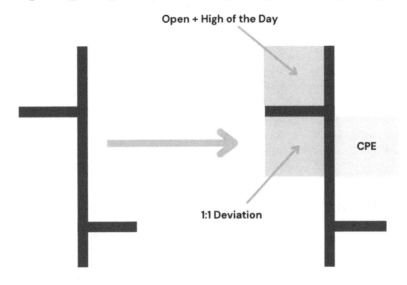

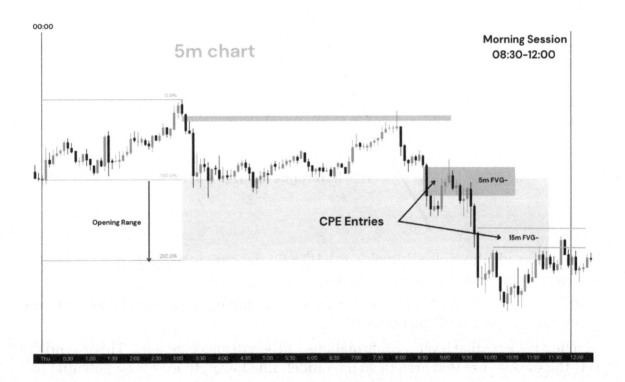

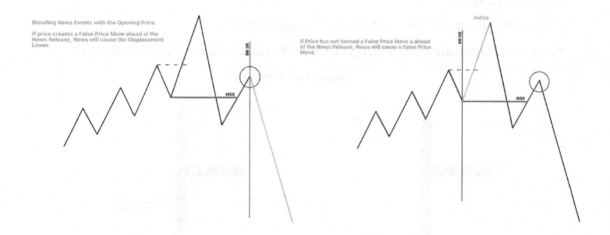

Blending News Events with the Opening Price.

If price creates a False Price Move ahead of the News Release, News will cause the Displacement Lower.

If Price has not formed a False Price Move a ahead of the News Release, News will cause a False Price Move.

Top Down Analysis

Assuming this impulse is created on a weekly, I want to identify key levels within a significant impulse. An ideal reference points are usually FVGs within a strong displacement leg.

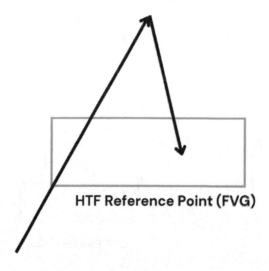

HTF Reference Point (FVG)

When we identify a clear impulse on a HTF (in this case weekly) we want to identify a clear reference point within the impulse.

Now, ideally on a timeframe lower, (daily for example) we can look for two impulse confirmations or clear displacement.

Once price it's that level, a confirmations will be a displacement leg. This essentially sets the stage to use that area to go on a timeframe lower, to look for a potential buy entry.

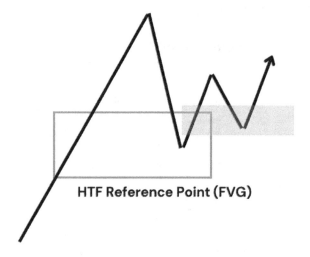

HTF Reference Point (FVG)

Inside the reference point, looking for a displacement (FVG after reaction).

Now, what's the point of a HTF breakdown if you can't enter This is probably the EASIEST entry model used when anticipating a bias for the day A clear move below the 12 am Eastern price into a key level from the prior day (s).

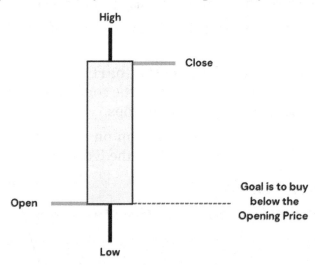

Breaking down the daily candle, once we identify a potential bias, we can simply look for a buy bias below the midnight opening price.

This could be a retracement into a reference point on 4h, 1h from the prior day (s).

Step 1: Identify the Major Trend (4H Chart): Begin your analysis by looking at the 4-hour (4H) chart to identify the major trend. The major trend will give you the overall direction in which you should be trading.

4h HTF Order Flow

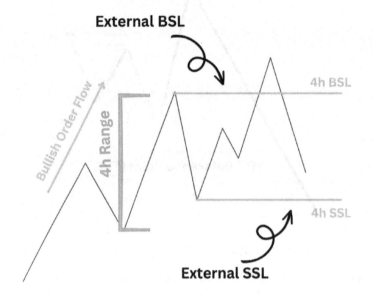

External BSL

Bullish Order Flow

4h Range

4h BSL

4h SSL

External SSL

Step 2: Locate SSL and BSL levels (4H Chart): Identify significant SSL and BSL levels on the 4H chart. These levels will play a vital role in your trading decisions.

Example: You identify a SSL level for NQ at 15,000 and for ES at 4,400 on the 4H chart.

Step 3: Move to the 1-Hour Chart (1H Chart): Now, switch to the 1-hour (1H) chart to get a closer look at price action within the context of the Order Flow. Look for key areas of consolidation, buystops, and sellstops.

Example: On the 1H chart, you notice a run on sellstops. Internal liquidity was taken on NQ, indicating a potential reversal to the External BSL (4H).

1h MTF POI and Liquidity Sweep

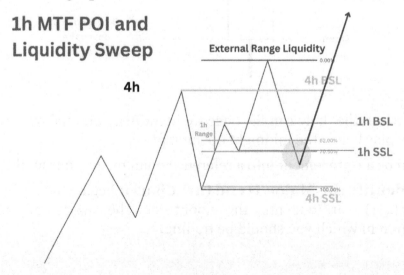

4h

External Range Liquidity

0.00%

4h BSL

1h Range

1h BSL

62.00%

70.00%

1h SSL

100.00%

4h SSL

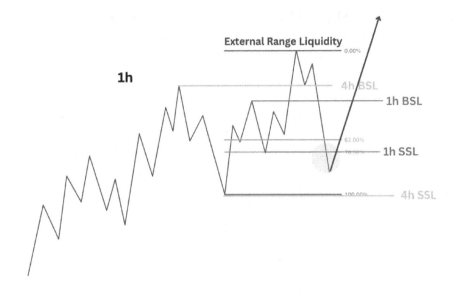

Step 4: Analyze the 15-Minute Chart (15M Chart): Move down to the 15-minute (15M) chart to further refine your entry and exit points. Look for confluence with SSL/BSL, SMT Divergence, FVG.

Example: On the 15M chart, you see a test of discount FVG, confirming potential reaction to the 4h External BSL.

Step 5: Confirm Entry on the 5-Minute Chart (5M Chart): Use the 5-minute (5M) chart for timing your entries. Look for price action signals that align with your analysis from the higher timeframes.

Example: On the 5M chart, you see a bullish OB after run on sellstops, signaling a potential long entry.

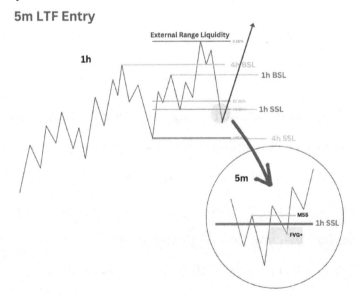

Step 6: Execute on the 1-Minute Chart (1M Chart): Finally, use the 1-minute (1M) chart to fine-tune your entry and set your stop-loss and take-profit levels.

NQU2023, 4h, CME O15327.25 H15342.50 L15255.75 C15313.00 Vol117.739K

1. Within this Displacement start doings Top Down Analysis for entries.

2. You want to follow a chronological order of 5, 4, 3, 2, 1 Minute Charts.

3. If you find a FVG on a 5 Minute, you don't have to go lower.

4. If you find a FVG on the 2 Minute, you don't have to go lower.

5. Once you find a FVG, you do not go any lower.

6. If you can't find a FVG on the 1 Minute, there is no trade.

Risk Management and Discipline

Trading in the financial markets can be an exciting and potentially lucrative endeavor. However, it is important to understand that trading also comes with its fair share of risks.

Trading involves the risk of financial loss. It is important to remember that there are no guarantees in trading and that the market can be unpredictable. Market volatility can lead to rapid price movements, which can result in significant gains or losses.

Emotional factors such as fear and greed can influence decision-making and lead to impulsive trading actions.

External events, such as geopolitical tensions or economic news, can impact the market and increase volatility.

Proper risk management is important for traders to protect their capital and minimize potential losses. Here are some key principles of risk management:

- **Setting a risk tolerance:** Determine the maximum amount of capital you are willing to risk on each trade. This will help you maintain control over your losses and prevent excessive drawdowns.

- **Position sizing:** Calculate the appropriate position size for each trade based on your risk tolerance and the size of your trading account. This ensures that you are not overexposing yourself to any single trade.

- **Stop-loss orders:** Implement stop-loss orders to automatically exit a trade if it reaches a predetermined level of loss. This helps limit potential losses and protects your capital.

- **Regular review and adjustment:** Continuously monitor and reassess your risk management strategies to ensure they align with your changing market conditions and risk appetite.

One common mistake that traders make is overleveraging their positions or engaging in excessive trading activity. Let's explore why these practices should be avoided.

Overleveraging refers to using a high amount of leverage in relation to your account balance. While leverage can amplify potential profits, it also magnifies losses.

Excessive leverage can quickly deplete your trading account if a trade goes against you. It is important to use leverage responsibly and within your risk tolerance. Always consider the potential downside and the impact of leverage on your overall risk exposure before entering a trade.

Overtrading refers to excessive buying and selling of securities, often driven by impulsive or emotional decision-making. Overtrading can lead to increased transaction costs, reduced focus, and increased risk of making poor trading decisions.

It is important to have a well-defined trading plan and stick to it, avoiding the temptation to enter trades based on emotions or short-term market fluctuations.

Importance of Patience and Discipline in Trading

Successful trading requires patience and discipline. Let's explore why these qualities are essential for traders.

Patience

- Patience is the ability to wait for high-probability trading opportunities and not get caught up in the excitement of the market.

- Waiting for the right setup can help you avoid entering trades based on impulse or emotions, increasing the likelihood of success.

- Patience also involves waiting for trades to play out according to your plan and not exiting prematurely due to fear or greed.

Discipline

- Discipline involves following your trading plan and adhering to your predetermined risk management strategies.

- It is important to stick to your trading rules and not deviate from your plan, even in the face of market fluctuations or unexpected events.

- Discipline helps you maintain consistency in your trading approach and reduces the likelihood of impulsive or emotional decision-making.

Remember that the number of years you've been trading doesn't automatically make you the best. It's not like time magically turns us into trading wizards. What actually matters is our approach to life and how much we do to be become successful. Whether you've been trading for 5 years, 20 years, or only 2 years, it doesn't set the ultimate benchmark. It's not like having two decades of experience automatically means you're the ultimate trading guru. It's not about just watching the clock tick away. So, what's the real deal? Well, it's about how we live our lives and how much we're hungry for success. Our discipline and drive are the secret sauce. I mean, you can argue all day that experience is everything, but it's not the starting point for greatness. Discipline is like the guiding star in the night sky. It's what keeps us on track, even when the markets are acting all crazy. You see, trading isn't just about making quick decisions and hoping for the best. It's about having a plan and sticking to it, no matter what.

Think about it this way: imagine you're on a road trip. You've got a map, a route planned out, and a destination in mind. Now, if you start taking random detours every time you see something shiny on the side of the road, you're probably not going to reach your destination anytime soon. It's the same with trading. Discipline means having a trading strategy and sticking to it, even when the market is throwing curveballs. It's about not letting emotions dictate your moves. When you're disciplined, you're less likely to make impulsive decisions that you'll regret later. Let's say you've set a stop-loss for a trade to limit potential losses.

Now, the market starts moving against you, and it's tempting to remove that stop-loss in the hopes that things will turn around. But discipline kicks in and reminds you that sticking to your plan is crucial. You keep that stop-loss in place, even if it means accepting a loss. In a way, discipline is like a habit. The more you practice it, the more it becomes a natural part of your trading routine. And trust me, it pays off. You'll make more informed decisions, stay calmer during turbulent times, and ultimately increase your chances of success. So, bottom line, it's not just about the years you've clocked in the trading world. It's about your outlook and how determined you are to make it big. Experience is important, sure, but it's not the spark that lights up the trading success fire.

Remember, there are many successful traders who have relatively little experience. What they do have is a strong understanding of the markets, a sound trading strategy, and the discipline to stick to their plan. If you are new to trading, do not let the lack of experience discourage you. You can still be successful if you are willing to learn, take risks, and never give up.

I wanted to share a piece of advice that has really helped me in my trading journey, and I think it could be valuable for you too.

You know, in trading, it's easy to get caught up in the excitement of chasing every potential trade, fearing that we might miss out on opportunities. However, I've come to realize that it's not about chasing trades; it's about making well-informed decisions, right?

So, here's my mantra: "You don't need to chase trades, and you don't need to be afraid to miss them." The most important thing is to ask yourself a crucial question before entering any trade: "Why am I considering this trade?" Ask this every single day! If you have a clear and confident answer to that question, then go ahead and take the trade. But if you find yourself hesitating or unsure, it's a sign that you should probably sit this one out. Believe me, this works 100% Remember, trading is all about discipline and strategy. By focusing on the "why" behind each trade, you'll ensure that you're making decisions based on a well-thought-out plan rather than FOMO. So, don't let the fear of missing out or the temptation to chase every trade cloud your judgment. Trust in your analysis and follow your trading plan. If you can answer the "why" question confidently.

Guidelines:

1. Stick & Stay with Your Bias Only.

2. Execute only with that bias in mind.

3. If you are Bearish, only stick to shorting.

4. If you are Bullish, only stick to longing.

5. You do not have to capture the large moves, but rather work with your biased expectation so that you do not "flip flop" back and forth between biases and confuse yourself!

Day Trading is NOT Everyday Trading

You think you will be able to do this every day, but that is a misunderstanding... Why?

You are falling in love with WINNING instead of being PROCESS-ORIENTED

Falling in love with "being correct" and "being better than the rest" is a trap

The truth is it does not need to happen every day.

Find comfort in NOT taking trades.

Understand the potential risks in trading every day because of the markets being open.

You are too focused on the money.

Not every day will give you a high probability opportunity.

Chapter 15

Market Structure For Precision Technicians

ICT market structure refers to the way the market behaves and shifts based on various factors such as institutional order flow, imbalances, and key levels. It represented in a series of either higher lows and higher highs - bullish, or series of lower highs and lower lows - bearish.

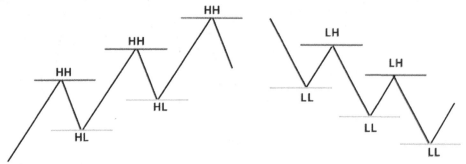

Market Structure Concept

The actual turning points that include high and lows within it (Intermediate highs and lows).

The market trades in a generic pattern or rhythm and it is easy to read if you are aware of the basic structure price tends to move in.

1. Generally, the market trades from short term low (STL) to short term high (STH) back to a new short-term low (STL). As these STL's and STH's form, they will develop a "market structure" of price action.

2. Any short-term low (STL) that has higher short-term lows (STL) on both sides of it is considered an Intermediate term low (ITL).

3. Any short term high (STH) that has lower short-term highs (STH) on both sides of it is considered an Intermediate term high (ITH).

4. Any Intermediate term low (ITL) that has higher intermediate term lows (ITL) on both sides of it is considered long term low (LTL).

5. Any Intermediate term high (ITH) that has lower intermediate term highs (ITH) on both sides of it is considered long term high (LTH).

Interbank Traders do not view Market Structure with Retail's method.

Interbank Traders view Price in terms of Liquidity and Imbalances.

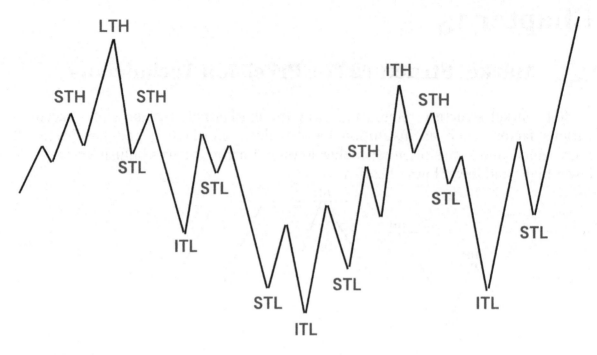

1) The highest time frame will act as a Long-term Perspective

- This time frame will show you Higher Time Frame Levels which will offer Trade Setup Opportunities.

- Trade Ideas will be built upon levels derived from the Higher Time Frame.

2) The mid-level timeframe will act as an Intermediate-Term Perspective

- Following the Trade Setup Opportunity found on the HTF, Mid-level will give you more definition in terms of structure based on that HTF Level

- Managing Trades will be done via a mid-level time frame.

3) The lowest time frame will act as a Short-term Perspective

- Following the Trade Setup Opportunity found on the HTF and insights given with Mid-level, the short-term perspective will give you even more definition in terms of structure.

- Timing trades with entries will be done via the lowest time frame.

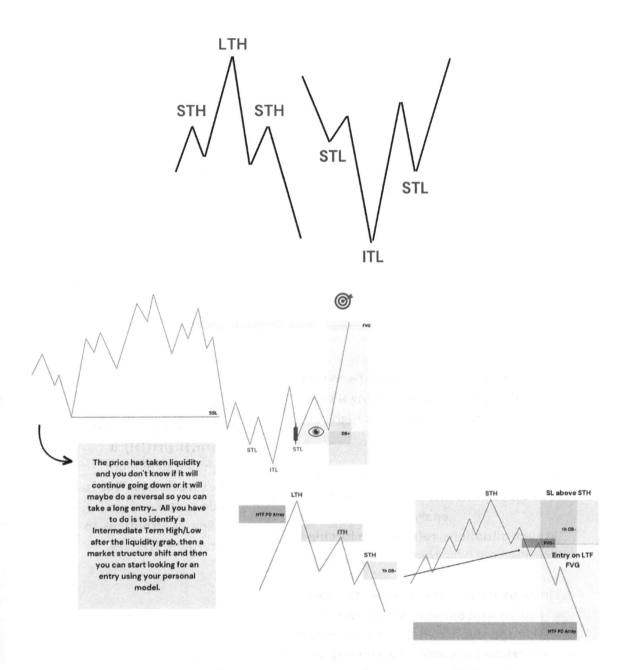

Intermediate Term High/Low – Any short-term low (STL) that has higher short-term lows (STL) on both sides of it is considered an Intermediate term low (ITL). Any short term high (STH) that has lower short-term highs (STH) on both sides of it is considered an Intermediate term high (ITH).

There are 2 Forms of Intermediate Term Highs

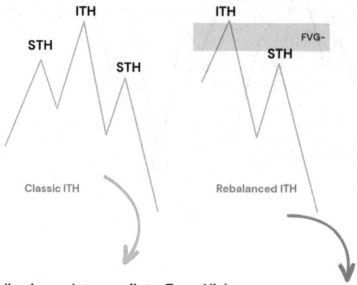

Following an Intermediate–Term High (ITH), we can consider taking a short position when a Short–Term High (STH) forms.

If the Intermediate–Term High is broken, it implies potential inaccuracies in our analysis.
In such situations, refrain from forcing the trade.

Instead, wait for the market structure to realign with our anticipated direction. This approach is vital for safeguarding your trading account and avoiding undue pressure on the market.

If you observe a Rebalanced Intermediate Term High (ITH), it signifies significant market weakness. This is akin to the market revealing its intentions to Interbank Traders.

If you see a Rebalanced ITH, that is telling you that the market is VERY weak. That is the market "tipping it's hand" towards Interbank Traders.

To effectively recognize Market Structure in a manner akin to that of an Interbank Trader, it's imperative to first grasp the prevailing market narrative.

The narrative guides us towards assessing liquidity conditions. Specifically, a liquidity draw serves as the foundation for establishing our daily bias.

Key questions arise:

• What is the current market narrative?

• Is it going higher for Buy Side Liquidity or to Rebalance a SIBI?

• Is it going lower for Sell Side Liquidity or to Rebalance a BISI?

FAILURE TO UNDERSTAND MARKET STRUCTURE LIKE AN INTERBANK TRADER,

WILL LEAD YOU TO FALL VICTIM TO FALSE MARKET STRUCTURE BREAKS.

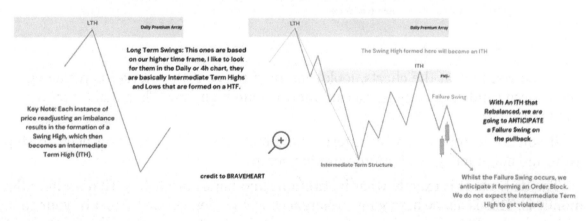

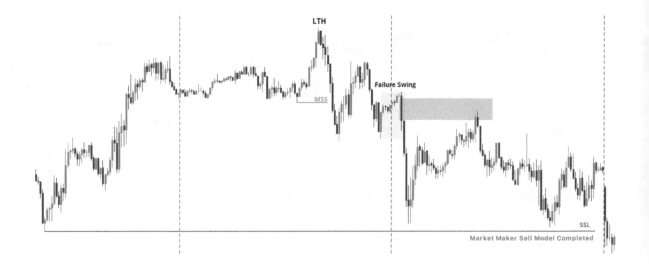

LTH

MSS

Failure Swing

SSL

Market Maker Sell Model Completed

Before you start trading, there are two crucial questions that you must answer to gain insights into the market direction:
1. Where does the price want to go? BSL or SSL?
2. Is the price more likely to go up or down before rebalancing?

Whenever an imbalance is filled, it creates an ITH/ITL (Intermediate Top High/ Top Low). These levels are formed when the balance is filled in the market.

If the ITH is not higher than two STHs (short-term highs), it indicates that the market is very weak.

Smart money focuses on imbalances, rebalancing, and liquidity as key factors.
When you observe the imbalance being filled and the price forming a new high, that high should not be broken if you have a bearish perspective.

Likewise, when the imbalance is filled and the price establishes a low, that low should not be breached if you have a bullish outlook.

When you look at the charts, look each time to see if the market is retracing an imbalanced candle. Classify this as an intermediate high/low. Then make sure prices don't violate it.

If you are bearish and your intermediate high is broken, then you need to step aside and not enter again. Wait for another setup.

The daily chart is exactly what institutions and banks are using. That's where the money is. This is also where your preferences will be determined. Most of your time and study should be focused on determining where the daily chart will be for the next day, two, or week.

Market Phases

There are 3 phases in the market:

- **Accumulation phase:**

Accumulation is the process of opening a large position by a market maker without significant price movement against the direction of this position.

- **Manipulation phase:**

The release of negative news makes weak players panic. They become very predictable. Namely, if the market falls, these players begin to massively sell everything, which is responsible for a large increase in supply.

The first manipulation leaves several questions: "What kind of demand can absorb the current volume?", "Who is on the other side of the deal?".

Weak players tend to often miss bull market formation points. After which they are overcome by greed, they begin to get nervous, which brings with it the thought that the current trend is passing by. That is why the "crowd" begins to buy everything.

Remember, **market weakness manifests itself in moments of an uptrend, strength in downtrend.**

- **Distribution phase:**

Distribution is the reverse process of accumulation.

ICT frames things based on a top down approach starting from the daily because that's where banks and institutions trade off. Number one question is what the current market narrative is.

Does the market have a reason to go up for BSL or to rebalance an imbalance (or FVG, Volume Imbalance)? Or is it likely to go lower to sweep Sellside liquidity or to rebalance an imbalance (or FVG, V.I.)? Imbalance, rebalance and liquidity, that's all they're doing.

The daily is where your bias is going to be determined. That's what makes or breaks your trend continuation. So, the majority of your time should be where that daily chart is going. If you're trading against what the daily chart is likely to do, you are absolutely asking for failure. That's not to say that you can't go long when the daily will go lower, but why would you? Why would you swim against the tide? If you line up with the daily, you will avoid a lot of mistakes.

From Narrative to Market Structure:

How Market Structure is built:

Market profiles will assist in market structure analysis concepts. Are we trending, in a reversal pattern or in a consolidation preparing for a breakout scenario? It helps you determine if we are bullish or bearish.

Below you see two examples of how market structure is built. To the left you see a market rally into a key (Higher Time Frame) resistance level followed by a Smart Money Reversal (SMR) and then a decline (which can be a retracement or a reversal dependent on if we've taken HTF external or internal liquidity) and to the right the opposite. Here the decline reaches into a key (HTF) support level. These support and resistance levels are your so called "PD arrays" (ICT Core Content month 4) and you have to use the highest timeframe to identify those levels. Without key support and resistance levels you're not going to get a directional bias regardless of what trading model you're using.

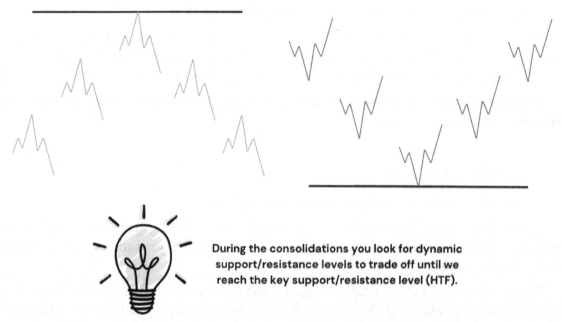

During the consolidations you look for dynamic support/resistance levels to trade off until we reach the key support/resistance level (HTF).

Swings consist of consolidation and expansions until we reach a key support/resistance level where the smart money reversal (SMR) takes place. The SMR takes place at the top by either a turtle soup or a failure swing (CC month 5 ep. 5). Same goes for the support level. You can anticipate an entry at the SMR after we hit the key support/resistance level.

The consolidations are the building blocks that we work with. During a consolidation you look for dynamic support/resistance levels to trade off until we reach the key support/resistance level (HTF). Those levels are very clear. So as price declines, you want to see these swing lows being formed and every swing low that forms there will be a discernible OTE at the retracement.

Which timeframes to use to break down market structure depends on the type of trade(r)?

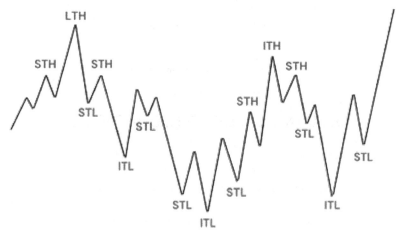

There are lots of different timeframes, and that can be overwhelming. Your primary objective is to know the timeframe that you're trading. That depends on what type of trader you want to be, as disposed in the image above. You see 3 timeframes per type of trade(r):

- HTF: trade idea based on this, directional bias and manage trade.

- Middle timeframe: manage your trade.

- LTF: short term, for timing your entry and looking for early reversal signs, so you know it's time to take profits.

Position Trading	Swing Trading
Long-term: Monthly	Long-term: Daily
Intermediate: Weekly	Intermediate: 4h
Short-term: Daily	Short-term: 1h
Short-term Trading	**Day Trading**
Long-term: 4h	Long-term: 1h
Intermediate: 1h	Intermediate: 15m
Short-term: 15m	Short-term: 5m

TIMEFRAME SELECTION
Monthly Chart – Position Trading
Weekly chart – Swing Trading
Daily Chart – Short-Term Trading
4h or less – Day Trading

DEFINING SETUP FOR YOUR MODEL

Trend Trader: Trading only in the direction of the Monthly and Weekly Chart direction
Swing Trader: Trading the Daily Chart intermediate term price action
Contrarian Trader: Trading reversal patterns at market extremes
Short-Term Trader: Trading the weekly ranges for 1-5 days in duration
Day Trader: Intraday trading with exits by 2:00pm NY Time

Long term high/long term low	A high that has two lower intermediate term highs next to it. A low that has two higher intermediate term lows next to it.	What makes a swing point a long term swing? Long term highs/lows are formed at Key HTF PD Arrays. Swing level where Liquidity has been taken. Long Terms levels are connected to Time. For example London session has the highest probability of creating the high or low of the day.
Intermediate term high /intermediate term low	1. A high with two lower short term highs next to it/A low with the higher short term lows next to it. 2. A high that fills an imbalance/a low that fills an imbalance.	If an ITH is not higher than 2 short term highs (or an ITL not lower than 2 STL), that is telling you that the market is very weak (strong) and the algo is tipping it's hand to the people that look at it like this. Smart money traders look at it like this. Bearish: LTH/ITH should be respected. Bullish: LTL/ITL should be respected. If not, your trade idea is probably flawed. Don't force that trade again just wait for market structure to get back in sync with what you're expecting; something bearish.
Short term high /short term low	Anything else that isn't long or intermediate term	

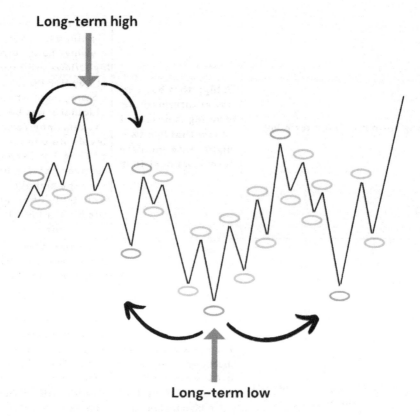

Long-term high

Long-term low

[Blue dots: are ITH/ITL, Orange arrows: those ITH/ITL are LTH/LTL. Green = STH/STL]

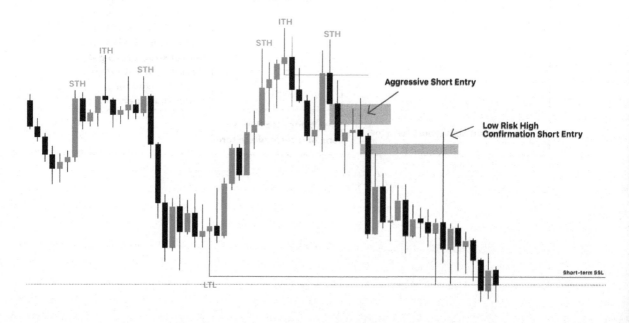

If Price is Bearish, we want to see price spend little time above highs, create shallow runs on highs, reject, and/or Respect Premium Arrays. We also want to see DISPLACEMENT LOWER. Violating discount arrays and/or LT,IT,ST LOWS.

Below you see 2 charts. The daily timeframe and the price action between the red lines from a 1h perspective. The daily is the parent of the 1h price structure so minor price swings are subordinate to it.

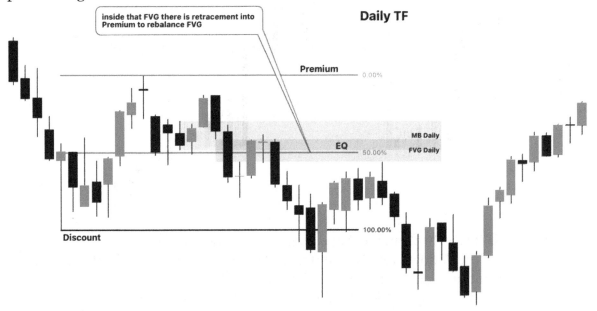

[On this daily you see the dealing range and a retrace into premium (just above EQ to rebalance that FVG)]

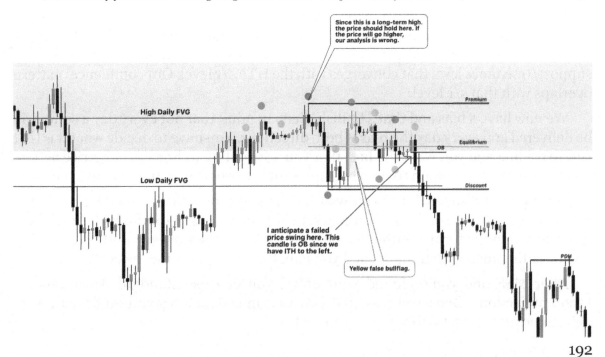

As you see you will have 2 possible entry points, an aggressive entry and a low risk high confirmation entry as displayed below.

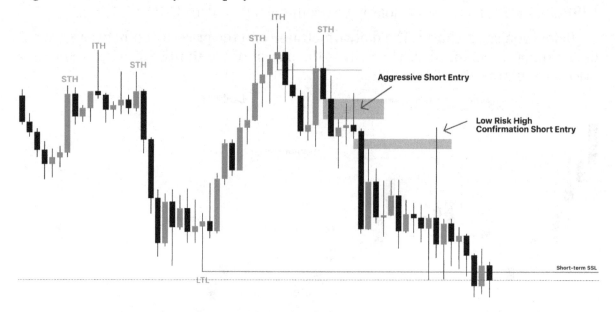

Once a ITH/ITL is broken, you have a significant break in market structure (BMS/MSB). Once we break down and take out the STL and ITL or just a ITL/ITH, then we have a significant break in market structure. This is more significant than just simply going into a chart and saying okay well it took out a short-term low there it is.

Your entry should be based on the lowest of the 3 timeframes.

Now let's assume we are a swing trader; market structure is bullish and we've traded off of a higher timeframe support level and we had a market shift to the upside on the highest timeframe chart. Our midlevel timeframe has allowed us to find a key support/resistance level that converges with the HTF s/r level. Our confluence: pattern overlaps with that s/r level.

We now have a bias and that's bullish. Keep in mind that not every day a setup will be delivered and every day the bias is both directions. You have to decide what it is that you're trading and you want the bias that you are holding to line up with price action, you can't force price action to do what you want it to do, you want to get in sync.

During the Killzone (time!) you wait for the key support level to be hit (as in the example below) and you look for a market shift there (based on the highest of the 3 timeframes) in the form of either a stop run or a failure swing (cc month 5 episode 5) and after that market shift happened you look for an entry on the lowest timeframe.

After MSS and you've found your entry, you can use standard deviations for target projections. Once we break that ITL, we can use the fib standard deviations to determine price targets from this consolidation.

193

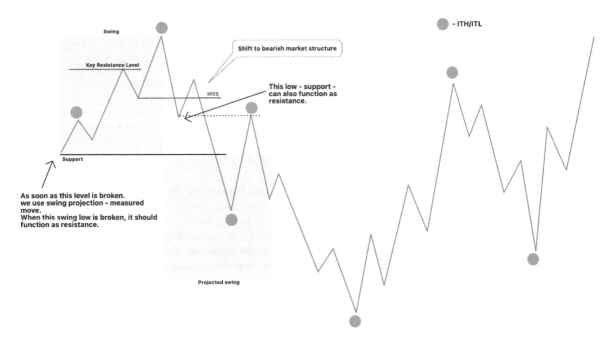

[You see the yellow price swing on the left. As soon as the low is taken out, you can use the swing projection for targets]

Above , as you can see, I drew the FIB from the ITH at the top to the LTL at the bottom of the range. Why anchor the FIB like this? This is not random of course. Because that's the up move, so the swing, from where the decline starts. It's the retracement swing up that fails that starts to decline. The projection is -2.0 STDV.

Once you are in trade, use institutional order flow to know if the move is still good. When you're bearish, all of your up close candles should keep price from going higher than that. So they are your resistance. For bullish price action, down close candles should support price.

Multiple Time Frame Analysis Tips and Tricks

Where should your focus be?
The Highest of the 3 Time Frames.

How do you manage trades?
Manage your trade with both a Long-term Perspective and an Intermediate-Term Perspective.
Long-term perspective will give you the Directional Bias
Intermediate-term perspective will show you how to manage that trade following the Long-term Perspective.

How do you enter Trades?
The Short-term perspective will be used to entry signals.
First you need to study the Market Structure on the Long-term and Intermediate-Term Perspective
Then the Short-term perspective will give you entry signals based on what you derived.

How do you find High Probability Trades?
The Highest Probability Trades will be found following the Long-term Perspective direction.
The Highest Probability Trades will be framed on the Highest time Frame.
Frame your trades on Key Levels (Order Blocks, Fair Value Gaps, Liquidity Pools)

What is the Market Profile?
Knowing if we are in a Consolidation Phase or a Trending Phase will assist with Market Structure Analysis.

On an Intermediate Perspective, if Price is drawing towards Buy Side Liquidity.

EVERY DOWN CANDLE IS BEING USED FOR BUYING.

Down Candles will hold as Support.
Up Candles will break as Resistance.

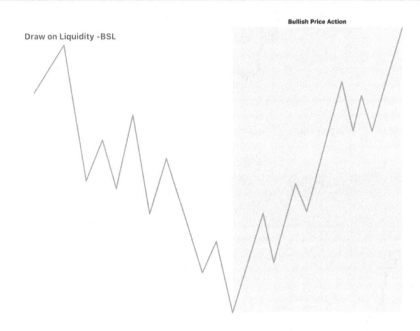

Draw on Liquidity -BSL

Bullish Price Action

NQ1!, 1h, CME O13990.75 H13992.75 L13900.00 C13918.00 Vol6.763K

Previous Day High
Broke resistance level
Previous Day High
Broke resistance level
Broke resistance level

BSL 13934.50
13918.00
14000.00
13800.00
13700.00
13600.00
13500.00
13400.00
13300.00
13200.00
13100.00
13000.00
Weekly OB+ 12957.50
12900.00

10   12:00   11   12:00   14   12:00   15   12:00   16   12:00   17   12:00

Do NOT lose the desire to hold the trade.

Interbank Traders understand that Down Candles will be used as Buying Opportunities. IF YOU UNDERSTAND THAT PRICE WILL WANT TO REACH THE BUY SIDE LIQUIDITY.

Every down candle is the chance for Smart Money to accumulate new long positions.

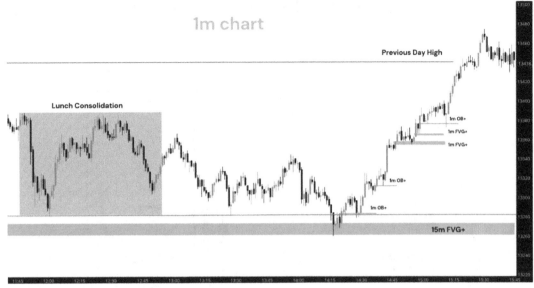

Questions to ask before you enter on an Order Block:

1. Does Price want to reach higher?

2. Does Market Structure support your Order Block?

YOU CAN ALSO USE AN IMBALANCE AS SUPPORT INSTEAD OF THE ORDER BLOCK.

High Probability Order Blocks have an FVG paired with them.

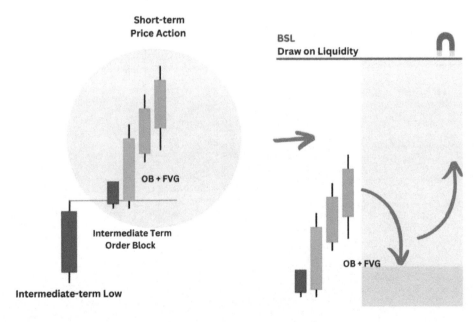

[Credit to Braveheart]

High Probability Order Blocks are blended with Time Theory.

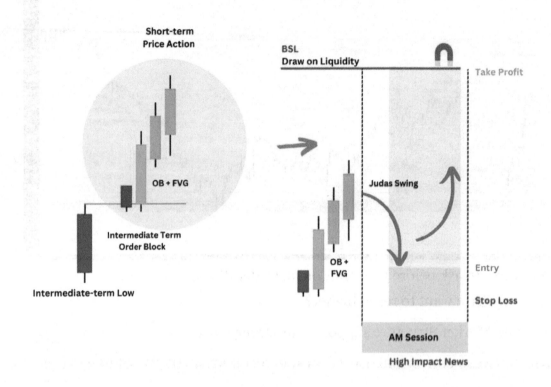

Chapter 16

Multiple Setups Inside Trading Session

Daily BIAS is a concept that helps determine the main direction of price movement for the day.

Here is 3 step process to determine BIAS:

Structure

To effectively map structure and identify liquidity areas, it is important to consider the premium and discount levels of external markets along with the impulse structure. Here's how you can approach it:

1. Analyze External Markets: Start by analyzing the premium and discount levels of relevant external markets. This involves comparing the current price of the market you're trading with the corresponding price in related markets. Identify any significant premium or discount levels that may impact the market you're focusing on.

2. Identify Impulse Structure: Study the impulse structure within your chosen market. Look for strong trending moves, price rejections, or breakouts that indicate a clear direction. These impulse movements provide valuable clues about the underlying market sentiment and can help identify potential liquidity areas.

3. Map Structure: Use your analysis of external markets and impulse structure to map out key structure levels in your chosen market. These levels may include support and resistance areas, swing highs, swing lows, or consolidation zones. Structure mapping helps identify areas where liquidity is likely to be concentrated.

4. Look for Liquidity: Focus on the areas of structure where liquidity is likely to be present. These are areas where significant buying or selling orders are expected to be executed. Liquidity can be found at key support and resistance levels, breakouts, or areas of price congestion.

5. Evaluate Premium/Discount Levels: Consider how the premium or discount levels in external markets may impact liquidity and price behavior in your chosen market. A premium level in an external market may attract sellers or create resistance, while a discount level may attract buyers or create support.

6. Trade with the Flow: Use your understanding of liquidity and structure to trade in the direction of the prevailing market flow. Look for opportunities to enter trades at favorable liquidity areas, aligning with the impulse structure and the premium/discount levels.

7. If no displacement through the structure, we can expect reversal. It is important to understand that Displacement is a key in determining true direction. If we see displacement through the structure, we are going to expect that price is reaching

Liquidity

Price movement in the market is influenced by the concept of liquidity and imbalances. Liquidity refers to the availability of buying or selling orders in the market. Understanding these factors can help traders identify potential areas of interest and make informed trading decisions.

Price in the market is constantly driven towards areas of liquidity and imbalances. Let's explore the significance of structure and imbalances in this context:

1. Structure: It provides a framework for understanding the behavior of market participants. Structure can act as a roadmap for identifying key areas of interest, such as support and resistance zones, trendlines, and chart patterns. These areas often attract liquidity and can influence price movement.

2. Imbalances: This can lead to price moves that seek to rectify the mismatched supply and demand. Imbalances can arise from factors such as large institutional orders, news events, or shifts in market sentiment. We often look for imbalances as they can indicate potential trading opportunities and areas where liquidity may be concentrated.

When considering potential trades, we often look for areas where liquidity is expected to be high, such as near significant support or resistance levels, breakouts from consolidation patterns, or areas of price congestion. These areas can provide opportunities for entering or exiting trades with favorable risk-reward ratios.

Order Flow

Order Flow analysis is a crucial aspect of understanding market dynamics and gaining insights into the actions of smart money or interbank traders.

Order Flow analysis involves observing the flow of buy and sell orders in the market and identifying which order flow is being respected.

Institutional Order Flow (IOF/OF) - is a flow of big capital orders to buy / sell, delivering the price to areas of interest of big capital.

It can help traders determine the direction of the market and decide whether to enter or exit a position.

At the time of **the bearish Order Flow**, lower lows and highs are updated, then price takes the liquidity (sell stops). During the period **of the bullish Order Flow**, the situation is mirrored to the bearish one, higher highs and lows are updated, then price takes liquidity (buy stops).

Big players can create zones of interest in the market, and when the price approaches these zones, place large orders to buy or sell to move the price in the right direction.

As soon as the price reaches the zone of interest and orders of big players are triggered, this can lead to a change in the direction of the Order Flow in the market. For example, if the price has reached the zone of interest to sell, large players can start placing large sell orders, which can lead to a change in the direction of the flow of sell orders.

Smart Money traders who take into account order flows can determine which direction the market is moving and enter into trades in the direction of the actual Order Flow. This allows traders to "mimic" the moves of the big players and reduce their risk as they work in the direction of strong Order Flow.

Institutional order flow is a crucial factor in determining market liquidity. Large orders placed by institutional investors can move the market, leading to significant price movements. It can also lead to increased volatility, which can provide trading opportunities for individual traders.

Order Flow Logic

It is important to understand the logic of the Order Flow. This is a manipulative move of the price of large capital to gain a position due to liquidity in the form of stop losses.

That is, the entire impulse of candles (without pullbacks), which took liquidity, we consider as an Order Flow.

At the time of the formation of the Order Flow, large capital **has 2 open positions for buying and selling**. One is manipulative, in order to capture liquidity and then the main position is opened.

The Order Flow is activated after the price leaves the OF zone and holds above it. In the Order Flow, we form order blocks, from which we are already looking for entry points to the position. **The price will then test (mitigate) the Order Flow zone** in order to close the manipulative position, which is unprofitable and bounces in the opposite direction.

As a rule, **the Order Flow on a higher timeframe looks like an order block.**

Order Flow Formation

To determine **a bearish Order Flow**, we look at the following signs:

1. The ascending structure has broken or there has been a liquidity grab along the trend.

2. Grab of liquidity to buy.

3. Formed a new lower low and high.

Below in the chart is an example of the formation of a bearish Order Flow

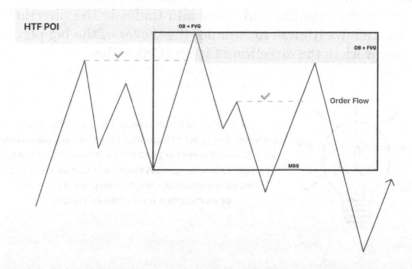

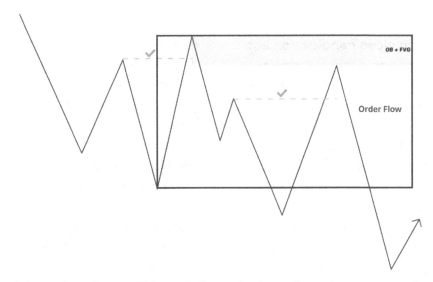

The bearish Order Flow will be confirmed when the price starts to break through the internal liquidity to buy and touch the bearish zone of interest.

The logic of the bearish Order Flow. Large capital makes manipulative trades in order to take liquidity in the form of sell stops, and at this moment large capital opens a second sell position. The price needs to return to the order flow zone in order to close unprofitable buy positions, then the price bounces off the order flow.

Down close candles can act as support levels for price movements. If price remains above the low of a down close candle, it indicates that the market is supporting that level and suggests a bullish bias. Additionally, a break above a short-term high following a down close candle can further validate the bullish sentiment.

An order block is a change in the state of delivery in the market. It's not about the candle itself, but rather the shift in the market's behavior from buy side to sell side or vice versa. This change occurs when the opening price of a candle is violated, indicating a shift in the market's direction and focus on either buy side or sell side liquidity

The breakaway gap is a gap when you want to see an energetic price run away from an area you anticipated prior to it running away.

It usually indicates a shift in market structure and is often accompanied by a strong price movement.

To determine **a bullish Order Flow**, we look at the following signs:

1. The descending structure has broken or liquidity grab along the trend

2. Grab liquidity for short.

3. Formed a new higher high and low.

An example of the formation of a bullish Order Flow

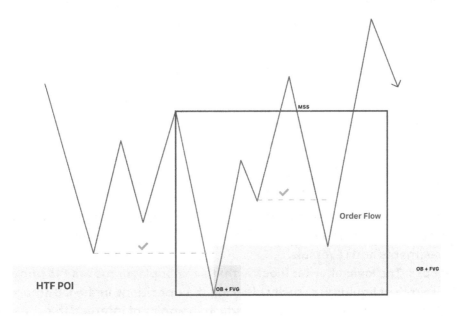

Confirmation is similar to bearish. When the price starts to break through internal sellside liquidity and touch the bullish POI zone or take external liquidity, and as soon as the price pulls back and exits the order flow zone, Order Flow is activated.

The logic of the bullish Order Flow. Large capital makes manipulative sells in order to take liquidity in the form of buy stops, and at this moment large capital opens a second position for longs. The price needs to return to the order flow zone in order to close unprofitable sell positions, then the price bounces off the order flow.

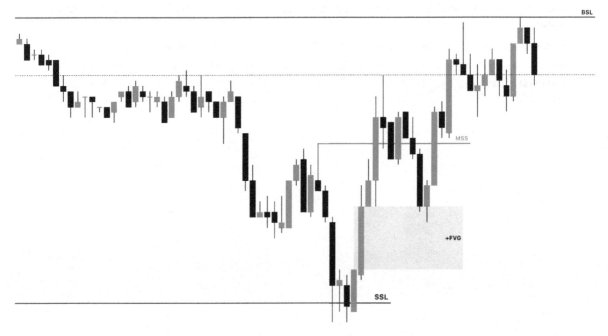

Order Flow is essentially a place on the chart where we can see the "traces" of big capital, where it gained its positions. When approaching (retesting) the price of the Order Flow zone, we expect a price bounce, which gives the price direction in which direction to trade.

An extended version for Order Flow is Order Blocks, with which we look for entry points to trades. It is unprofitable to enter from the Order Flow zone itself, the stop loss is already too big.

Idea of BIAS

1. Market structure: ICT identifies different phases of the market cycle, such as accumulation, manipulation, and distribution and uses them to anticipate potential price movements and reversals.
2. Order blocks: The logic of order block is that a major player moves the price up or down in search of liquidity, actually blocking their positions in the OB area and making them unprofitable. To close a trade in the point of interest, they need the price to return to the order block, after which it will continue to move in the opposite direction.
3. Liquidity pools: These are areas where there is a high concentration of resting orders, such as stop losses, limit orders, or option strikes. We can use liquidity pools to identify where institutions may target or avoid in order to fill their orders or manipulate the market.
4. FVGs: These are gaps between the current market price and the fair value of an asset, which is determined by using a longer-term moving average. We can use them to determine the market bias and direction, and to identify potential reversal points.
5. Top down analysis: This is a technique of analyzing multiple time frames, from higher to lower, in order to identify the dominant trend, the key levels, and the optimal entry and exit points.

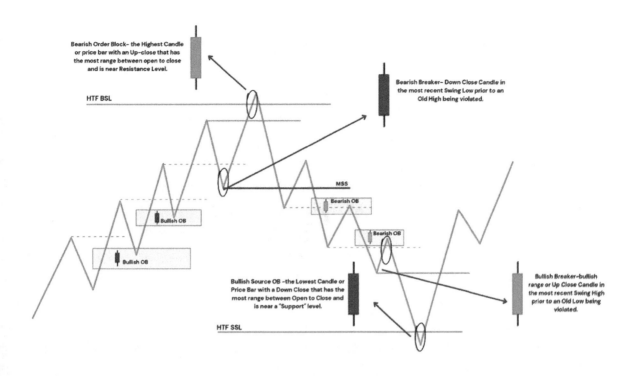

Bearish Order Block- the Highest Candle or price bar with an Up-close that has the most range between open to close and is near Resistance Level.

Bearish Breaker- Down Close Candle in the most recent Swing Low prior to an Old High being violated.

HTF BSL

MSS

Bearish OB

Bullish OB

Bearish OB

Bullish OB

Bullish Source OB -the Lowest Candle or Price Bar with a Down Close that has the most range between Open to Close and is near a "Support" level.

Bullish Breaker-bullish range or Up Close Candle in the most recent Swing High prior to an Old Low being violated.

HTF SSL

NQ1I, 1W, CME O15690.00 H15811.00 L15661.50 C15800.00 Vol371.051K

21/7/2023
NQ1! | W

Nov 2022 Mar May Jul Sep Nov 2023 Mar May Jul Sep

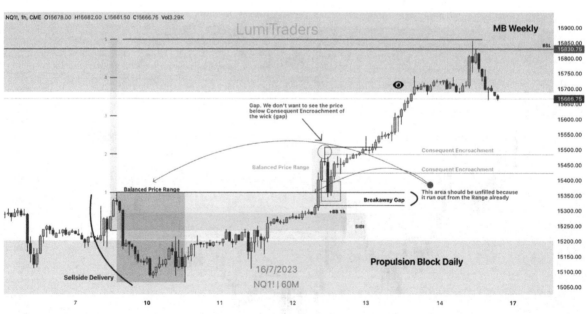

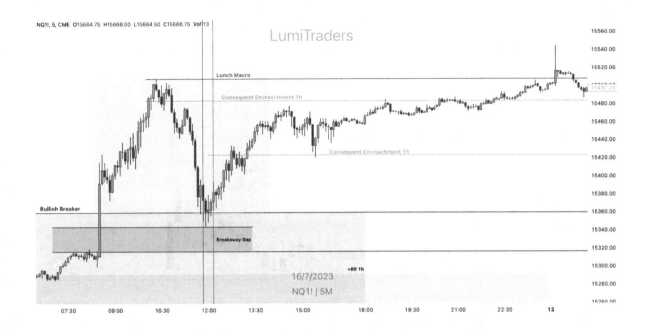

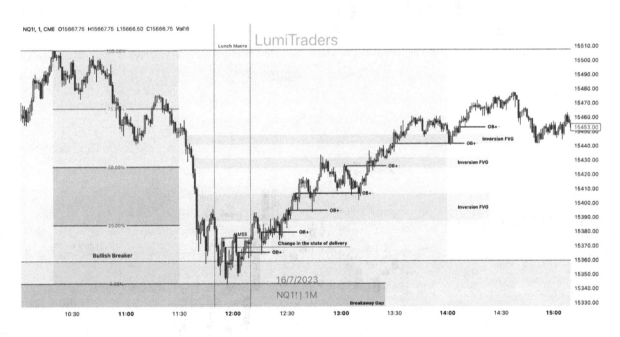

The main idea of BIAS is to determine where the daily candle will move, based on the liquidity grab and the one that has not yet been grabbed.

The main questions you should be asking yourself to determine BIAS are:

1. **What was taken?**

2. **Where can this lead?**

3. **What hasn't been taken yet?**

It is important to note that once the target is reached, the market BIAS should be revised again , as the reaction from the liquidity pool at that level is uncertain.

Daily BIAS is a fundamentally important tool in your trading, as a correctly defined daily price move direction will give you a clear understanding of which positions to consider and complement the information received during trading sessions.

<u>**It is crucial to accurately define the Daily BIAS through proper backtesting, as inexperienced traders may make mistakes in determining it.**</u>

Understanding the Daily BIAS allows us to recognize that price movements are not random but rather have purpose and direction.

DAILY INDECISIVE CANDLESTICK

The presence of a Daily Indecisive Candlestick, characterized by a small body and large wicks, can suggest a potential reversal in the context, indicating that the next candle may be opposite to the previous one.

However, it's important to note that the Daily Indecisive Candlestick should not be solely relied upon for determining the BIAS or opening trades. It serves as a small hint in defining the BIAS but should be supported by other factors and analysis.

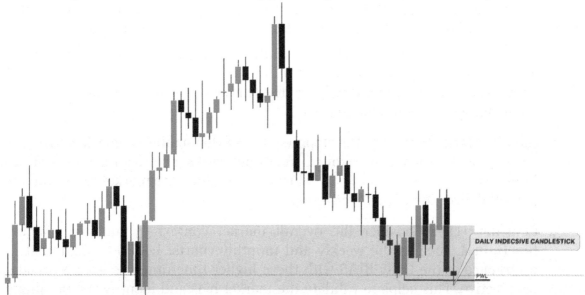

In this example, you can see that the price is in **1D POI, DAILY INDECISIVE CANDLESTICK** took **Previous Week Low**, in this context, we can assume that the next candle will indeed be reversal.

Just having a DAILY INDECISIVE CANDLESTICK doesn't mean anything.

As result,

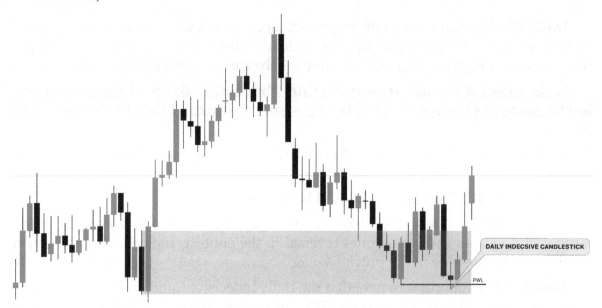

To determine the Daily BIAS, you need to follow a systematic approach that incorporates multiple factors. Here are the key steps to determine the Daily BIAS:

1. Analyze Market Structure: Start by analyzing the previous day's price action and identifying key market structure levels, such as support and resistance areas, swing highs, and swing lows. These levels provide important reference points for assessing the market bias.

2. Identify Market Structure Developments: Look for significant market structure developments, such as breakouts, trendline breaks, or price rejections at key levels. These events can provide valuable clues about the market's bias and the potential direction of price movement.

3. Consider HTF: Consider the overall market context by analyzing higher timeframes, such as the weekly and monthly charts. Look for alignment or divergence of the Daily BIAS with these higher timeframes to gain a broader perspective. This helps to validate the market bias and identify the dominant trend.

4. Evaluate Key Market Participants: Evaluate the behavior of key market participants, particularly institutional players. ICT emphasizes understanding the psychology and intentions of big market players and using that information to determine the market bias. Pay attention to volume and price action around key levels to gauge the involvement of institutional traders.

WHENEVER PRICE CLEARS OUT LIQUIDITY, THERE IS ALWAYS A POSSIBILITY OF A CONTINUATION.

HOWEVER, IF WE SEE PRICE CLEAR LIQUIDITY AND A SWING HIGH FORM [3 CANDLES], THIS SETS UP A RETRACEMENT.

If a Retracement is bound, the next following days are expected to be Bearish.

If we are expecting Bearish Days, we apply the Power of 3 Concepts.

Also, incorporate the Premium vs Discount Concept to see how far the retracement will occur. Look for an area where Price may have a willingness to trade towards.

INCORPORATING THE POWER OF 3

ANTICIPATING THE UPCOMING DAYS AS BEARISH, NOW WE CAN INCORPORATE THE POWER OF 3 INTRA-DAY

There are 2 Opening Prices we focus on:

00:00 AM and 8:30 AM [NEW YORK TIME]

We want to see the price trade above the Opening Price to act as Manipulation. This will act as a Judas Swing, and it is COUNTERING where the price will want to go.

- You need to mark the opening price at midnight 00:00 New York time .

- If you are bearish , ideally you need to see the market above the opening price , this will be manipulation . Manipulation is a move above a key level when we are bearish. The name of a swing that goes above the opening price is called a Judas swing . It also works the other way around when you're bullish.

- Most of your analysis should be on the daily chart (1D) . Where is the price likely to go? Where the expansion will bring the price up or down? This is the main thing to pay attention to because it will determine your BIAS .

- Higher time frame gives you frameworks . As in the video example (episode 16), the 15 minute FVG fills up, but the 5 minute one doesn't. The 15 minute timeframe provides the foundation, it provides the context.

The algorithm races from the discount to the premium zone and vice versa. Within this logic, the market seeks liquidity in the form of: BSL, SSL or imbalance, or creating an imbalance, FVG, or return to FVG. This is what all algorithms do and they do it based on time and then price.

When we trade above the old high, the old high becomes the discount zone. This is where the old highs that were broken become support. That's why sometimes the books are right and your analysis will be right on specific key highs and lows. Note that they are not always consistent, and this is the problem. So, you need to know what makes an old high or old low a real support/resistance.

The old broken high will act as support if there is FVG open for filling.

Point of interest

POI in is a point of interest of a big player, where he or she accumulates his or her trades. The big player will "protect" their entry area.

A POI can be found on any timeframe and chart as prices are fractal. The chart moves according to the same rules on any timeframe.

Types of POIs

POIs can be represented as follows:

1. EQL and EQH

2. Liquidity Levels

3. FVG

4. Order Blocks

5. Breaker Blocks

6. Mitigation Block

7. Rejection Blocks

Which POI zones are the strongest?

There is no concept of which of the POI levels are stronger and which are weaker. Each of the levels as a whole is strong in itself.

There are cases when there are several levels of interest in one area at once - for example, an OB and a FVG can be observed at the same time. In this case, it is worth choosing a level according to the R/R - the more profitable it is, the more preferable it is to choose one or another POI.

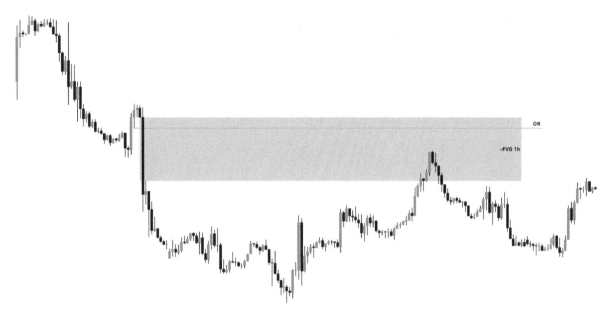

Which POI to choose?

It is also important to wait for confirmation on the LTF. For example, we are looking at the 1h, and on the 1h we have two bearish POIs - the FVG and the OB. Even an experienced trader may ask questions - how to understand which of the zones we should trade? Which of the two zones will be stronger?

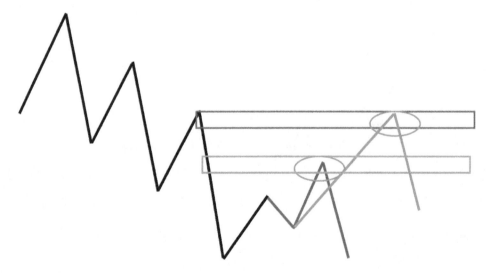

Which of the two POIs is stronger? Both zones are generally strong, and it is worth waiting for confirmation on the LTF.

How to find an enter using the POI?

Aggressive players can enter immediately from the POI, with a small stop loss and an aggressive entry into the trade. But it would be best to use different timeframes and look for an entry on the LTF.

Timeframes to use:

1. 15m – 5m

2. 1h – 15m

3. 4h – 1h

4. 1D – 4h

Consider the example above. We saw a OB and FVG on the 1h chart, in the direction of a long-term trend.

Now, let's switch to the 15m, and draw a 50% of the FVG:

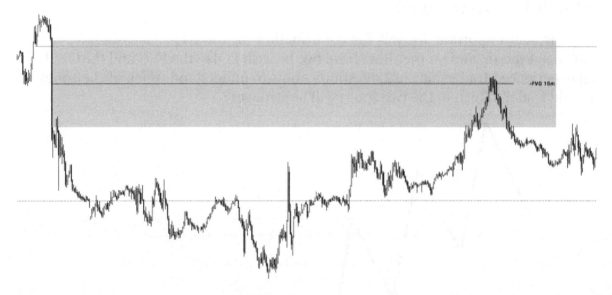

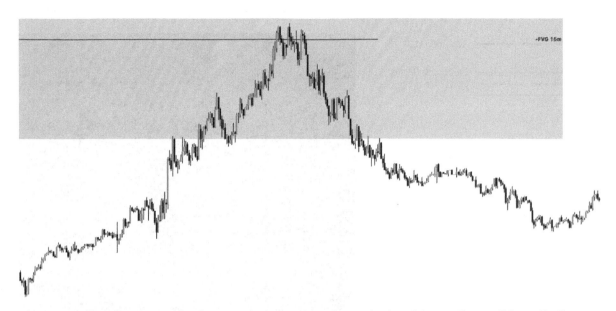

Drop from POI on the lower timeframe. The R/R in this trade could easily be set from 1/10+.

In general, the use of bundles of higher and lower timeframes is one of the secrets of Smart Money. By combining them, we can achieve a better risk-to-reward ratio.

Yes, someone may say - short stops are more likely to be taken! But that's not the case here. Here, the lower our risk, the better for us. It is most reasonable to set the risk at 1-2% of the deposit, with a target profit of 10-20% of the deposit from the trade using this concept.

Optimal Trade Entry

LEVELS	
O	Profit Scaling
0.5 - 50%	50% Equilibrium
0.62 - 62%	Possible Entry #1
0.705 - 70.5%	Possible Entry #2 - Best one
0.79 - 79%	Possible Entry #3
-0.27 - -27%	Target 1
-0.62 - -62%	Target 2
-1 - -100%	Symmetrical Swing
-2 - -200%	Final Target

*Optimal Trade Entry represents the best places to get into a trade and they can be identified by utilizing the Fibonacci drawing tool. When price has bottomed or topped in a certain area, we usually make a nice and deep retrace before going further in the other direction. This is called the optimal trade entry (OTE) since it's the ideal spot to enter a trade for high R/R trades. To be more specific, price retraces to the area between the 62% (0.62) and 79% (0.79) Fibonacci levels on your Fibonacci tool. With 70.5% being the middle of that and essentially being the sweet spot.

Now, these Fibonacci levels don't magically work everywhere. Like every other concept, you must combine this with other concepts to work. The OTE is an essential tool to find high R/R entries. The reason for this is that when price retraces this deep, you're close to your invalidation or stop loss, and so you automatically get high R/R trades because you enter close to your invalidation level.

*A limit order should be placed in the area between 0.62-0.79 levels.

*0.705-0.79 - this zone is considered as a Discount zone in case of an uptrend and Premium zone in case of a downtrend.

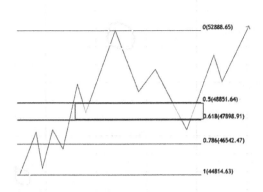

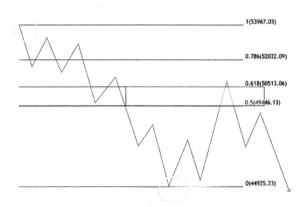

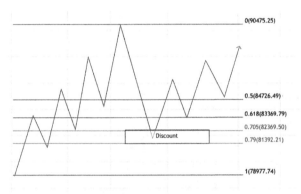

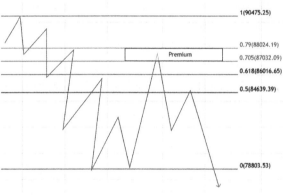

ES1!, 5, CME_MINI O4088.00 H4088.50 L4088.00 C4088.50 Vol13

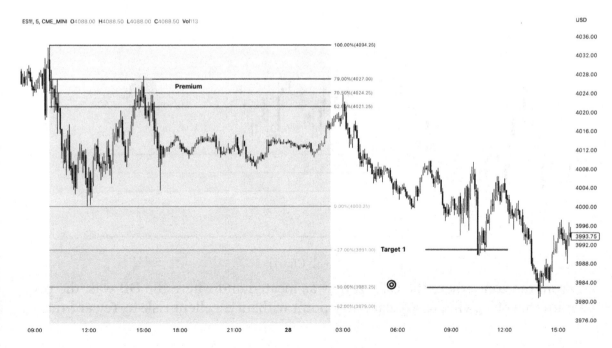

To implement the OTE strategy, follow these steps:

1. Determine the current market structure, whether it has a bullish or bearish bias. This is crucial as Fibonacci levels work best within a trending market.

2. Identify significant swing highs and lows to draw the Fibonacci grid. These highs and lows are often visual prominent and easy to label.

3. Use the Fibonacci retracement tool to assess the correction potential in an uptrend (from bottom to top) or downtrend (from top to bottom).

Why is this happening?

The golden rule of trading - after the main move in the market, a pullback will certainly occur. Nothing can grow indefinitely; you need to have price pullback in order to collect liquidity from below.

The 50% growth level is the most important and sooner or later the price will want to return there. Other than 0.5, 0.62 and 0.79 are important, most technical analysis users leave their stops behind these grid marks.

[4h Chart]

From the zone where the OTE zone was located and where the OB was, the price went up sharply, giving us a great entry point with an excellent risk-to-reward ratio.

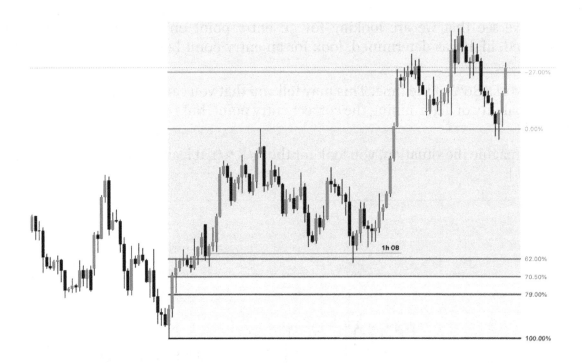

Finding an Entry Point

1. Determine the structure on a 4-hour timeframe

2. Determine the structure on a 1-hour timeframe

3. We define the structure at 15m and 5m.

4. An example of an ascending structure: from the swing low, we drag the Fib Retracement Tool to the swing high, in the direction of move. When we have up trend, we pull the Fib Retracement Tool from the low to high.

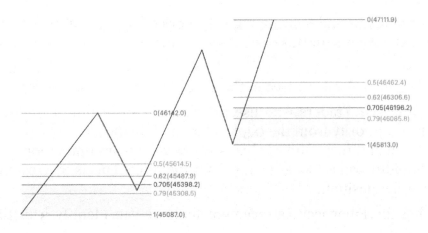

And we see that we are looking for an entry point on the pullback. Low was determined, high was determined, look for an entry point below the 0.5 zone on the Fib.

This works 80% of the time. This may tell you that you can enter positions with an 80% probability of determining the correct entry point, but risk management must be followed.

Now imagine the situation, you look for the R/R 3/1 at least [that is, either earn 3% or lose 1%].

We see a swing low and a swing high. The price bounced off the 0.705 zone, the move continued upwards, in this case, it was in the 0.705 zone that your entry point was.

Usually the pullback takes place in the zone between 0.62 and 0.705.

Why these levels? Traders who use the classic TA (Technical Analysis) in their trading work as a priority from the 0.5 level of the Fib, they leave stop orders behind the levels of 0.62 and 0.79, and so this is where a large accumulation of liquidity is located. All liquidity will act as a "magnet" for the price. This is where a major player will gain his or her position.

By utilizing the Fibonacci Retracement tool, we can identify 3 distinct trading correction levels:

1. the Premium zone - represents the price correction range situated above the 0.5 (50%) level in the context of a downward momentum. Traders pay attention to this zone when considering selling opportunities.

2. the Discount zone - The Discount zone refers to the price correction range located below the 0.5 (50%) level in the case of an upward impulse. Traders observe this zone for potential buying opportunities.

3. the Equilibrium zone - The Equilibrium zone denotes the price range where the asset's average price is located. In other words, it represents the fair price zone or the level of balance between buyers and sellers.

Traders and market makers seek opportunities to buy at a Discount and sell at the Premium zone. As a result, traders often disregard the 0.236 and 0.382 Fibonacci levels in their analysis and instead wait for the price to move above or below the equilibrium level.

Following the Fibonacci retracement grid rules, it is drawn based on the impulse movement, starting from the initial swing point (assigned a value of 1) and extending to its logical conclusion (assigned a value of 0).

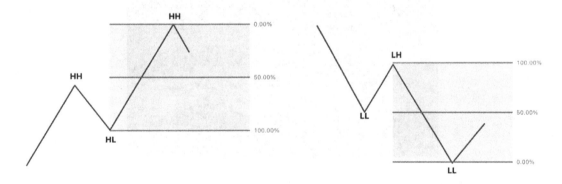

According to the rules, this OTE goes from the beginning of a trend to its end. If it is drawn correctly, we get possible correction targets, from these levels we can enter the trend, or use them as targets.

In the screenshot below, using the TradingView example, these are the values set to set up this Fibonacci. Colors are naturally customizable to your preference.

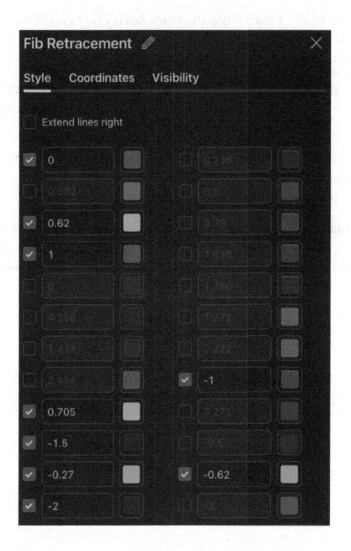

The OTE zone is located in the Premium zone if we consider a short position, and in the Discount zone if we consider a long position.

OTE includes correction levels 0.62 (62%); 0.705 (70.5%); 0.79 (79%) are the levels with the highest probability that the price will turn in the opposite direction.

First of all, focusing on the premium / discount zones, since the price does not always enter the OTE zone, sometimes it is enough for the price to adjust by 0.5 (50%) in order for the major players (institutional money) to gain or lose a position.

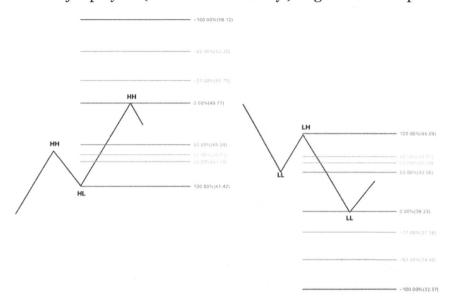

Please note that the Fibonacci levels themselves do not act as support or resistance, and the price does not bounce off the levels themselves. We use the Fibonacci retracement to search for "Liquidity Blocks" such as imbalance (FVG), order block (OB) and so on.

How to Select the High and Low of a Dealing Range

To select the high and low points of a dealing range, follow these steps:

1. Run a Fibonacci retracement tool from the highest high to the lowest low within the dealing range. This will help establish the overall range of price action.

2. Pay attention to areas where the algorithm consolidates. These consolidation areas indicate fair value and are important in determining the proper dealing range.

3. Consider the nearest high when the 50% Fibonacci level aligns with the common consolidation area. This will help identify the appropriate high point of the dealing range.

4. Select the pullback as the low point of the dealing range. This ensures that the range encompasses the relevant price action and aligns with the areas where algorithms are active.

Exploring the Algorithm's Preference for Premium and Discount Markets

Algorithms tend to favor buying in a discount market and selling in a premium market. Understanding this preference is key to getting in sync with the algorithms and maximizing our trading profits.

- Premium Market: The premium market refers to the price range above the equilibrium level. Here, the algorithm considers the asset to be overvalued and looks for opportunities to sell. As traders, we need to be cautious when trading in this range and consider taking profits or entering short positions.

- Discount Market: On the other hand, the discount market represents the price range below the equilibrium level. In this range, the algorithm considers the asset to be undervalued and looks for opportunities to buy. As traders, we should be on the lookout for potential buying opportunities in this range.

Analyzing the Behavior of the Market Above and Below Equilibrium

Premium Market Behavior: When the price of an asset reaches the premium market, it tends to sell off and move back towards the equilibrium level.

Discount Market Behavior: Conversely, when the price of an asset reaches the discount market, it tends to bounce back and move towards the equilibrium level. This buying pressure occurs because the algorithm considers the asset to be undervalued. As traders, we should be on the lookout for potential buying opportunities in this range.

Within each market, we can further break it down into its own premium and discount areas. This allows us to have a more detailed understanding of the range. For example:

- Premium within the Premium Market: This is the top part of the premium market. It represents a higher value within the premium range.

- Discount within the Premium Market: This is the bottom part of the premium market. It represents a lower value within the premium range.

- Premium within the Discount Market: This is the top part of the discount market. It represents a higher value within the discount range.

- Discount within the Discount Market: This is the bottom part of the discount market. It represents a lower value within the discount range.

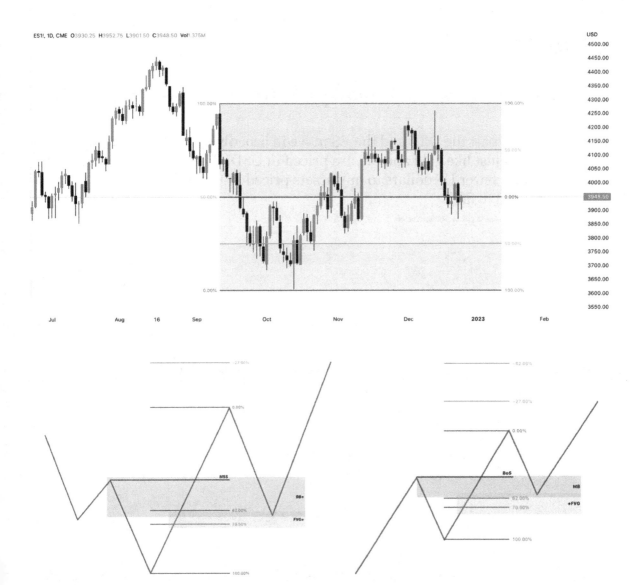

Chapter 17

Intermarket Relationships & Intermarket Analysis

For the most part the DXY and the ES move in broadly opposite directions. Stocks in the S&P 500, just like gold and oil, are priced in USD. When the USD is increasing in value, it takes fewer US dollars to buy assets priced in US dollars ... so the prices of those assets tend to fall.

There are also times when the S&P 500 and the US dollar both move up together. These are usually times of economic recovery ... when everything is going right.

US Dollar Index

DXY an index of the value of the US dollar against other currencies, which was created by JP Morgan in 1973.

The DXY is essentially a measure of the value of the US dollar relative to a basket of other major currencies, including the euro, yen, pound, and Canadian dollar. As such, it can provide valuable insights into global economic trends and investor sentiment.

Thus, given the presence of the euro, the dollar index contains currencies represented by 24 states.

The correlation between the Dollar Index (DXY) and indices can be explained through the risk-on and risk-off scenarios.

When the Dollar Index is moving higher (risk-off), it usually indicates that foreign currencies and index futures have more freedom to drop and have a hard time rallying higher. On the other hand, when the Dollar Index is moving lower (risk-on), it supports the rise of indices and foreign currencies.

It's important to note that market conditions and other factors can influence this correlation, and it may not always hold true.

Why is this happening?

The growth of the US dollar index causes a decrease in the price of assets in dollar pairs, while the drop and consolidation of the index causes assets in dollar pairs to strengthen, therefore, ES/NQ/YM. begin to grow.

There are three scenarios for the behavior of the DXY and the reaction of ES/NQ/YM:

1. Scenario #1 - DXY falls, ES/NQ/YM rises.

2. Scenario #2 - DXY rises, ES/NQ/YM falls.

3. Scenario #3 - DXY consolidates, ES/NQ/YM rises.

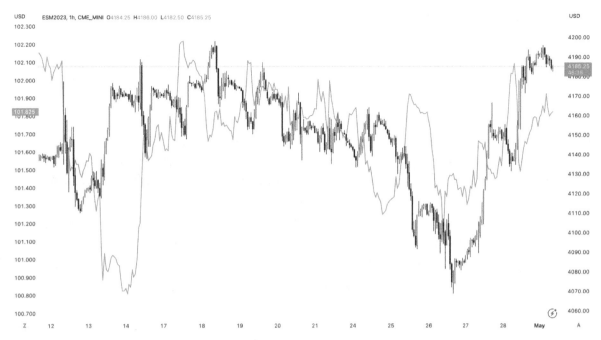

Traders who are able to understand the correlation between the DXY and indices can use this knowledge to identify potential trading opportunities. For example, as I mentioned above, if the DXY is trending higher while the ES is trending lower, this may suggest that investors are becoming more risk-averse and moving away from equities. Traders who recognize this trend may be able to take short positions in the ES (YM, NQ, etc.), anticipating further downside.

On the other hand, if the DXY is trending lower while the ES is trending higher, this may indicate that investors are becoming more bullish on equities and willing to take on more risk. Traders who recognize this trend may look for long opportunities in the ES.

When the dollar index strengthens, meaning the value of the U.S. dollar increases relative to other currencies, it can have a negative impact on the e-mini S&P futures market. This is because a stronger dollar can make U.S. exports more expensive, which can lead to a decrease in corporate earnings for U.S. companies. As a result, the stock prices of these companies may decline, causing the e-mini S&P futures market to go down.

On the other hand, when the dollar index weakens, meaning the value of the U.S. dollar decreases relative to other currencies, it can have a positive impact on the e-mini S&P futures market. A weaker dollar can make U.S. exports more competitive, which can lead to an increase in corporate earnings for U.S. companies. As a result, the stock prices of these companies may rise, causing the e-mini S&P futures market to go up.

Seasonal Tendencies

"There is a time to go long. There is a time to go short. And there is a time to go fishing."

- Jesse Livermore.

Seasonal tendencies are not absolute, but they can serve as a roadmap or a treasure map, giving traders an idea of what to normally expect in price action during a specific time of year. They are based on historical data and can help traders anticipate market movements, but they should not be relied upon entirely, as market conditions and other factors can influence the actual outcome.

Seasonal tendencies can be useful for futures and forex trading, but it's important to remember that they are not guarantees and should be used in conjunction with other analysis tools and techniques.

Seasonal trends: This is not a panacea. If your analysis is consistent with the seasonal trend, then you will trade the most probabilistic models.

December – January

In the last and first months of the calendar year, all markets tend to be in a state of consolidation with the least favorable price behavior for the formation of trading patterns. Such price action is dictated primarily by the busy schedule of holidays and bank holidays, when liquidity leaves the markets. During these periods, most traders take vacations or spend more time observing and testing new trading patterns.

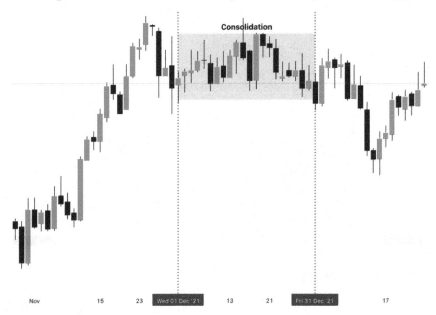

February – April

Since February, markets have come out of consolidation, moving and trending, which suggests more favorable price action. This is due to the fact that smart capital enters the market in large volumes. During these periods, the market has the most optimal and HIGHLY probabilistic trading models.

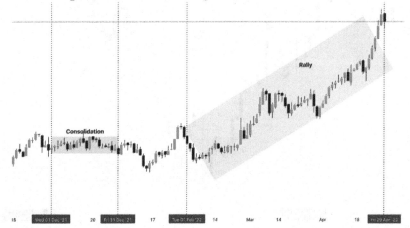

May – August

The popular saying "Sell in May and go away" is justified by the fact that smart capital takes profits on its positions before the summer period of low volatility. As a result, the market forms a downward trend and subsequent consolidation during the so-called "summer depression". During these periods, most professional traders take vacations, especially in August.

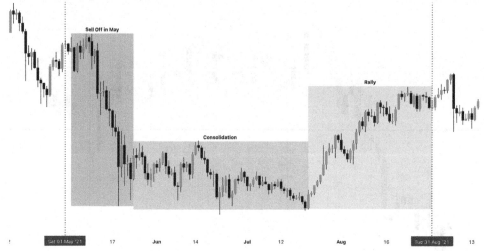

September - November

In the last quarter of the year, the market starts moving again. While the stock market tends to go up. During these periods, most professional traders are actively trading. Then a new cycle begins.

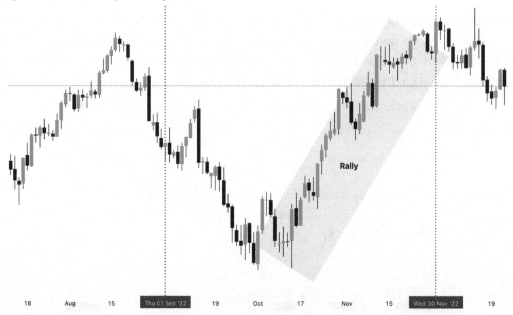

S&P500 E-MINI / OPEN-CLOSE

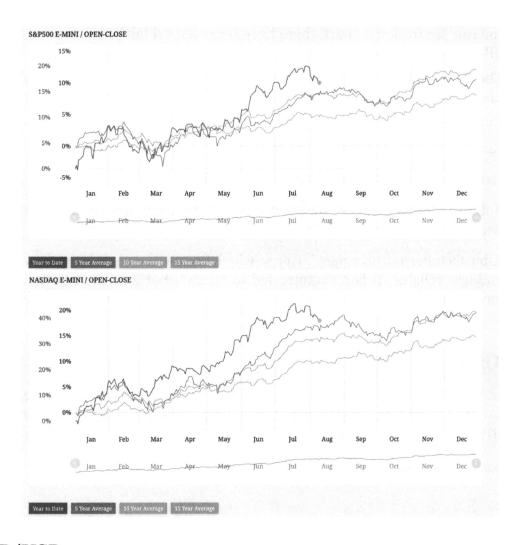

Year to Date | 5 Year Average | 10 Year Average | 15 Year Average

NASDAQ E-MINI / OPEN-CLOSE

Year to Date | 5 Year Average | 10 Year Average | 15 Year Average

EUR/USD

EURO FX / OPEN-CLOSE

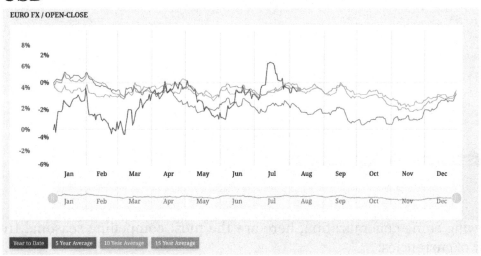

Year to Date | 5 Year Average | 10 Year Average | 15 Year Average

As you can see from the chart, there have been several fairly stable trends for the EUR/USD pair over the years:

1. The Euro typically forms a bottom in mid-February and then moves higher into mid-March. A pull back then occurs then we see another climb into the end of April.

2. Another low in June which climbs into late July/early August.

3. Usually a decline from early August to early September.

4. Early to late September is a good time for the Euro, and then usually sees a decline in early October.

5. After October our averages diverge which means the signals are less concise and less reliable. It is recommended to be aware of data inconsistencies that happen for some timeframes that do not allow for definitive observations to make trading decisions.

GBP/USD

Since the pounds have been trading against the US dollar for the longest time, there is quite convincing data on the seasonal trends of trading this pair in Forex. Unlike JPY, there is a direct link between GBP futures and the corresponding Forex.

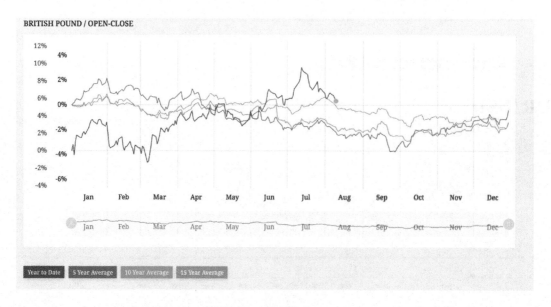

Allowing some generalization, here are the most compelling seasonal trends for this pair of currencies:

239

1. The Pound typically forms a bottom in early to late March and then moves higher into the end of April.

2. Early May to mid-May is usually a bearish time.

3. A bottom typically forms again in mid-May we see a move higher into early August.

4. Price usually peak early in August and decline into early September.

5. Averages re-align to form a top in early November and the price slides into mid-to-late November. After this the averages diverge again.

Dollar Index

The first time frames looked at are the 5, 10 and 15 year seasonal trends. Therefore, we are only looking for common points where all three time frames bottom or top at similar times of the year.

By looking at multiple time frames, and finding commonalities, we can extract the strongest Dollar Index seasonal trends.

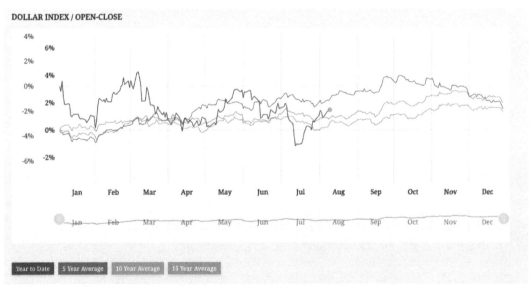

Over the three time frames studied we can extract the commonalities to find usual tendencies in the USD over the last 5, 10 and 15 years:

1. Start of the year to mid-February has an upward bias.

2. Typically tops out in the middle of February and declines into mid-March.

3. Last half of March is usually strong and then sells off into late April.

4. Beginning to middle of May is a strong time for the USD, but then falls into a short-term low by the end of May.

5. End of May to Mid-June may see some price appreciation.

6. Middle of June usually marks a short-term high and the USD declines into the end of July.

7. Rally from beginning of August to early September.

8. Early November to late-November sees a rise.

9. Late December is a bearish time.

Chapter 18

FOMC, NFP Study

- FOMC days: The Federal Open Market Committee (FOMC) is the committee that sets interest rates in the United States. FOMC meetings are held eight times per year, and the day of the meeting is often a taboo day for trading. This is because the FOMC's decisions can have a significant impact on the market, and traders may be more likely to make impulsive decisions on these days.

- Non-farm payroll (NFP) days: The NFP report is a monthly report that measures the number of jobs added to the US economy. NFP reports are released on the first Friday of every month, and they can also be taboo days for trading. This is because the NFP report can have a significant impact on the market, and traders may be more likely to make impulsive decisions on these days.

Why Avoid Thursday & Friday of NonFarm Payroll (NFP) Weeks?

ICT recommends avoiding trading on Thursday and Friday during non-farm payroll (NFP) week. This is because there is a lot of heavy manipulation that goes on that week, and the market tends to be really unfavorable. ICT advises that as a new developing student, it is important to know that those market environments are not the same as the week after NFP. There's a lot of wait and see type conditions, and you can hurt yourself. During NFP week, the market is likely to consolidate, gyrate around in a small, meaningless, aimless range, waiting for the news to drop. Therefore, it is not a good idea to trade during this time.

- Increased volatility: These days often see increased volatility in the markets, which can make it difficult to trade profitably.

- Liquidity issues: Liquidity can be an issue on these days, as many traders are hesitant to trade in volatile markets.

- The potential for false moves: These days can often see false moves, which can trap traders into taking losing trades.

ICT also advises avoiding trading London open after FOMC events that create whipsaw.

- Manual intervention by the institutions.

- Seek and destroy profile on Thursday (Friday) expected.

- After large expansion move.

- Fridays when Thursdays met HTF objective.

Seek and Destroy Market Profile

Buy Stops Blown Out

BUY STOPS ORDERS

Buy Stops triggered.
Short taken out.
New longs on breakout trade active

BUY STOPS ORDERS

SELL STOPS ORDERS

Sell Stops triggered.
Long taken out.
New shorts on breakout trade active

SELL STOPS ORDERS

Sell Stops Blown Out

- High resistance liquidity conditions :

When price is constantly moving up and down in a range on DXY, we want to see what side of the market when it comes to Futures moves easier or more freely. Pair that up with Market Structure, Narrative and/or Bias. It is very important to identify the Markets Condition and act accordingly. Sometimes staying on the sidelines and speculating is the best thing to do. Sometimes price might not follow these rules and that creates high resistance liquidity runs.

Think of high resistance as an area that was already induced so the market has less incentive to return while low resistance is where untouched liquidity rests (sequence of higher lows and lower highs).

- Precision will be skewed.

- PD arrays may not be as reliable as normally would.

243

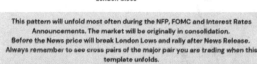

RANGE TO NEW YORK OPEN/LONDON CLOSE RALLY

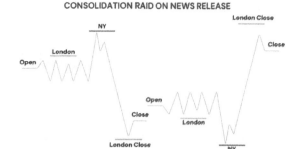

CONSOLIDATION RAID ON NEWS RELEASE

This pattern will unfold most often during the NFP, FOMC and Interest Rates Announcements. The market will be originally in consolidation.
Before the News price will break London Lows and rally after News Release.
Always remember to see cross pairs of the major pair you are trading when this template unfolds.
Forex: If Dollar is dropping and EURUSD pair is consolidating EURJPY will be buying if Dollar is DROPPING, GBP is RALLYING and EUR is CONSOLIDATING: Wait for GBP to hit a PD Array level and EUR will give a range to NYO/LC rally setup. If majors are consolidating but crosses are moving, wait for the crosses to hit key PD Arrays and come back to majors, and trade to the direction of the crosses.

This pattern will unfold most often during the NFP, FOMC and Interest Rates Announcements:
- After opening price, market will consolidate before the News.
- During the News releases price will drop to induce traders and take stops (this move might not be that big below the consolidation but it has to break the consolidation)
- After clearing the stops and inducing, price will move into true direction You have to identify Key support level or order block below the consolidation. See if price will reject at support/resistance within 5 minutes after News release, if it won't reject then leave the trade because you might be wrong in your analysis.

Taboo Trading Days and Market Manipulation

In the world of trading, there are certain days that are considered taboo for trading. These are days when market conditions can be unpredictable and potentially volatile.

One example of a taboo trading day is a Monday following a non-farm payroll report. Non-farm payroll reports are released on the first Friday of every month and provide important data on employment trends in the United States. If there is no holiday in the beginning of the week or prior to Wednesday, Mondays can be particularly volatile due to increased movement in the market.

Another taboo trading day is when there is a holiday on Monday, Tuesday, or Wednesday of a non-farm payroll week. In this case, Thursdays and Fridays after the non-farm payroll release become the focus for trading, as market movements can be significant during these days.

Analyzing Market Manipulation During Significant Economic Reports

Market manipulation is a common occurrence during significant economic reports. One example of this is the FOMC event. The FOMC event is a two-stage event that takes place at 2 o'clock in the afternoon. The first run after the event is often considered a fake move, designed to lure in unsuspecting traders. It is important to be aware of this manipulation and not get caught up in the initial run.

During the FOMC event, it is common for the market to move in the opposite direction during the conference portion. This can be compared to a tsunami, where the water moves away from the beach before the big wave hits. Similarly, the market may move in one direction initially before reversing during the conference portion. It is crucial not to be caught up in these big moves and to be aware of the manipulation that can occur during these events.

Chapter 19

Model Diagrams

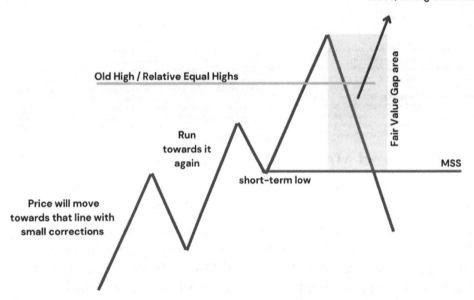

You need to see it go below that level with displacement and an energetic move, taking out a short-term low.

Old High / Relative Equal Highs

Fair Value Gap area

Run towards it again

MSS

short-term low

Price will move towards that line with small corrections

If you have an old fair value gap above the market, and the market is trading below it and moving upward, when it trades into that fair value gap, it doesn't have to completely close it. Anywhere between the old FVG is acceptable. You can simplify it by considering the low of the fair value gap as your trigger point, similar to how you treat the relative equal highs. Once it takes out the low of the fair value gap and trades within it, go back through that leg and identify the trigger and the displacement leg. This will help you find the fair value area for your trade.

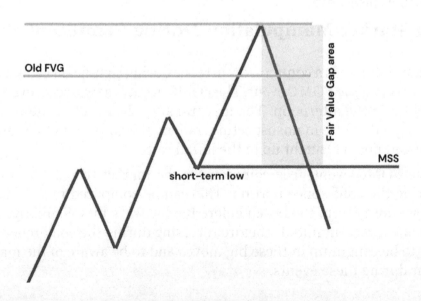

Old FVG

Fair Value Gap area

MSS

short-term low

Remember, missing a move in the market doesn't result in a losing trade unless you use a flawed logic that leads to a losing trade. If today the setups we expected didn't form, but it doesn't mean the market is against us. It's just a missed opportunity and dwelling on it won't make any money or change the outcome. Instead, focus on learning from the experience and developing a mindset that can handle setbacks.

Trading is about studying, observing, and recognizing repeating patterns in price action. It's not about blindly following instructions to buy or sell. ICT teaching method might not suit everyone, but it's based on logical analysis of charts. Avoid toxic thinking and negative self-talk. Accept missed opportunities as part of the learning process. Stay positive, study, practice, and be prepared for the next opportunity.

ICT 2022 Mentorship Model

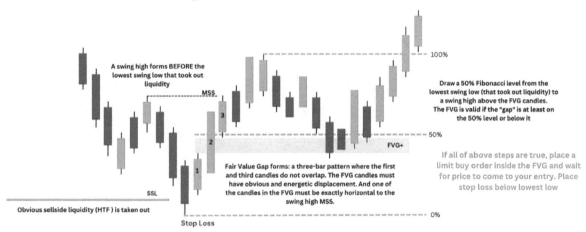

1. Price trades through major Buyside or Sellside Liquidity (Asian High/Low, London High/Low, Previous Day(s) High/Low, etc.).

2. Price reverses direction and creates a Fair Value Gap (FVG) with Displacement (Displacement must exist. This signifies there is Institutional sponsorship to the move).

3. Swing (high or low) must be exactly horizontal to one of the three candles in the FVG. This swing is now a Market Structure Shift (MSS): a. The Swing High/Low can occur either before the liquidity grab or afterwards. Either way is valid.

4. Draw a 50% Fibonacci line (two options): a. Start at swing that took liquidity to a swing on the other side of the FVG. b. Start at a prominent swing after liquidity taken swing to a swing on the other side of the FVG

246

5. The gap in the FVG candles must be on the Equilibrium line (50%) or on the side of the Liquidity (i.e. the better side).

6. Place Limit Order inside the FVG at the Equilibrium or on the better side of Equilibrium.

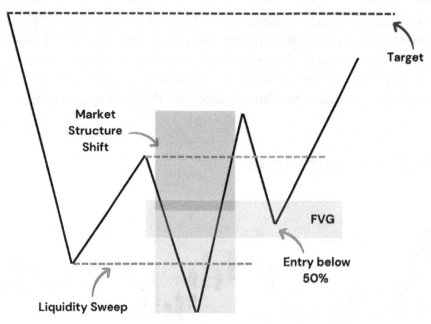

1. Liquidity grab. (Old highs/lows or other HTF PD Arrays

2. Displacement

3. Market Structure Shift (MSS)

4. FVG/OB above or below 50% fib of the Displacement Range

5. Return to FVG or OB.

6. Solid Risk Reward Ratio.

The displacement low is the short-term low being broken, and the displacement high is the old high. The range between these two points is called the displacement range.

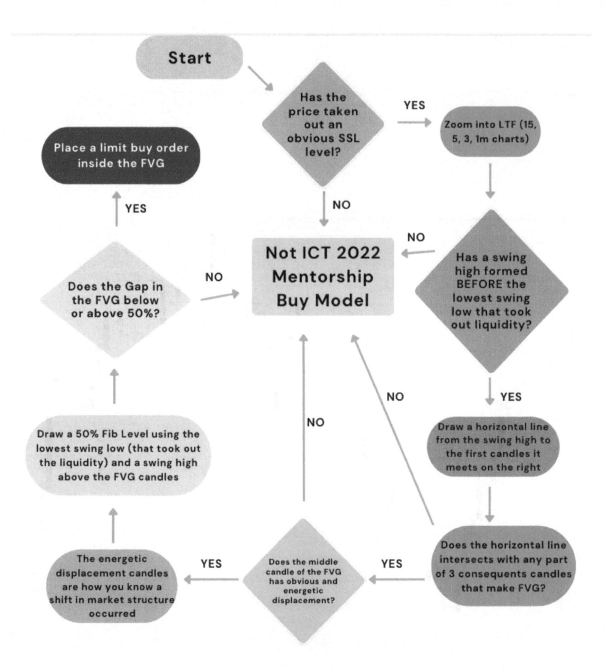

[Credit to Infinity Trading – Twitter: @infinitytradeIO]

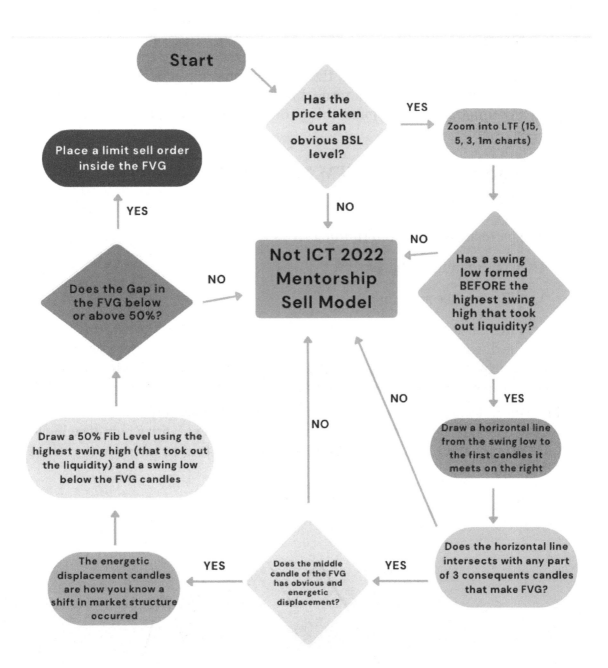

[Credit to Infinity Trading – Twitter: @infinitytradeIO]

The ICT ATM Method

The ICT ATM model is similar to the 2022 mentorship model but it is a stand-alone price action pattern. The pattern capitalizes on stop hunt. *You can find this setup on any timeframe. Remember this is only a setup, you have to frame context behind every setup.

Introduction To The ICT ATM Method:

- ATM is an independent pattern.

- The pattern benefits from running stops.

- Used on 60 minute charts.

- Very Easy to see and trade.

*Scan Price on 1h Chart for a key high that forms with the short-term swing low broken to the downside. Ideally if it is part of a continued swing higher – with a pair of swing highs broken – prior to the Key High formation. We are going to wait for price to retrace to the swing low broken prior to the Key High forming.

*Price on 1h Chart for a key low that forms with the short-term swing high broken to the upside. Ideally if it is part of a continued swing lower – with a pair of swing lows broken – prior to the Key low formation. We are going to wait for price to retrace to the swing high broken prior to the Key Low forming.

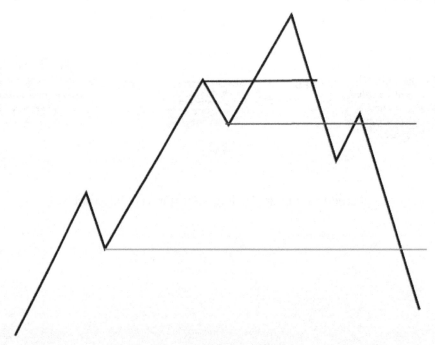

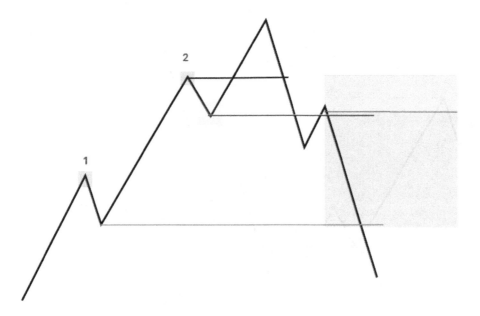

After breaking the structure and taking 2 Short-Term Lows, you need to wait for the pullback to Breaker Block and enter the position.

Stop Loss: High or Breaker Block.

Take Profit: Below Second Short Term Low.

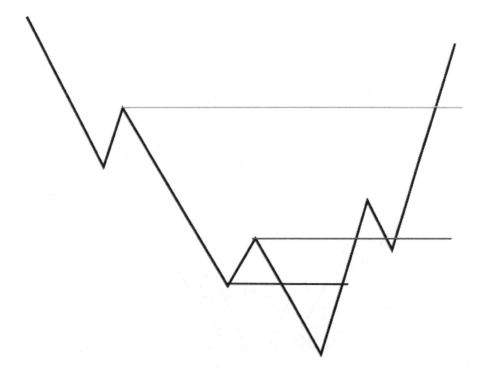

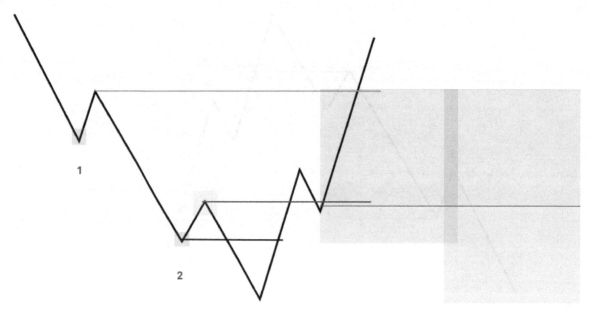

After breaking the structure and taking 2 Short Term Highs, you need to wait for the pullback to Breaker Block and enter the position.

Stop Loss: Low or Breaker Block.

Take Profit: Above Second Short Term High.

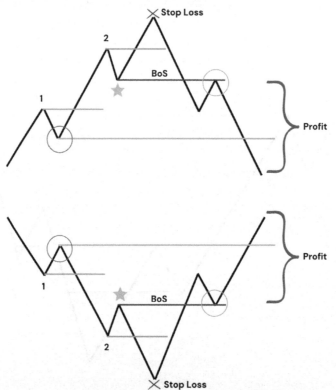

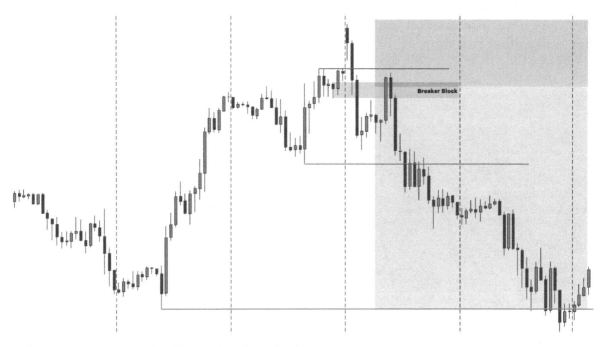

Market Maker Sell Model - MMXM

Credit to TheInnerCircleDragons

Let's talk about the market maker sell model. I want to specifically focus on the buy side. So, let's take a look a diagram below, this is the buy program inside of the market maker sell model.

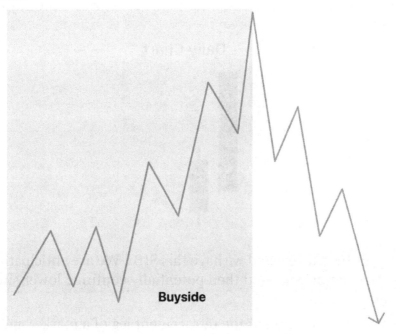

For market maker sell model, we look for HTF bearish conditions. If the HTF is trending lower, the market maker sell model will be a retracement higher and will generally either run stops or rebalance.

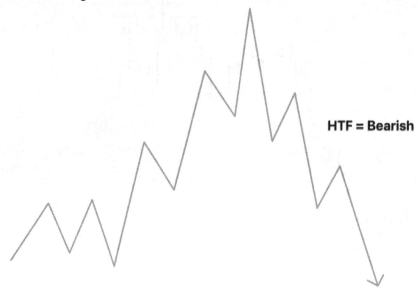

HTF = Bearish

Once the buy program ends of the market maker sell model, the sell program will commence to take price back below the initial consolidation.

It's very important for us to know what the HTF draw is likely to be. Generally the best trades using the market maker sell model in a HTF bearish environment will be on the sellside within the sell program.

However, we can still counter trend trade to the HTF within the buy program of the market maker sell model.

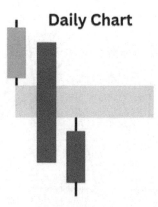

Daily Chart

We see the daily time frame and we have this SIBI. We are anticipating price to run higher to close this inefficiency and then potentially continue lower since we are in a higher time frame bearish trend.

We anticipate a buy program as the retracement leg of a market maker sell model.

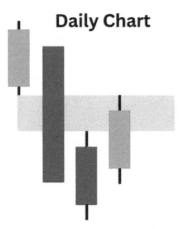

Daily Chart

The algorithm will reprice to the sellside imbalance. And this whole retracement higher looks like this on 1h time frame:

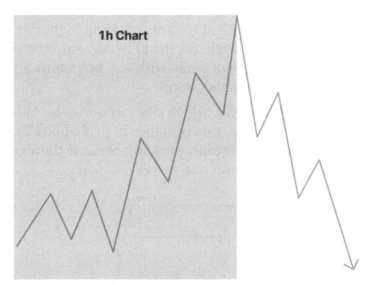

1h Chart

This is the buyside delivery within a smaller retracement on the daily time frame. Before the price reaches the higher time frame premium level of this SIBI. Let's simplify it: this upward move on the daily time frame represents a buying program within the market maker sell model on the buyside of the curve.

I want to focus on the buy program initially and see how we can capitalize on the movement higher during this retracement into the sellside imbalance on the daily time frame.

So, we have our initial consolidation and we have higher time frame level (PD Array). Again, it can be any higher time frame level: FVG, OB, BB, MB, BSL, etc. It could be any of the number of arrays that we can see in price. It's all dependent on what we can currently see in price at the time.

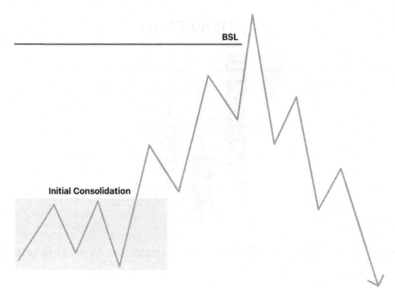

We focus on a run on BSL, and then we are repricing higher in our buy program to purge the liquidity above the old high. So, it will be buy stops resting above that old high. Smart money will pair short positions with the buy stops and then distribute their positions below the initial consolidation.

If we see a higher time frame level, which sits just above an old high where there are buy stops and BSL resting above, this is higher in probability that we are likely to see a market reversal and the end of the buy program because the algorithm is efficient, it will always look to kill two birds with one stone.

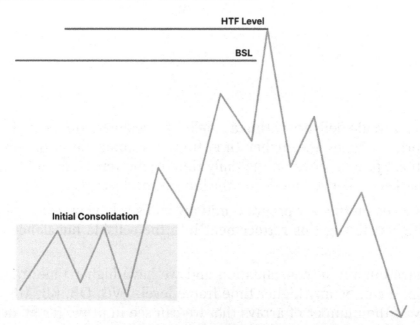

1m Chart

The two main parameters that the algorithm is going to look to do is to seek liquidity and to rebalance inefficiencies where you often going to find an old high that rests below an inefficiency. And the algorithm will often draw to this area and it will serve you very well if you keep this analogy whenever you're looking for setups in the market.

Now let's focus on the left side of the curve.

From the initial consolidation low to the HTF level where we expect price to reach for. This is known as the BDR – Buyside Delivery Range.

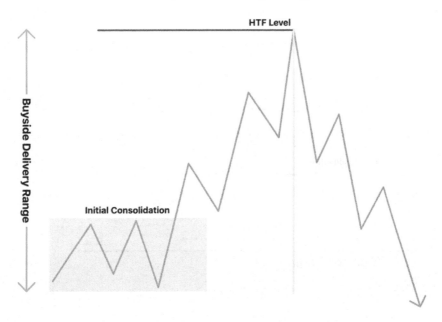

The initial consolidation will be our point of origin and we're anticipating price to go up to the HTF level. We should then expect a reversal and the initiation of a sell program to run the engineered sellside liquidity below the initial consolidation.

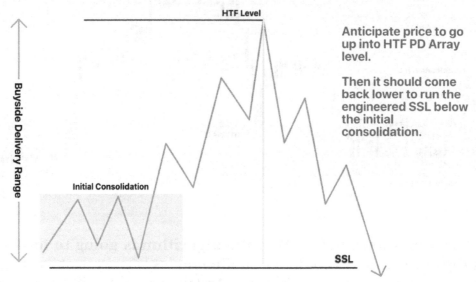

Once we have identified our point of origin and we have identified our potential draw on liquidity on the HTF, we can then grade our buy side delivery range in 25% quadrants.

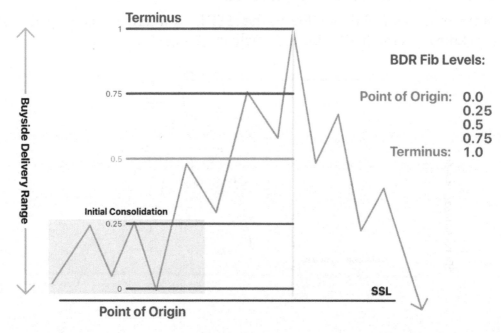

259

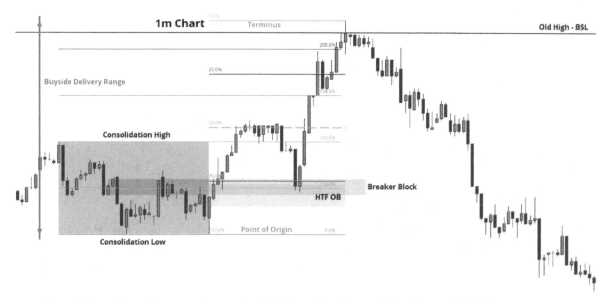

We will anchor the FIB from the high to the low of the buyside delivery range.

The initial consolidation will generally form in the lower quadrant. Between the first and second quadrant, we will see our first stage of accumulation or a return to the consolidation.

We generally look for price to do one of two things:

1. It will either drop lower to rebalance an inefficiency in the expansion leg that moved away from the consolidation.

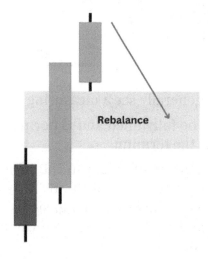

2. It will look to run sell stops or SSL.

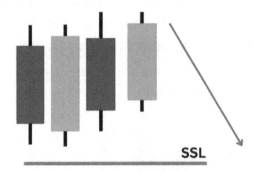

At the 50% level, we will generally see a measuring gap.

A measuring gap will not be fully filled and is normally a reflection of the halfway point between the origin and the terminus.

If we take a fib from our point of origin to the measuring gap and project one deviation higher, we should get the high of the BTR. If this overlaps with a higher timeframe level and or buyside liquidity, this gives us a good indication that this is in fact a measuring gap and gives us extra confirmation that we are set around equilibrium 50% of the buyside delivery range.

Between 2nd and 3rd quadrant we normally expect our second stage of re-accumulation. We are looking to either rebalance an inefficiency below the market in the form of a BISI or we are looking to seek sellside liquidity in the form of sell stops below an old low or relative equal lows.

1. **It will either drop lower to rebalance an inefficiency in the expansion leg that moved away from the consolidation.**

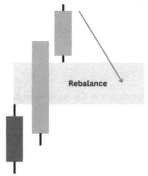

2. **It will look to run sell stops or SSL.**

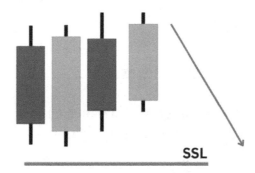

We will see an explosive move higher from the final stage of accumulation and into Terminus, which would be our buyside objective or a higher timeframe level. This would prevent traders from entering the market on a retracement, and it also reduces the time for traders to close positions that are underwater.

Let's look at the initial consolidation again and we'll get into a little bit more detail of how we can use the initial consolidation to give us measurements on how high the buy program can reach.

We have our initial consolidation high and we have our initial consolidation low.

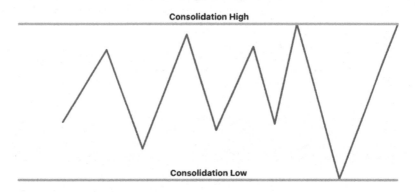

It is known as the consolidation range. If we take the consolidation range high and the consolidation range low and we use a fib and then anchor it to the high and the low, we want to get the midway point between the consolidation range and reject half a standard deviation above the consolidation range high.

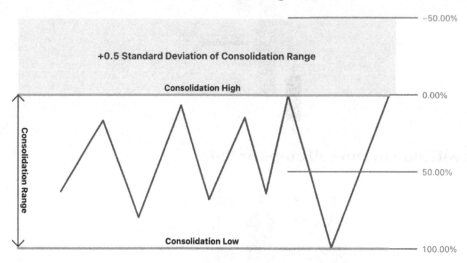

If we take our consolidation range and we project deviations using our FIB tool higher, we will be interested in level that near Terminus.

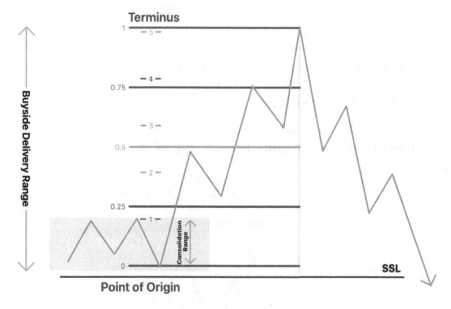

How do we use this information?

Swing points will often form around these deviations. We can use these deviations to anticipate highs and lows inside of the buyside delivery range within the buy program.

If these deviations overlap with the grades of our buyside delivery range, this is where we are likely to see our highest probability setups form.

If we see a deviation that is above buyside liquidity, say we have an old high to the left and it's in close proximity to this higher time frame level, we have a strong probability of a buy program high.

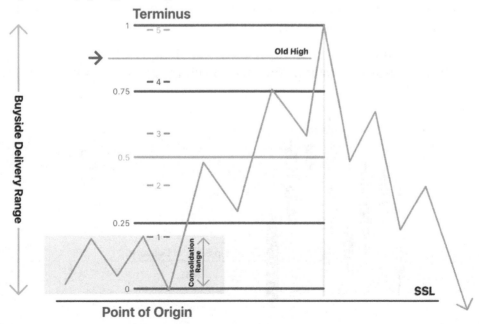

From the initial consolidation before anything has printed to the right, we can already reference using these deviations to project a theoretical terminus, which we can then use to grade our buyside delivery range. So, we can identify the highest probability areas of where setups will form before price even prints.

Now let's discuss the sellside of the MMSM.

On the right side of the curve, we have the sellside delivery. Again, we look for the market maker sell model when the higher time frame is bearish.

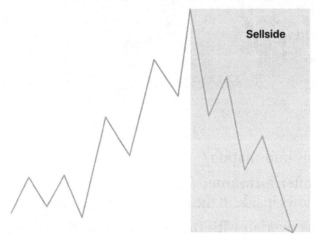

On the 1h time frame, the smaller fractal is the sell side delivery of the market maker sell model.

Once price has left the initial consolidation and our buy program was underway, offering buyside delivery to our higher timeframe level, we then have a reversal known as a smart money reversal or an SMR.

What is a smart money reversal? It is a change in state of delivery. The algorithm goes from a buy program to a sell program or a sell program to a buy program.

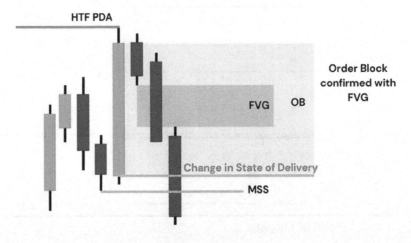

In the case of the market maker sell model, we are going from a buy program to a sell program to a sellside delivery.

We have type one reversal where we run above an old high and tap into a higher timeframe level.

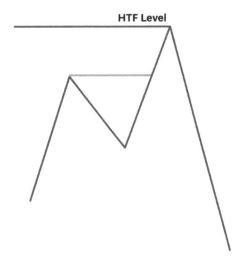

We then reverse breaking below an old swing low. This is known as a breaking market structure.

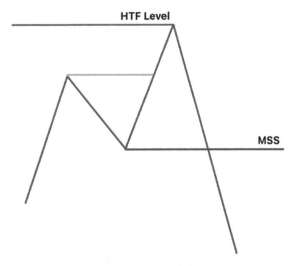

The type two reversal is we have reached a higher timeframe level. We have this high which failed to go above its previous high, giving us a lower high. And then running back below, swing low, giving us our break in market structure.

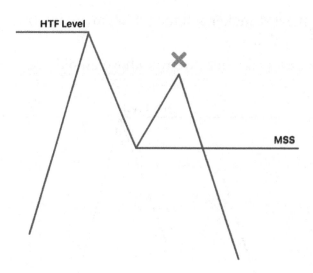

The ideal reversal pattern we are looking for is a type one reversal where we make a higher high and then break below an old swing low.

For extra confirmation, we want to look at a correlated asset class and we want to see an SMT divergence between the two. When asset one makes a higher high, we look for a correlated asset class to make a lower high. If they are inversely correlated, then we would look for one to make a higher high and its correlated pair to make a higher low.

We would only refer to this type of reversal pattern if it's correlated asset was showing an SMT divergence by posting a higher high.

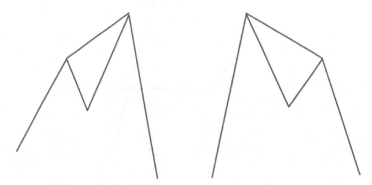

Let's look at type one in a little bit more detail.

When we see a break in market structure after we have run a short term high and rejected from a higher timeframe level, we are looking inside of the expansion leg that broke market structure to see if we can see a FVG.

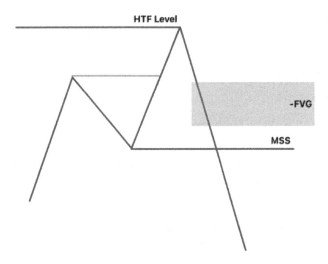

This is what it would look like on the chart where we have an old swing high which we run through sweeping the buy stops above this high, rejecting from the higher timeframe level and then running back below this swing low, causing a break in market structure.

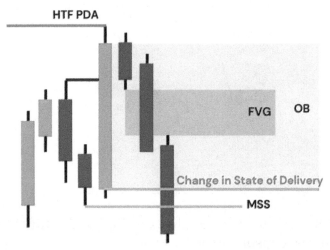

The break in market structure is confirmed with this FVG. If this FVG is not present, we don't class this as a valid break in market structure. We don't have to close below the swing low in order for it to be classed as a valid break in market structure if we still have the FVG present.

However, it is higher in probability if we do see a close below the swing low when price runs through the opening price of the last close candle that ran the buyside liquidity.

This becomes an order block and when its open is violated, we have a change in state of delivery.

This order block and the change in state of delivery is confirmed with the presence of the FVG inside of the expansion leg that traveled through the opening price of this order block.

The algorithm will then reprice lower to attack, sell side liquidity or to rebalance an inefficiency below the market.

When price has reached its HTF level and we have taken out buyside liquidity in the form of an old high to the left, we can now start looking for targets on the left side of the curve. We know that our initial consolidation is going to be our likely draw since the higher timeframe is bearish.

The sellside liquidity will rest below the initial consolidation lows. This would be our initial terminus as a target. From the point of origin to the terminus will be our SDR or our expected range for sellside delivery.

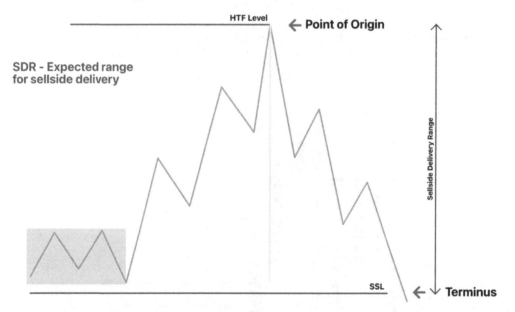

We are anticipating price to go lower after the SMR and we are targeting the sellside liquidity below the initial consolidation.

Just like on the left side of the curve where we could grade our range, we can now do the same for the sellside of the market maker sell model. Again, this would be our SDR levels and our FIB tool.

We would anchor our fib from point of origin, which would be the high of the market maker sell model to the initial terminus below the initial consolidation, and we would get a graded range of 25% increments.

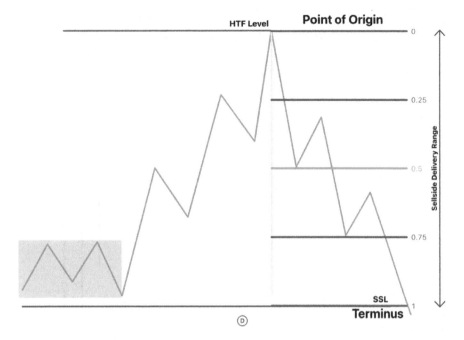

How far below the initial consolidation can price go? Well, the initial consolidation would be our first target. But we can use calibration techniques to assess how far low we can go.

Calibration techniques are going to involve a number of things:

1. We look for range below the initial consolidation.

If we have our consolidation range or we have our consolidation high and our consolidation low, we want to look for point range below the initial consolidation in increments of 5, 10, 15 and 20 points (NQ) or 2, 5, 7, 10 points (ES/SP500).

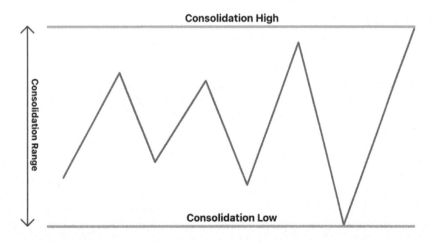

2. The second thing we want to look for is if a higher timeframe level will be in close proximity to one of the point range levels.

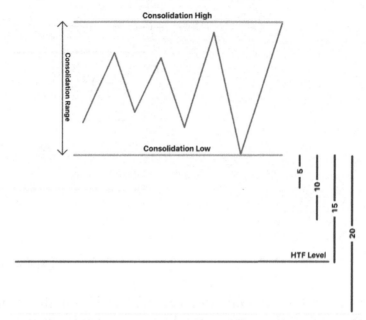

Once the buy program is completed, we can start taking measurements to assess how far the sell program can potentially deliver price.

If we take the swing low, which is the last swing low before the reversal and we take the swing high, this is our manipulation swing that ran the buyside liquidity above this high and into our higher timeframe level.

This occurs after the final stage of re-accumulation and it tricks buyers into longs. The market moves explosively in this direction. This is known as the manipulation leg of the SMR. This will form an intermediate term swing with a short-term high to the left and a short-term high to the right.

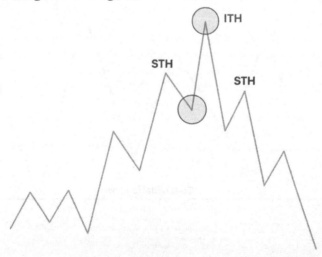

If we take the swing low through the swing high and we project standard deviations of this swing lower, we can look for potential targets that the algorithm will reach for to complete its sell program.

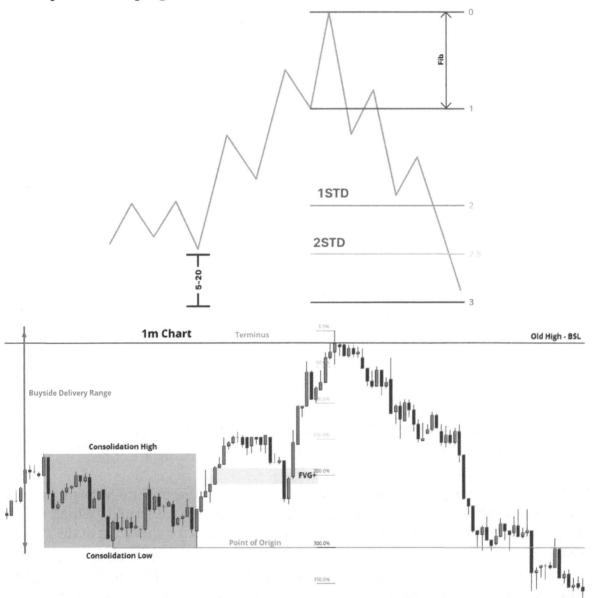

If one of these deviations aligns with between 5 and 20 points (NQ) below the initial consolidation and it also overlaps with a higher timeframe level. This is a very strong confluence of where the market may want to reprice to 2 to 2.5 standard deviations of the manipulation swing is common.

When these standard deviations also align with other arrays, this is a high probability of a distribution area.

1 to 2STD of the manipulation swing is also another good area to look for re-distribution.

If we also take the first swing low after the SMR and use fib from its low to the short-term high and if we project deviations lower, this can give us extra confidence again, especially if it lines up with a higher timeframe level and another standard deviation.

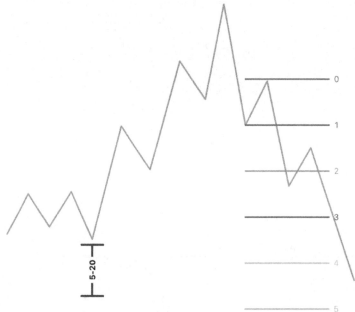

Now we have our calibrated terminus, which aligns with a higher timeframe level of 5 to 20 points (NQ) range below the initial consolidation. And we've used a different swing measurements.

If we now grade this from our point of origin to our new calibrated terminus and we divide that range in our 25% increments, we now have a calibrated grading range. The first stage of distribution is likely to occur around the first quadrant of the graded range.

Around this area we are also likely to see a breakaway gap (BG), which is an unfilled FVG. Again, at the 50% grade, we are likely to see our measuring gap, which will be an unfilled FVG at the midpoint of the range. This measuring gap will give us extra confidence that our calibrated terminus was correct.

We will normally see our second stage of distribution around 3rd quadrant of our graded range. This is known as the silver bullet (SB).

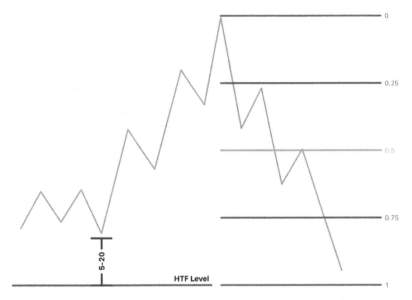

Reverse all of this for the buy side of the market maker buy model.

So, in the upper area, after our change in state of delivery, we have our first entry, which is going to be our low risk sell. And this is going to occur after the change in state of delivery has been confirmed.

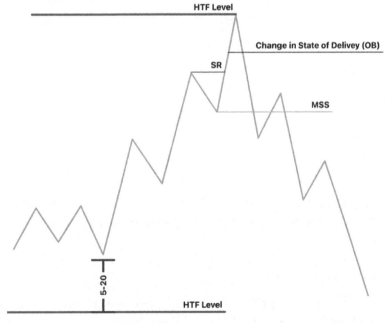

The change in state of delivery will be confirmed with displacement and time.

This is what our Change in Stated of Delivery would look like, where the buy program has completed its buyside delivery and we have rejected the higher.

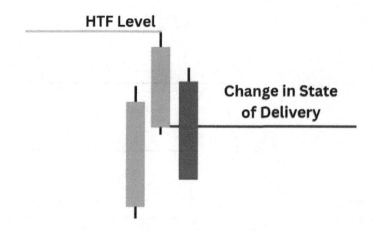

HTF Level

**Change in State
of Delivery**

Time frame level and ran below the opening price of the last up close candle, which becomes our bearish order block.

The low risk sell will be a retracement back into the order block and then we would see a move lower. As a sellside program continues on a LTF, you will see FVG inside of this order block.

This will be a high probability FVG. It doesn't need to come in to rebalance that. It can often just key off the low to the opening price and run lower, leaving that FVG open. We can travel higher into the order block, but we do not want to see the mean threshold of the order block breached on a closing basis.

We next have our MSS where we've had a run on the sellside liquidity below the second stage of accumulation. This gives us our break in market structure. Again, we do not need to close below the low in order to have a valid break in structure.

If we break below the second or final stage of re-accumulation, this is much more significant than smaller break inside of the manipulation swing that run stops.

The highest probability valid structure break is going to be the second stage or the final stage of re-accumulation. FVG found inside of the expansion leg that broke structure is going to give confirmation of the valid structure break.

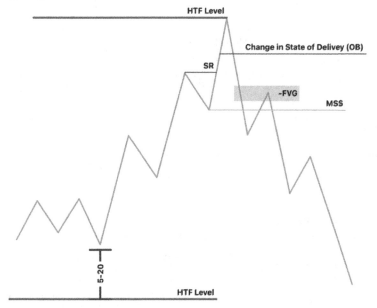

Our first stage of distribution where we return to the FVG inside of the leg that broke structure, and we will mitigate at the breaker, which is the down close candles that rests inside of the final stage of accumulation.

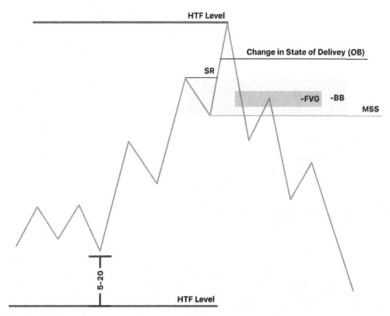

Next, we have a second structure break and then a continuation lower to seek the next sellside liquidity below the first stage of accumulation.

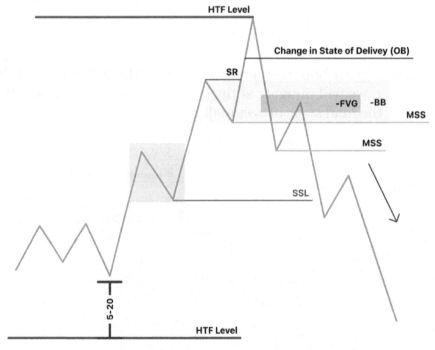

After we have run the sellside liquidity below the first stage of accumulation, we will begin our second stage of re-distribution on the right side of the market maker sell model within our sell program. We will run the sellside liquidity below the first stage of accumulation.

As a side note, there can be more than two stages of accumulation or distribution cycles. It all depends on what price is presenting at the time and what we can see on our charts.

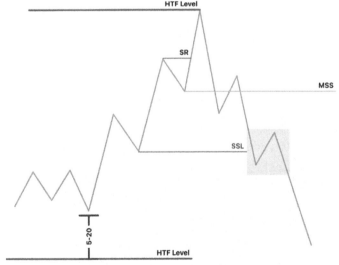

We have a break in market structure. We return back up into a FVG or we see a run on stops above a short-term high, and then we mitigate inside of a distribution block. The distribution block will be the down close candles inside of the stage of accumulation.

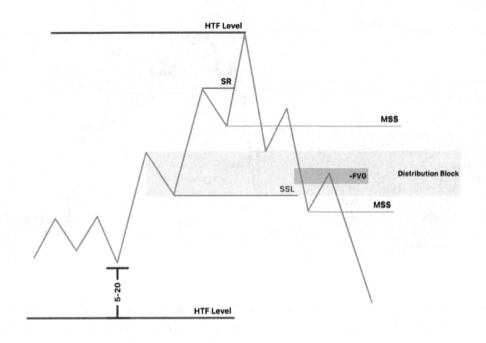

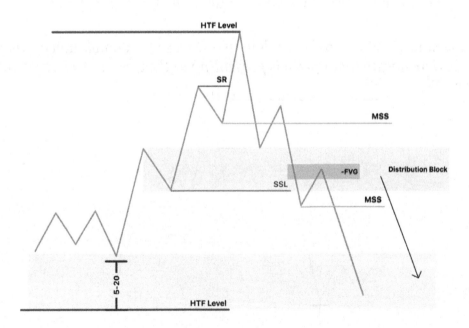

We continue lower to seek the next stage of sellside liquidity below the initial consolidation and ultimately to our calibrated terminus. The distribution cycle essentially consists of these four things:

1. We run liquidity

2. We rebalance or we run stops.

3. We mitigate within an area on the. Left side of the curve.

4. We continue lower to seek liquidity.

This is our guide:

Phases

1. Buy Program = Net Long

- Original Consolidation = Engineers Pending SSL > Pending BSL.

- Accumulation = Buy Orders (Through Accumulation at Discount Market) > Sell Orders.

2. Smart Money Reversal = Institutional Reference Point utilized for one or multiple of the following:

- Mitigation of Long positions.

- Rebalancing an Old Imbalance - Sell-Side Imbalance Buy-Side Inefficiency.

- Buy-Side Liquidity Raid where:

Limit Orders in the form of Buy stops (protecting long positions) are paired with Institutional Short orders / Long exit liquidity.

Limit Orders in the form of Buy orders (interest of selling below a specific level) are paired with Institutional Short orders / Long exit liquidity.

*Once at Reference Point, Expect a Market Structure Shift / Market Structure Break = Change in the State of Delivery | Buy Program -> Sell Program

3. Sell Program = Net Short

- Distribution (1st leg) = Sell Orders > Buy Orders.

- Redistribution (2nd leg) = Sell Orders > Buy Orders.

- Terminus / Completion = Orders added to Institutional Positions during.

Hedging and SMR are now paired with the Original Consolidation Liquidity.

Sell Model - Understanding

Identify the Following:

1. HTF IOF = Bearish.

2. DOL = Lower.

3. Initial Curve = Buy Program with Accumulation / Re-Accumulation.

If we are in HTF Bearish OF, the expectation is that Price will respect HTF Bearish PDAs. Once we have identified our draw, we would want to see a major Institutional.

The Sell Model's purpose is to deliver Price efficiently to our HTF Draw, while also generating Liquidity Pools Below the Market Place (during Buy Curve, generating protective sell stops under old lows) that would later be used to pair Institutional Orders post - SMR. The Idea would be for us to be in alignment with OF in order to capture parts) of the move.

Once the Smart Money Reversal has been Identified (MSS / MSB), we would look to apply one of the Entry Models:

1. 2022 Model

2. OFED

3. Breaker + Fair Value Gap

Chapter 20

Daily Rebalance Theory

As I mentioned above, seasonal trends are periods of the year when markets or particular asset classes will most likely move. Historically, they have led to large price fluctuations. An example is that May is usually the month when the market drops for index futures and stocks.

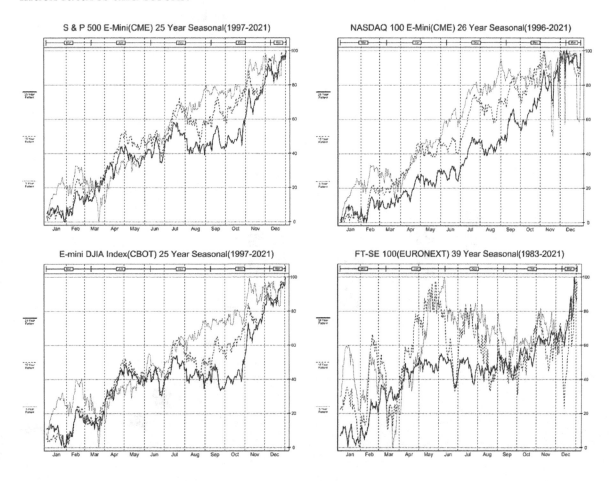

Don't predict low or high, you will only lose money!

The algorithms work on New York time , and it starts at midnight. Markets are controlled and driven by algorithms. At 08:30 New York time, the time comes when the algorithm starts looking for liquidity.

The stock market opens at 09:30 New York time. In the 1-hour timeframe between 08:30 and 09:30 we expect bearish sentiment to move higher to find short setups.

At 09:30 it's time for manipulation and it creates a small opportunity when it looks like the market is going to do something. But in general, this is the opposite of what it looks like on the chart, and retail traders see this as a breakout, meaning that the price is rising.

When we are bearish, we are saying that the market will rise to the premium zone. For one of two reasons:

1. Take the old high or highs to take BSL so that the smart money can compete with them on their short positions.

2. They are going to sell on these buy stops in order to then buy cheaper SSL. This would be their pool of liquidity to offset/allocate short positions.

In the example 15-minute chart below, we see a great run of the "power 3" setup. At 08:30 the price rises above the BSL and this is what we have called a Judas swing/manipulation.

5m chart

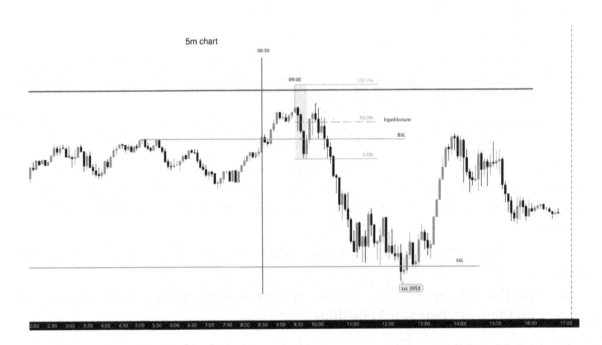

Immediate Rebalance

An immediate rebalance occurs when the market quickly adjusts to a new price level, often after an imbalance or inefficiency in price action. It typically happens within a short time frame, such as within a few candles, and can result in a rapid price movement.

An immediate rebalance, as explained by ICT, occurs when the market reprices back to a specific price level, such as a weekly gap low, and then quickly fails to continue in that direction. This can be seen when the market moves up through a level, then down through it, and attempts to test it again but fails immediately.

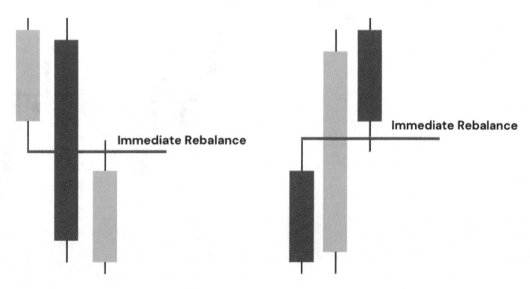

For example, if a candle's high is immediately followed by a trade down to that candle's high, it would be considered an immediate rebalance. This quick adjustment can be like rocket fuel, causing the price to take off rapidly.

Chapter 21

View Price with Institutional Perception

Never buy above old highs, never sell below old lows.

Step 1. Identify market profile:

Are we in a consolidating market or are we trending? This model works extremely well in a rangebound market. Can you see that this whole PA is rangebound?

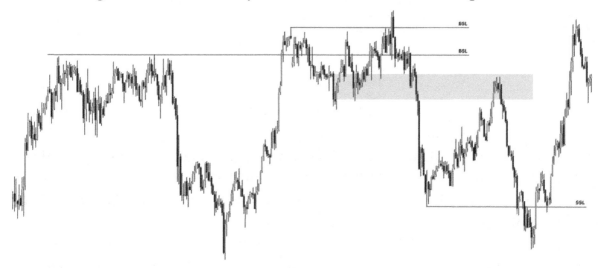

Step 2. Run on BSL followed by a breaker:

You see the BSL (EQH) being taken. Then price breaks down. That last down close candle is the start of the run on the buyside liquidity is the bearish breaker. Once price breaks through that down close candle you wait for price to revisit and sell. That in itself is a complete trading model. You'll find it on every timeframe. Just frame the model on the timeframe and duration you would like to trade. If you want a lot of setups, you can trade them on 15m multiple times a week. Once you go below the SSL you're out (partials or full close). Your stop should be above the breaker block or the bearish OB just above the breaker.

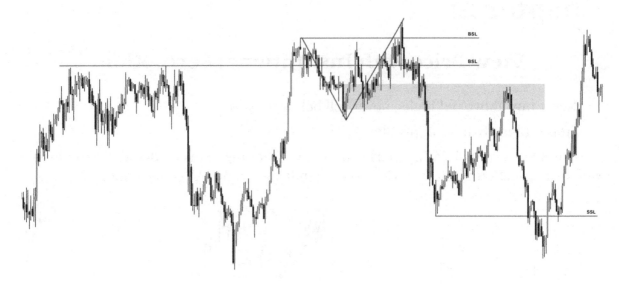

Step 3. The confluence that SMT divergence offers for the Smart Money Reversal:

This model is based on: if the market is going to have these internal turning points at major ITH/ITL, there should be some kind of signature or fingerprint there, reoccurring phenomenon. It's always there in a rangebound market.

Above the EQH, what can we do to anticipate this turning point? **Look for SMT before it happens.**

In this example, the SMT is the confluence that the HH on ES is only a fake out (or turtle soup, stop run). It shows that the markets are under a heavy distribution coming into the marketplace. So checking the relationship with correlated pairs is important. NQ made that lower high and ES made that slightly higher high. This is indicating that there's a lot of selling going on in NQ. The fact that the NQ is not able to get back up and trade above its old high like ES did, is tipping its hand that these 2 pairs are likely to go down because they're closely correlated. If we see that NQ is making that LH that means to me that that HH on ES is a "fake-out" (turtle soup, run on stops) and we can anticipate a reversal here. So the underlying signature here is you want to look for REH/REL or old highs/lows in a consolidating market and then look at a closely correlated asset.

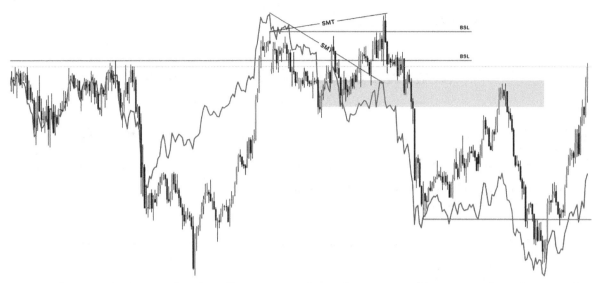

Understand that only the divergence doesn't necessarily mean there's a trade. Narrative is a key. We anticipate the BSL going to be tapped. You have to grow into this, you have to train yourself to know there's a turning point. The breaker is also a great entry point.

Cross pairs only make major moves when we are in an underlying consolidation as a whole like look at the dollar index. If that's consolidating, your mind as a trader should start thinking 'we are in an environment that the crosses will have big moves'. If the FED's holding dollar in a narrow range, you immediately start going through and finding the strong and the weak pairs. Find a strong versus a weak currency and trade the cross pair.

As I have already mentioned, I use ES, NQ, YM, and DXY for SMT analysis.

Chapter 22

General Range Trading Rules

1) The high / low that led to a sweep of the opposite side

This one is a bit trickier to spot, as you might try to use the first high as range high, but the midrange is not quite lining up. The relevant high here is the one, that led to the sweep of the range low.

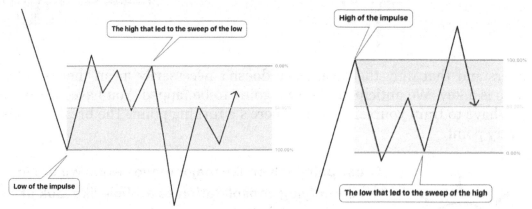

2) The high / lows before the sweep of the same side

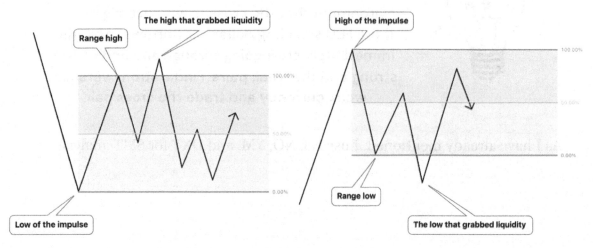

3) Equal Highs & Lows

This one should be obvious, as equal lows and highs are usually easy to spot and give clear targets that get swept most of the time.

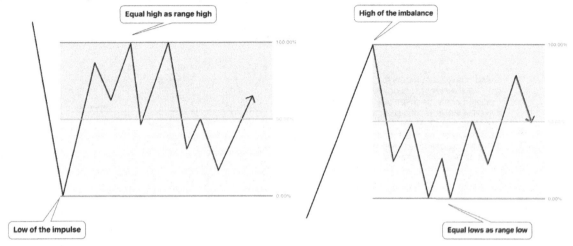

4) Previous daily, weekly, monthly range

This one is a great way to spot daily, weekly, or monthly ranges. Simply zoom out to the desired time frame and take the high and the low of the candle. Some people take the wicks, others only include the bodies of the candles. Again, just have a look what works best with the midrange and go from there.

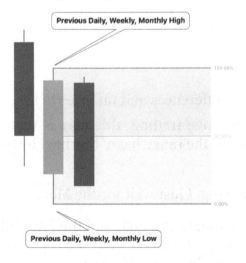

Monday Range

The Monday Range is the price range between Monday´s highest and Monday´s lowest price. Wait for a range to form, spot run on buystops or sellstops to give you clear invalidation, trade it to the opposite side of the range.

MONDAY RANGE

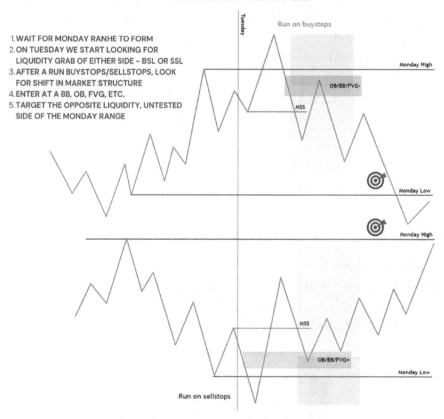

1. WAIT FOR MONDAY RANHE TO FORM
2. ON TUESDAY WE START LOOKING FOR LIQUIDITY GRAB OF EITHER SIDE – BSL OR SSL
3. AFTER A RUN BUYSTOPS/SELLSTOPS, LOOK FOR SHIFT IN MARKET STRUCTURE
4. ENTER AT A BB, OB, FVG, ETC.
5. TARGET THE OPPOSITE LIQUIDITY, UNTESTED SIDE OF THE MONDAY RANGE

But there are also some differences and nuances to it:

Different from general range trading, this play is more time-dependent, as you can´t trade it on Mondays, as the range hasn´t formed by then.

Here is an approach:

- Monday is for observing, I just wait for the Monday Range to form.

- After Monday close, I mark the high and the low. Still, not trading yet, as I´m waiting for on side to get taken out AND be back inside. (Price moving too far away and not breaking back inside the range makes it more difficult to spot possible plays right away).

- After a run on buy or sellstops happened, I start looking for positions.

293

- Price back inside usually gives a relatively high probability, that the opposite side of the range gets taken out next sooner or later. I´m looking to enter after a shift in market structure.

Some weeks only one side gets taken out and turns into support/ resistance, or price just expanded so far away from the Monday Range, that it´s either unlikely to come back, or is too far away to set proper invalidation points after it got back inside (at least for this setup). Whenever this is the case, I just stay away from this play - or check for different pairs.

Here is an example: low got swept, what marks an HTF area of interest for longs. It´s lining up with Monday low, that got swept forming equal lows. These got taken out followed by a MSS and a rally to the highs.

As HTF order flow is bearish in this example, chances are high this could be a bearish continuation range. As we don´t know, it´s best to TP at the midrange (50% of the range) to make it risk-free.

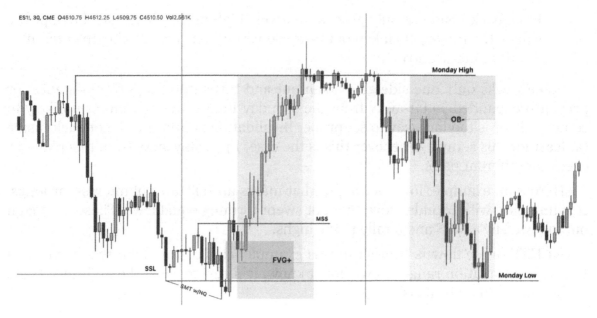

Daily Range

The concept around trading the "Daily Range" builds up on basically two narratives:

1. Asia Session is consolidating.

2. Asia Session is trending with a clear direction.

Asia Session in consolidation	London takes BSL or SSL, then reverses	NY Reverses clearing BSL/SSL from London Session
Asia Session is trending with a clear direction	London follows Asia's directional trend	NY continues or reverse at London Close

The most important thing to keep in mind, no matter where you are trading, is how each session is framing the context of the following session: **Asia Session** —> creates bias for —> **London Session** —> creates bias for —> **New York Session**

London Open Kill Zone	NY Kill Zone
Usually gives the clearest + biggest Swing: London Swing	Most likely reverses or retraces LOKZ at some point
High Volatility and high volume	Often manipulated or influenced by economic news
Has the highest probability for forming the low/high of the day	NYKZ often takes BSL/SSL from LOKZ
Judas Swing	

Example one: Asia Session is consolidating (10-15 points (ES/SP500) as a rule of thumb):

1. Asia ranging —> **Consolidation**.

2. London takes out BSL/ SSL from Asia (Asia High/ Low) aka the "Judas Swing" —> **Expansion targeting the opposite side**.

3. Price sets low/ high within LOKZ and reverses ("London Swing") —> **Reversal**.

4. New York session is some kind of **Retracement**.

Example two: Asia Session is trending (>15 points (ES/SP500)):

This one can be tricky, as LOKZ will likely be a bit more difficult (or let´s say less clear) to enter in my opinion.

In this scenario, I usually try to avoid trading and wait for NYKZ to give better opportunities.

The reason behind this is the following: Asia trending means a reversal during LOKZ is a bit less likely. So, what I do is, I wait for NYKZ to develop and enter on a clear break of the previous trend and try to play the reversal/ retracement towards clear London BSL/ SSL.

1. Asia trending bearish.

2. LOKZ opens inside Asia Premium, then follows the directional trend of the Asia Session.

3. NYKZ reverses and takes BSL from LOKZ and the Asia Range.

Chapter 23

New Week/Day Opening Gap (NWOG/NDOG)

NWOG: A New Week Opening Gap is a real dynamic fair value level; it is a range between two specific price points (close on Friday and open on Sunday). Between these two price points there is uncertainty and uncertainty builds opportunity. Where there is a difference on opinion there is a trade, that's the reason why NWOG works, that's a real liquidity void. The algorithm delivers price to these levels to offer fair value and encourage new business.

You need to know that NWOGs are a tool used by ICT to understand better where the price could go to / go be pushed away from. The algorithm refers to **older inefficiencies & liquidity voids**. A **real** Liquidity Void is a total absence of buying and selling, such as the NWOG. When the market moves away from it, it can refer back to old NWOGs for weeks and even months.

How to find NWOGs & highlight them on a chart

Go into a **Lower time frame** (do not use the 1D chart), but for example 5min chart. Sign the range between the Sundays opening price & the closing price on the Friday Prior.

You can see the NWOG only on the **"Regular Trading Hours"** (not on the Electronic ones)

To find the mid-point of the NWOG (aka Consequent Encroachment): Use **Fibonacci**, anchor it from Friday Closing price to Sunday opening price - the 50% is our mid-point - our Consequent Encroachment.

How to use NWOGs:

- Think about NWOG like you would with a FVG.

- The price is likely to re-visit them and react to them somehow.

- The price is also respecting of C.Es of NWOG.

- It's recommended to record at least the five most recent NWOGs for reference.

- When several NWOGs are located close together, the market often enters a range-bound phase.

NDOG: New Day Opening Gap Difference between 5pm Close Price & 6pm Open Price.

C.E. - Consequent Encroachment or "middle point" of any Gap or Inefficiency.

The difference between two consecutive candles' closing price and opening price is called the gap. A gap occurs when prices skip between two trading periods, skipping over certain prices. A gap creates a void on a price chart. Price gaps are simply areas on the chart where no trading has taken place.

ICT: "Having the prior 4 weeks NWOG on your chart gives you an X-ray view of how the algorithm will refer back to old areas of real FAIR VALUE".

It is important to understand that the Up-gap acts as a support zone and the down gap acts as a resistance zone.

Why should we have NWOG/NDOG on our chart? Because institutions will want to fill the gap before big move. As I mentioned above this kind of gaps are strong support and resistance.

They are real point of interest for the market to want to gravitate back to and the market is designed and could do this because it allows the sentiment and interest on a large fund level for them to want to bring their orders into the marketplace which is really the primary driver for where the market drives against liquidity.

ICT Event Horizon PD Array

*ICT Event Horizon PD Array - Halfway between a NWOG and the closest NWOG is the Event Horizon. It will not allow price to escape the draw to the NWOG & it will create a surge towards the NWOG it got too "close" to but yet reached.

Measure High - Low of the NWOG of 2 closest NWOGs.

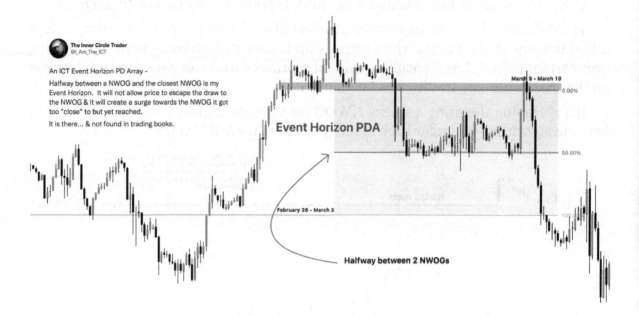

The Inner Circle Trader
@I_Am_The_ICT

An ICT Event Horizon PD Array -

Halfway between a NWOG and the closest NWOG is my
Event Horizon. It will not allow price to escape the draw to
the NWOG & it will create a surge towards the NWOG it got
too "close" to but yet reached.

It is there... & not found in trading books.

Event Horizon PDA

March 5 - March 10

0.00%

50.00%

NWOG High

February 26 - March 3

100

Halfway between 2 NWOGs

Chapter 24

Liquidity Void and Fair Valuation

<u>Fair Valuation</u> is only for the Market Maker and not for the trader.

When analyzing current price action ask yourself:

- Is price a Fair Value for Market Makers to go buy in?

- Is price a Fair Value for Market Makers to sell in?

When price returns **back** to an area of Fair Value that is a fair value for the Market Maker to either sell or buy at. Market Makers have to deal in terms of Fair Valuation for their short and long positions. They also have to do the same Fair Valuation for their exists on both sides of the marketplace.

On higher timeframes always ask yourself where does the Market Maker view Fair Value?

To ascertain Fair Value look for three things:

1. Find the total macro range of larger price move (Premium or Discount).

2. Where is the Equilibrium price point (of the larger price move) relative to the most recent trading range high and low?

3. Where are the reference points that Market Makers will aim for? (FVGs, Liquidity Voids, Order blocks).

Equilibrium

<u>Equilibrium</u> is the 50% (or middle point) line between a swing high and a swing low.

Mark out the Equilibrium on the current trading range. Then draw the Equilibrium on the next largest trading range. And the next. Etc. Is the current price in a Discount or Premium in all or many of them? Is price in the lowest or highest third?

When price is at Equilibrium you need to refer to where the most recent price swing took place. Because at Equilibrium (or Fair Value) price can go either direction. The easiest way to determine the most probable next direction is finding where market structure broke most recently:

Did price break a swing high most recently or did price break a swing low most recently? Also notice what part of the big overall range price is in. Is price is the lower part, upper part, or near the middle?

Pay attention to the bodies of the candle when price is around Equilibrium. Does the bodies of the candles stay on one side of Equilibrium while the wicks cross it? This gives hints that price may reverse after the wicks go across the Equilibrium.

Liquidity Void is when price makes a sudden movement in one direction over a large range (compared to recent candle size) in a short amount of time.

Liquidity voids occur when price moves sharply in one direction, leaving large candles that have little trading activity as price moves in one direction. Eventually, the price will return to close the liquidity void later.

Liquidity voids are long-body candles where the price has only been set one way, sometimes with a small gap between the larger candles.

The candles are characterized by large beefy bodies with tiny wicks:

- A Liquidity Void means price spent very little time trading at those prices.

Liquidity Void characteristics:

When price is on the other side of the Liquidity Void (after just creating it) then the Liquidity Void is considered Fair Value and the Market will want to come back to it because there was very little trading in it. But price doesn't have to trade back to the Liquidity Void immediately.

The Liquidity Void is Fair Value to the Market Makers because the algorithm seeks to rebalance inefficiently traded price ranges (which is the definition of a Liquidity Void).

Liquidity Void Trading: When price trades back into a Liquidity Void expect price to wick up and down as price fills the Liquidity Void. This is because Market Makers are selling their long positions or buying back their short positions in the range of the Liquidity Void that was accumulated beforehand.

Once the Liquidity Void is filled in look for farther up/down (farther in a premium or discount) Fair Value Gaps or ICT Order blocks where Market Makers will look to offset their positions, they got on the other end of the premium vs discount move.

Let's take a look an example below, the liquidity void will be filled in the future by a bearish price move that will cover the entire range and when this happens, the price will be balanced as the price will be offered on the buy side and on the sell side.

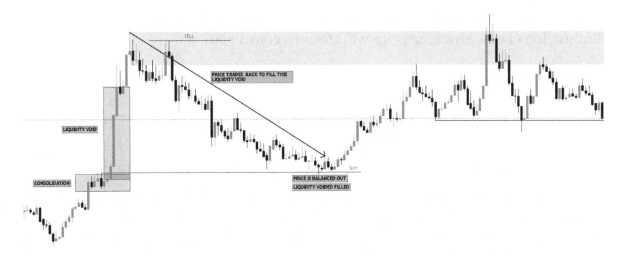

Now you expect the price to completely fill the void, sometimes it happens instantly, but sometimes it first goes higher, deceiving traders, and then completely fills it, as in the example above.

When price goes with gap so aggressively, we know there is a good chance that price will go further up. We can place a limit order to buy at the level of this gap.

Consolidation

When price moves in defined trading range (i.e. Consolidation) there is going to be Equilibrium:

- Equilibrium in itself is Fair Value.

- Look for price to continue trading in the direction of the strong move out of a consolidation.

If we see expansion then we know that prior to the expansion was consolidation. But we don't know how long price will stay in a consolidation.

Market Makers

The Market moves:

- From buy stops to sell stops and sell stops to buy stops.

- From Fair Value to Discount, Discount to Premium, Premium to Fair Value

The only reason why price is allowed to be delivered at higher prices is because the Market Makers are net long and it's in their interest in price to go higher. It doesn't matter how many Retail traders buy or sell. The price is going to be set by the Market Makers and they are going to do things to line their own pockets and not Retail traders.

It takes a perspective shift (remember the market efficiency paradigm that ICT taught) to view things from the Smart Money's perspective and not what Retail logic teaches.

Price action is not random. Market Makers specifically move price to where they want it to go and Market Makers control the reason why price goes in a direction. This is why if you mess up a trade or miss a move, don't worry about it. The market will give you another chance almost every day. Because everything repeats! Because everything is controlled by Smart Money (i.e. Market Makers).

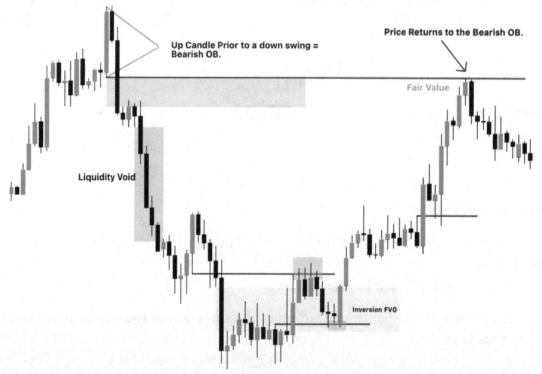

On the chart above, the price has broken through the previous high (breaking the structure) and returned to the Equilibrium zone. Been in this area for a long time. This is already an indicator. The price can stay here in consolidation for a certain amount of time, but we don't know how long the price will stay here. Also, if we take a large range marked in blue, we can conclude that the price is in the oversold zone now (discount zone).

Based on this, we decide where the price is more likely to go - short or long? I vote for long.

Notice, we returned to the Equilibrium zone of a small impulse, which may be a reason for market makers to open longs.

Down candle right before the up move through the short-time-high - bullish OB. Therefore, the price comes back down, reaches OB along with equilibrium.

That is, we have a high probability that the market will go from the discount zone to the premium zone.

We should consider the following couple of things:

- Overall range we trade.

- Equilibrium, relative to the last formed range.

- Liquidity voids and liquidity pools above old highs/lows.

The easiest way to understand the Institutional Order Flow is to understand that the markets are **moving from buy stops to sell stops, from sell stops to buy stops.**

From Fair Value to=> Discount, to Discount to=> Premium, to Premium to=> Fair Value.

The market moves between these three breakpoints: we have a Discount, or a Premium, or a Fair Value.

All of this together gives us clues as to what we are seeing in terms of Market Maker (MM) activities: they are accumulating, manipulating, or distributing.

Fair Value in Discount - MM buy.

Fair Value in Premium - MM sell.

Think in terms of where we are now in relation to the current range. Are we at the bottom? Are we near the low of the current range? Do we consider Equilibrium? Having determined the price in the current trading ranges, we can see where MM will increase the price. So when an expansion occurs, we know that there was a consolidation prior to that expansion.

After a sharp run in Price, the large candles that form are the least efficiently traded areas in the range. Sudden runs in Price will leave porous Price Action that tends to fill in at a later time. These tiny gaps can be viewed sometimes by opening a 1 minute or 5-minute chart. This is described as a void of market liquidity or Liquidity Void.

Fair Valuation is when price trades back inside its current range and return to levels it recently moved from – usually an order block for example. Smart money tends to unload longs in this area and at the same time establish new shorts or vice versa. This makes it a good location to either take profits from or enter into a new position.

Fair Value Gap is when price leaves a specific level and has only a small section of price action that is seen as one directional. These can present as very good areas for profit taking or new setups.

Chapter 25

How to Use Day of the Week and Time of Day

If we're bullish on market conditions, we look for an opportunity to go long when the low for the week is formed (likely to form before Tuesday's/Wednesday's London Open). The same is true for shorts.

Monday, Tuesday, and Wednesday are high probability days for high of the week or low of the week to be formed but look closely for Tuesday and Wednesday London open.

The Weekly High or Low forms 80% of the time between Sunday's /Monday's Open & Tuesday's London Open. When it fails, it will likely form between Tuesday's London Open and Wednesday's London Open. If it has not formed by Tuesday's London Open, then very likely to occur between Tuesday's London Open and Wednesday's London Open.

Monitor 4 hours after 00:00 or New York midnight, there is high probability of high/low of the day to form within those 4 hours.
You will see high/low of the day forming most of the time around 04:00 – 04:30am EST.

Market rallies up in the sell day after 12:00am EST to 02:00am EST.

05:00am EST most of the time expect to see a Judas Swing or and Divergence above/below the 02:00 – 04:00am EST price that will form a swing high/low to the direction of the market, for example if you are in a sell trade you will see a move back to the higher of the day that will form a swing high and continue down or we have SMT Divergence.

Mark the opening price of 05:00am EST and most of the time this price will setup New York Optimal Trade Entry in sync with High/Low that was formed in London. In New York most of the time price will trade back to 02:00am Price and give you optimal trade entry. When you don't see a Judas swing in London expect the Judas to form in 05:00am EST.

For a sell trade, most of the time high of the day will form in first **4 hours after 00:00 EST** (London open kill zone) but the ideal time window for a high to form is 02:00 – 05:00 EST and low of the day will form around 10:00 – 11:00am EST and vice versa for a buy trade (if you were selling from London open kill zones you need to close trades around 10:00 – 11:00am EST.

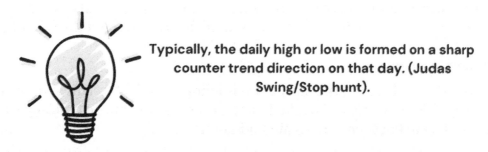

Typically, the daily high or low is formed on a sharp counter trend direction on that day. (Judas Swing/Stop hunt).

05:00 – 06:00 most of the time you will see a pause in price after London move or a Judas swing that will make a fractal to the direction of the market in lower time frame.

07:20 EST (20 minutes after the beginning of New York kill zone) is when futures contracts begin trading.

Start looking for New York trade setups from 07:20. For a buy trade you need to buy 10pts (ES/SP500) below the 07:20 open price and for a sell trade you need to sell

10pts (ES/SP500) above the 07:20 open price for New York trade.

LONDON CLOSE/LATE NEW YORK CLOSE (REVERSAL MARKET PROFILE)

- London Close kill zone: 10:00am -12:00pm (as late as 13:00 EST).

- Generally, the market will look to encounter profit taking around 11:00am EST as London traders close their trading day and NY traders are taking lunch.

- High/Low of the day can be formed in London close too.

LONDON CLOSE TREND TRADE (Classic reversal market profile)

- Trend trade entry to get in sync with the daily trend or long-term price swing. This will happen if price is trading to higher time frame optimal trade entry.

- This trade will form the high or low of the day and above/below London open high/low.

- Look for Higher time frame support and resistance level, this will happen if price didn't trade to support and resistance in London open.

For the London close trend trade sell, the day will start as classic buy day and reverse in London Close/Late New York and price will trade below London low.

- For the London close trend trade buy, the day will start as classic sell day and reverse in London Close/Late New York and price will trade above London high.

The London Close Killzone - the Price Action seen at London Close typically sees a retracement off the High of the day on Bullish days – and off the Low of the day on Bearish days. There is typically a 5-minute OTE Setup in these conditions. *They are very short-term moves.

ICT: "If we're Bullish and the daily close is going to be high relative to its opening in other words it's an up-close day, the London Close is going to be typically when the high today is formed between 10:00 am and noon".

Characteristics of London Close: London Close can create continuation points for swings that trade well into the New York afternoon hours.

Other times – The London Close can also be a Reversal Point for Price and what had been the direction of the day or week – can change during London Close.

New York Session - Buy below 05:00 and 07:00 EST open price and Sell above 05:00 and 07:00 EST open price.

Chapter 26

Daily Templates

THE LONDON SWING TO NEW YORK OPEN / LONDON CLOSE REVERSAL (REVERSAL MARKET PROFILE)

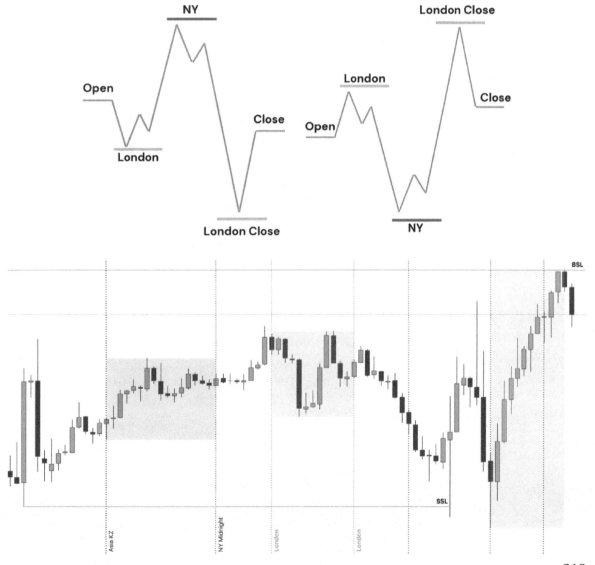

THE LONDON SWING TO NEW YORK OPEN / LONDON CLOSE REVERSAL (REVERSAL MARKET PROFILE)

The bullish version of this template always begins like a Classic Buy template with a decline below the opening price before price starts rallying. Once price drops, a buy entry forms, price rallies to a higher time frame Point of Interest (POI), e.g., a bearish order block (OB), into a Fair Value Gap (FVG), etc. If this happens during the New York session, it indicates a classic market reversal.

The template is used to either reach for a bearish order block on a higher time frame, for a turtle soup raid or to close a range. On a bullish day it will first create an initial low of the day during the London session, run up and create the high of the day during the New York session around the London Close, then run back down and clear the initial low that was created during the London session. Ideally it can pan out after the market is in exhaustion based on the higher time frame's dominant trend.

The strategy involves monitoring the market during the last hour of the London trading session (4 - 5am) and the first hour of the New York trading session (7 - 8am). During this time, traders look for signs of a trend reversal, such as a break of key support or resistance levels or a shift in trading volume. If a reversal is identified, traders will enter a position in the opposite direction of the prevailing trend.

One of the key advantages of this strategy is that it allows traders to take advantage of the momentum created by the overlap between the London and New York sessions. This can result in a rapid acceleration in price movement, which can be profitable if the trader is able to enter and exit their position at the right time.

However, there are also some risks associated with this strategy. For example, if the market does not reverse as expected, traders may find themselves in a losing position. Additionally, the increased volatility during the overlap between the London and New York sessions can also result in sudden price spikes or gaps, which can be difficult to predict and may result in unexpected losses.

The Classic Buy or Sell Day Template

This is the best template to make money since it is a wide range trending day that **unfolds mostly on Monday, Tuesday and latest on Wednesday during the London session.** The New York session will eventually give a retracement to continue with the trend that was set during the London session. The daily range will last for 7 to 8 hours once the profile is established.

THE CLASSIC BUY OR SELL DAY TEMPLATE

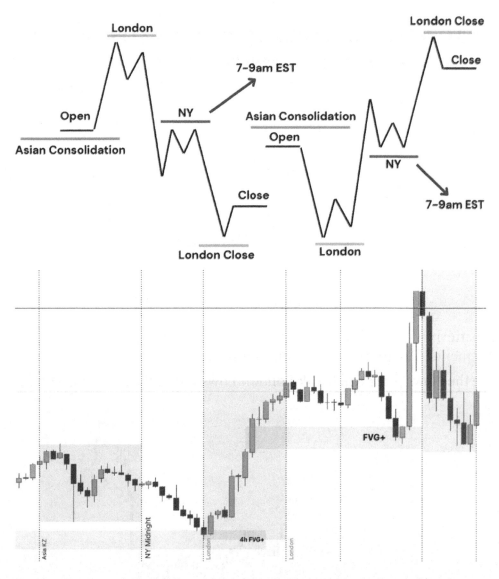

Mostly it will give a rally or drop from the daily opening price to the low or high of the day during the London session. The trend usually lasts into 11:00 EST.

On a classic buy day, always buy when the market drops at the right time of the day at key support level (buy below the opening price).

On a buy day, if price starts by trading above the opening price, do not fall for that and wait for it to trade below the opening price.

The distance from the open price to support will be 7 – 12 points (ES/SP500) on average. If the move from open price to support in London session is more than 12 points, wait for New York trade. If you can't trade London session, you can trade New York session to get in sync with London trade. Always take small profit of 5 – 7 points (ES/SP500) by 12:00.

RANGE TO NEW YORK OPEN/LONDON CLOSE RALLY

RANGE TO NEW YORK OPEN/LONDON CLOSE RALLY

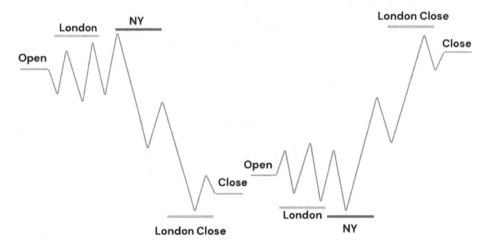

This pattern will unfold most often during the NFP, FOMC and Interest Rates Announcements. The market will be originally in consolidation.

Before the News price will break London Lows and rally after News Release.

CONSOLIDATION RAID ON NEWS RELEASE

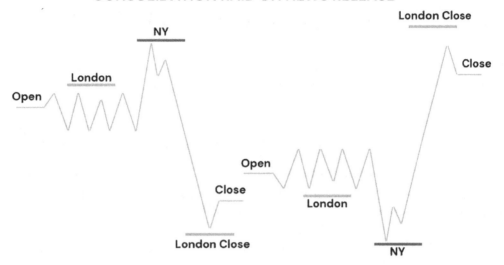

This pattern will unfold most often during the NFP, FOMC and Interest Rates Announcements:

- After opening price, market will consolidate before the News.

- During the News releases price will drop to induce traders and take stops (this move might not be that big below the consolidation but it has to break the consolidation).

- After clearing the stops and inducing, price will move into true direction.

You have to identify Key support level or order block below the consolidation.

See if price will reject at support/resistance within 5 minutes after News release, if it won't reject then leave the trade because you might be wrong in your analysis.

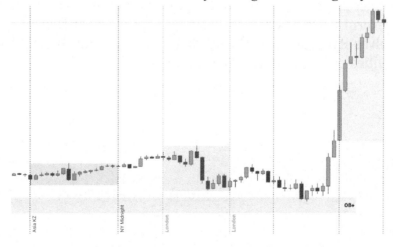

Chapter 27

Previous Day High and Low as a Liquidity Pool

One of the most accessible liquidity pools for traders to tap into is the previous day's high and low. Every day, the market tends to gravitate towards one of these levels, creating opportunities for traders to enter or exit positions.

The Previous Day's High and Low are one of the foundations for determining the daily bias and serve as significant liquidity pools that the market targets daily.

- The previous day's high acts as a level of resistance, where the market is likely to encounter selling pressure. Traders can look for opportunities to sell or take profits when the price approaches this level.

- Conversely, the previous day's low serves as a level of support, where the market is likely to find buying interest. Traders can look for opportunities to buy or enter long positions when the price approaches this level.

Taking note of the highest high traded in the previous trading day can serve as a valuable reference for short-term resistance levels if price reaches those levels again. Similarly, observing the lowest low traded in the previous trading day can offer significant support levels for the short term if price approaches those levels again.

It's not limited to just the previous trading day; you can also consider the previous three-day period to gather additional insights. By observing the daily highs and lows, you will be monitoring the precise levels that banks and institutions often pay close attention to for buying and selling interest.

The daily highs and lows have the potential to generate substantial moves, often ranging from 25 to 50 points (in this case we picture below of ES/SP500) per trade. These levels can act as important reference points and offer trading opportunities for capturing short-term price fluctuations. Those who monitor these levels closely can position themselves strategically in the market and potentially benefit from the buying and selling activities of larger market participants.

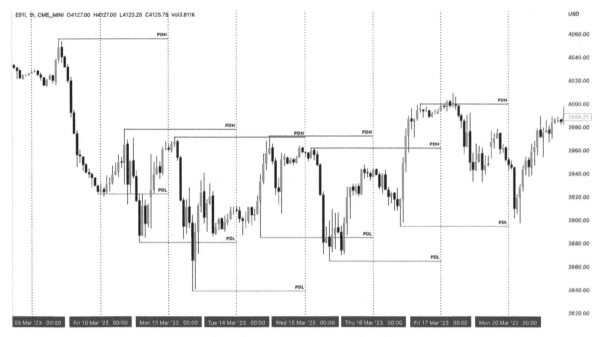

Bullish and Bearish Order Flow

In a bullish order flow, buyers dominate the market, driving prices higher. As a result, the market tends to seek buyside liquidity above the previous day's highs. Conversely, in a bearish order flow, sellers dominate the market, pushing prices lower. The market then seeks sellside liquidity below the previous day's lows.

After taking out Sell stops, we look for the next DOL. In this case this is the Equal Highs .

316

Identifying Buy-Side Liquidity Pools Above Previous Day's Highs

As I already mentioned above, previous day's high and low are the easiest draw on liquidity for traders. Every single day, the market tends to reach for the previous daily high or low, creating opportunities for traders to capitalize on these movements.

To identify buy-side liquidity pools above previous day's highs, we can follow these steps:

1. Analyze the daily chart: Start by looking at the daily chart of the currency pair or asset you are trading. This chart will give you an overview of the price movements and help you identify the previous day's high.

2. Look for inside bars: Inside bars are candlestick patterns that do not take out the high or low of the previous day. These patterns can indicate a potential reversal in the market.

3. Mark the previous day's high: Once you have identified the previous day's high, mark it on your chart. This will serve as a reference point for potential buy-side liquidity pools.

4. Identify potential buyside liquidity pools.

To analyze daily charts for potential trading opportunities, follow these steps:

1. Look for break of structure: Identify key support and resistance levels on the daily chart. Look for areas where the price breaks above or below these levels, indicating a potential change in market direction.

2. Identify daily POI (FVG, OB, etc.): FVGs occur when the price moves away from its fair value. These gaps can serve as potential areas of interest for traders. In the picture above, a daily fair value gap is present after a break of structure. This gap can be used as a reference point for trading decisions.

Identifying Sell-Side Liquidity Pools Below Previous Day's Lows

Every day, the market seeks liquidity, and one of the easiest liquidity pools to target is the area below the previous day's low. This means that traders often look to sell when the market breaks below the previous day's low. By analyzing daily candlestick charts, we can identify instances where the market has taken out the previous day's low. These instances serve as indications of potential reversals or opportunities to enter trades.

When the market breaks below the previous day's low, it suggests that there is a potential bearish order flow. This can be a signal for us to look for opportunities to sell, as the market may continue to seek sell-side liquidity.

Outlining New York Midnight Opening Price for Trading Decisions

When analyzing daily charts, it is important to observe how the market trades in relation to the New York Midnight opening price. If the market trades above it and then starts to decline, it can be an indication of potential bearish order flow.

However, if the market consistently trades and stays above the New York Midnight opening price, it suggests a bullish order flow. Traders can look for opportunities to buy, especially when the market breaks above the previous day's high.

The New York Midnight opening price refers to the price at which the market opens at midnight (12 AM) Eastern Standard Time (EST) in New York. This price serves as a reference point for traders and can provide valuable insights into market behavior. Traders often outline the New York Midnight opening price on their charts to visually separate each trading day. This helps in identifying key price levels and understanding the market's behavior throughout the day.

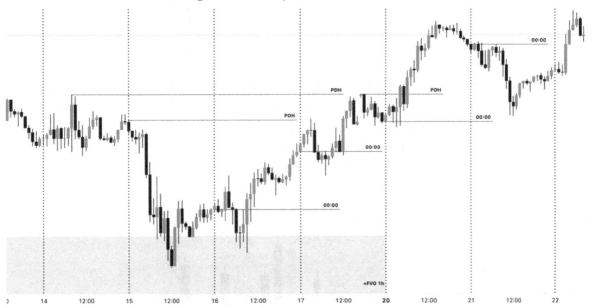

Trading Previous Day High and Low

Everyday ask yourself how price traded today, did we work the high/low of the previous day? Or the day prior to it or the day prior to that. Always refer to the last 3 days.

There are two circumstances when fading the move in Price beyond a Previous Day's range:

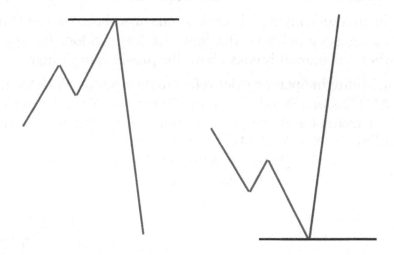

During Expansion Swings there are smaller retracements that typically create opportunities where the Previous Day's Low is raided then Price Rallies Higher.

In opposing Expansion Swings there are retracements that create opportunities where the Previous Day's High is raided then Price Declines.

Trading Previous Day's Low

In this example, we see Price moving Higher as part of a larger Expansion Swing. During a normal retracement lower - into a Fair Value Gap - Price finds Buyers under the Previous Daily Low (PDL).

Price trades under previous day's low

Using the Previous Daily Low and anticipating a Market Reversal after the PDL is raided - one can be a Buyer intraday.

We look for confluences of PD Arrays to support the idea of Buying under a PDL. We do not simply Buy under a PDL on sole basis Price moves beyond the Previous Day's Low.

Trading Previous Day's High

In this example, we see Price moving Lower as part of a larger Expansion Swing. During a normal retracement higher - after a Fair Value Gap was filled - Price finds Sellers above the Previous Daily High (PDH).

Using the Previous Daily High and anticipating a Market Reversal after the PDH is raided - one can be a Seller intraday.

We look for confluences of PD Arrays to support the idea of Selling above a PDH. We do not simply Sell above a PDH on sole basis Price moves beyond the Previous Day's High.

Price trades above previous day's high

Ultimately, it's all about HTF context. Weekly, Daily, 4h suggesting lower prices -> price trades up into a premium array during a retracement up -> trades above PDH ->we can be a seller.

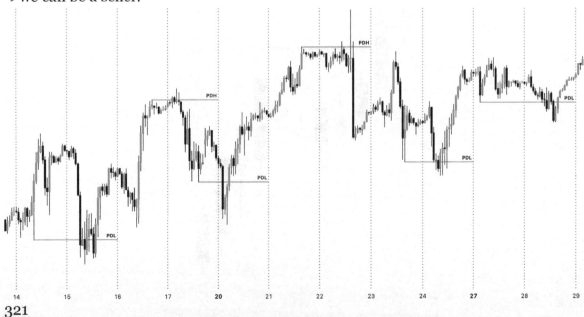

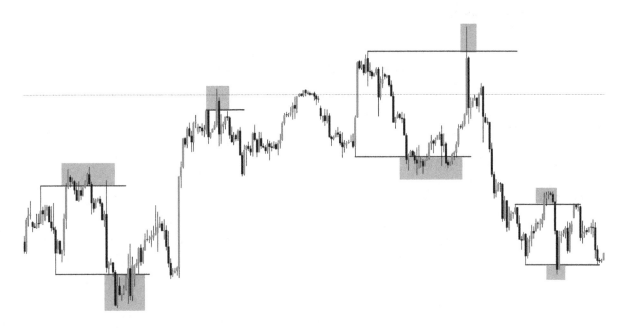

HTF institutional order flow will assist us, and when we look for a retracement, we look for price to trade below a PDL and into a discount array.

We look for confluences as to why we should buy below the PDL, we look for a discount array. We don't just buy below a PDL, there has to be context.

We have to look at what institutional order flow is indicating: we look at institutional order flow on the week daily and 4h suggesting prices will go lower, if we have that and prices trades into a premium array and it's during a retracement and gets to the premium array that's what you couple it with then if it trades above the PDH we can be a seller.

Chapter 28

Hours of Operation

One Setup For Life

PM Session Ranges :

PM Session Ranges

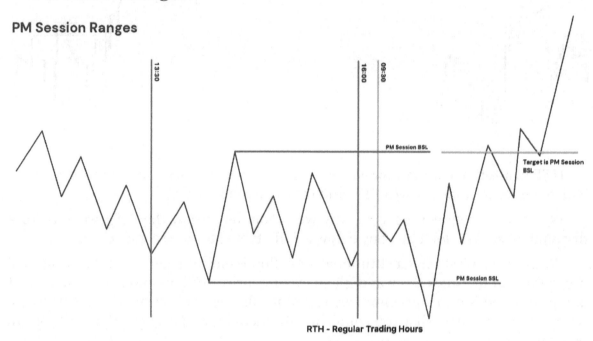

The PM session is scheduled between 13:30 and 16:00 EST.

During this window, we aim to identify the HH and the LL.

When analyzing PM Ranges, we focus on RTH (Regular Trading Hours), excluding any Overnight trading activity.

After the Opening bell rings at 9:30 EST, we have a 30-minute period known as the Opening Range.

If you have a bullish outlook (with a Higher Time Frame objective above the market), and we took out the SSL below the Lowest Low of the PM session, it is favorable.

Hint: We can consider the grab of the PM Session BSL/SSL as a significant liquidity area that can be utilized for the Silver Bullet or Judas Swing setup.

London Session Raid :

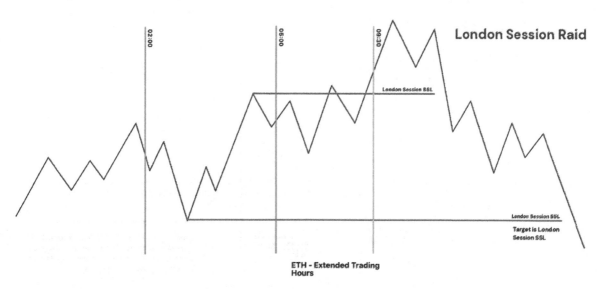

If we are not close to the PM range during the first 30 minutes after the Opening Bell, we look for the London Session Raid.

This refers to the range between 2:00 AM and 5:00 AM, which can be found on the ETH (Electronic Trading Hours) chart.

So far, this is our routine: During the first 30 minutes after the 9:30 Opening Bell, we assess our position relative to the PM or London session. There may be a run higher or lower, or the market may consolidate.

We then wait for the Displacement between 10:00 AM and 11:00 AM, which sets the stage for the Silver Bullet setup.

NY Lunch Raid :

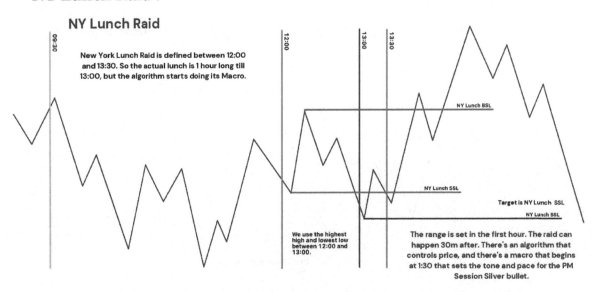

This is the range between noon and 13:30.

The lunch hour would usually be a period of consolidation (unless it's a big trend day). Many times, the price action during the morning session would be completely reversed during this time.

If it was not a trending day, the morning session would create the low, and price would rally towards the lunch highs and/or morning highs.

However, if it was a trending day, the price would continue following the direction set by the morning session. It would keep running into 15:00 and 16:00, representing the full daily range.

If the day was bullish, the price would move up during the morning session, then consolidate between 12:00 and 13:00. In the afternoon, between 14:00 and 16:00, it would repeat the same move as in the morning, but in a lower time frame.

AM Session Ranges :

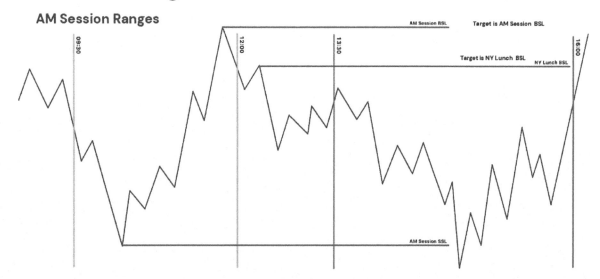

This is the range between 9:30 and 12:00.

We consider this in the afternoon, so we can always refer to it in the same trading day. In this case, me might anticipating a market reversal profile or something to that effect.

If we observe an elongated market where the NY AM Session of the current trading day is characterized by consolidation, and even the lunch hour shows consolidation or a directional movement, we can refer to the trading activity of the previous session, particularly the electronic trading.

Chapter 29

Core Content – ICT Block Types

Breaker Block

Breaker block is so-called an order block (OB) broken by a strong impulse without a pullback reaction. A prerequisite for the formation of a breaker block is to break the last high or low, depending on the trend.

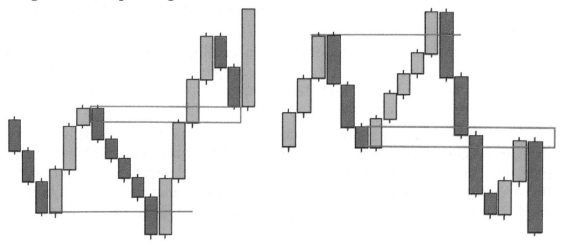

You can understand what a breaker block is by carefully studying impulse candles. If you find a bullish or bearish order block that has been broken, and liquidity has been removed from the high or low, then a reversal pattern - a breaker - will begin to form.

The purpose of a Breaker Block is to create a price movement with manipulation to gather liquidity towards important highs or lows, followed by a breakout in the opposite direction. During this process, a popular trading setup called Stop Hunt is formed. Stop Hunt involves manipulating the price to trigger buystops or sellstops orders.

STOP HUNT is a smart money practice that happens very often. Imagine this: the market moves straight to your stop loss, hits it, and immediately turns in the other direction - you are stopped out. The name of all this is to stop the hunt.

Smart money uses this method to take their positions at the price they want, in the best possible way for themselves. By manipulating the price, they will force you to go in a certain direction, and then swallow your position abruptly. It is worth being alert if the liquidity zone is very large and pronounced. There is a high chance that smart money will target this particular zone, especially if it is against the main trend.

The Breaker Block operates on a similar principle as OB, but the reaction from the BB occurs only after a strong impulse penetration. Once the Stop Hunt movement has manipulated liquidity and led to a trend change, large capital often returns the price to the breaker block zone for retesting. This is done to close unprofitable positions after manipulation.

To gain a better understanding of the Breaker Block, it is crucial to analyze the impulse candles on the chart accurately. For example, if we observe that a Bullish or Bearish OB has been broken through, taking liquidity from a high or low level, it may indicate a potential trend reversal, which is known as a Breaker Block.

BUT! Despite its name, a breaker block in trading is not necessarily a reversal pattern, it can signal the continuation of a trend. To determine the trend of the market, you need to consider the formation of higher highs (HH) and higher lows (HL) for a bullish trend and lower lows (LL) and lower highs (LH) for a bearish one. A breaker is formed after the formation of a new HH or LL during an impulse breakout of an order block.

Bullish and Bearish Breaker Block

Let's analyze the bullish and bearish breaker blocks separately:

Before **a Bullish Breaker** can form in the market, liquidity needs to be taken. To change the direction of the trend in the market, an impulsive update of the low is required, and to continue the uptrend, an impulsive grab of liquidity from the HL level is required. After the price moves in the opposite direction, an impulsive breakout of the OB should be expected.

329

Before **a Bearish Breaker** enters the market, liquidity is taken from the previous trend element. If the trend is down, then the momentum occurs at the LH level, and if the trend changes from rising to falling, then the momentum occurs at the HH level.

To confirm a bearish breaker, you need to wait for a change in the direction of price movement and an impulse breakout of the order block.

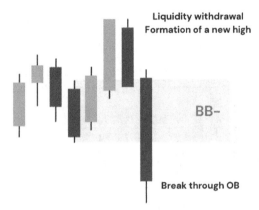

Let's think why breaker blocks work:

First, a major player knocks out stop-losses below a low to take a position. The buyers placed their stops there. Which need to be picked up. That is, a large player opens a sell position before this, just in the place where we will have a Breaker Block, initially it was OB in a downward direction.

There is a breakdown and holding above this low, thereby showing the situation that everything now we have the market intends to go in a downward direction. At this point, a major player has successfully entered a buy position by removing stops. We no longer have buyers, now there are sellers. And the price at this moment goes in the opposite upward direction. Sellers will set stop losses beyond a significant high. The task of a major player is now to take these stops beyond the high.

Right now, we still have OB in the downward direction, upon breakdown, the price impulsively breaks the structure, it is important that the price does not try to fight off this OB, otherwise, after the breakdown, we do not consider a BB. So, there was a breakdown with a change in the descending structure to an ascending one, now we have a breaker block formed from the former OB.

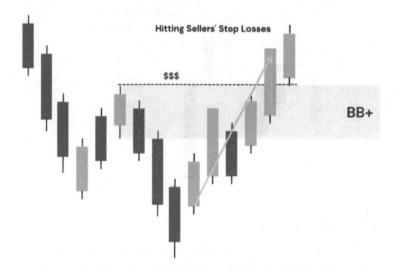

So now a major player has 2 positions, the first position was opened in the breaker block for short - it is unprofitable, the second position was opened for long in the place where liquidity was taken.

It is necessary to close the unprofitable sell position, so the price pulls back to the BB zone.

BUT! Despite its name, a breaker block in trading is not always a reversal pattern, it can signal the continuation of a trend. To determine the trend of the market, you need to consider the formation of higher highs (HH) and higher lows (HL) for a bullish trend and lower lows (LL) and highs (LH) for a bearish one. A breaker is formed after the formation of a new HH or LL during an impulse breakout of an order block.

A bullish breaker block is formed on a downtrend. After the upward momentum, speculators go long on the blue zone retest.

Bullish Breaker – a bullish range or up-close candle in the most recent Swing High prior to an Old Low being violated. It becomes valid once stops are taken below a previous low and breaks above the Swing High that contains the breaker candle.

To identify bullish breakers, traders must first identify a failed bearish order block. This happens when liquidity is taken to the downside, later causing the bearish order block to fail. Once identified, traders can take advantage of these bullish breakers by entering the market and taking advantage of price reversals.

<u>**Key Elements**</u> – Low – High – Lower Low – Higher High.

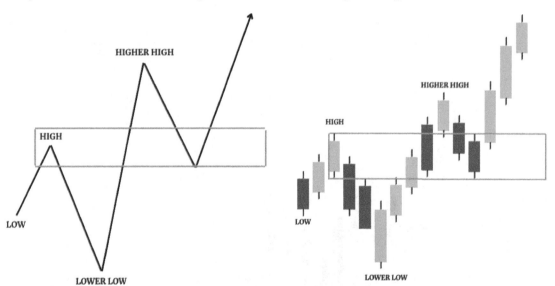

The diagram above illustrates a bullish breaker, which occurs when a bearish order block fails to act as a resistance level and liquidity is taken to the downside. This results in a market structure break, which confirms the bullish breaker, allowing price action traders to anticipate the trend to continue in the new direction.

Pay close attention to the "Higher High" as it holds great importance. When the price closes above this level, it suggests a strong desire for the price to keep rising. Similarly, take note of the "Lower Low" because it acts as a stop run and implies that the price is likely to move higher.

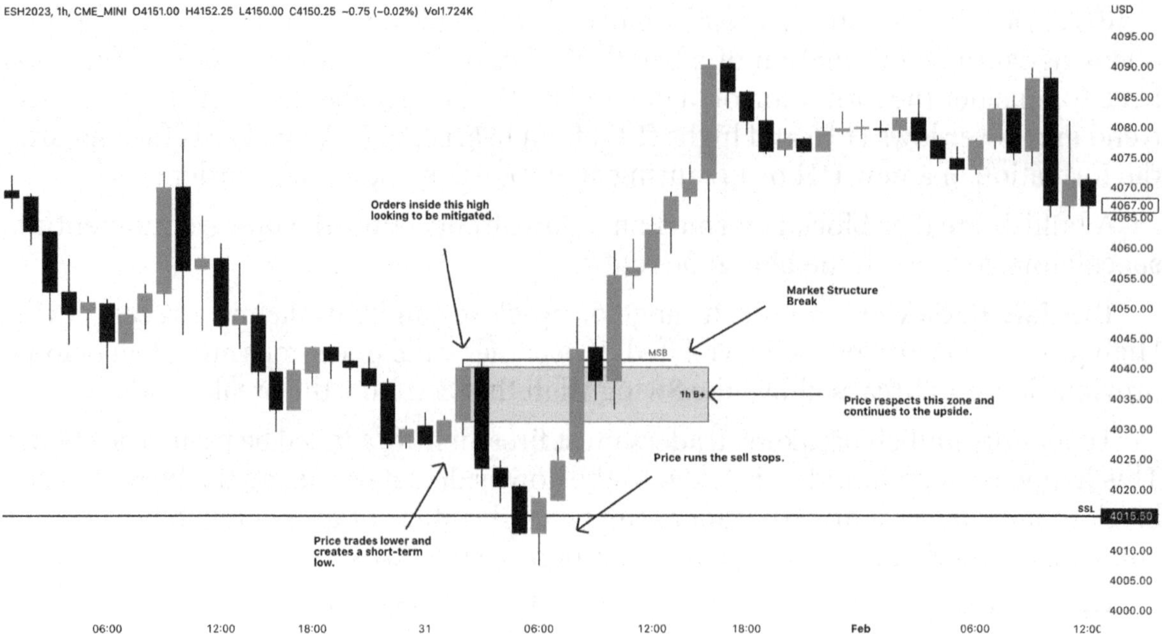
ESH2023, 1h, CME_MINI O4151.00 H4152.25 L4150.00 C4150.25 −0.75 (−0.02%) Vol1.724K
USD
Orders inside this high looking to be mitigated.
Market Structure Break
MSB
1h B+
Price respects this zone and continues to the upside.
Price runs the sell stops.
Price trades lower and creates a short-term low.
SSL
4015.50
4067.00
06:00
12:00
18:00
31
06:00
12:00
18:00
Feb
06:00

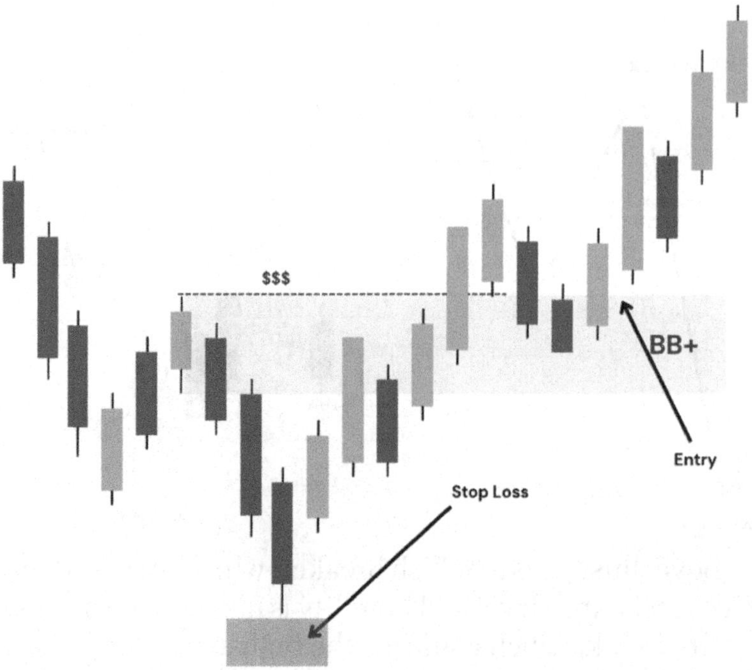
$$$
BB+
Entry
Stop Loss

An aggressive stop immediately below the breaker block. We will get an excellent risk-to-reward ratio. But such a stop will very often taking out. A conservative stop rarely attracts price, it is safer, but the risk / reward ratio with this order placement is less attractive compared to an aggressive one. Placing a conservative stop at short-term low.

Bearish Breaker – a bearish range or down-close candle in the most recent swing Low prior to an Old High being violated. It becomes valid once stops are taken above a previous high and breaks below the swing low that contains the breaker candle.

To identify bearish breakers, traders must first identify a failed bullish order block. This happens when liquidity is taken to the upside, later causing the bullish order block to fail. Once identified, traders can take advantage of these bearish breakers by entering the market and taking advantage of price reversals. Below is an example of a Bearish Breaker.

<u>**Key Elements**</u> – High – Low – Higher High – Lower Low.

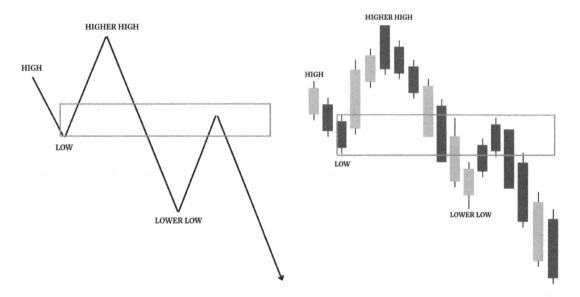

"Higher High" acts as a stop run, indicating that the price is likely to go lower. Similarly, the "Lower Low" plays a significant role. When the price closes below this level, it signifies a strong indication that the price intends to continue its downward movement.

334

We can consider only bodies to find a breaker because news candle can have long wicks or regular candle can have small body (in this case we can consider breaker as entire candle).

Breaker's task is to make a price move with manipulation to collect liquidity towards significant highs and lows, followed by a break in the opposite direction.

Advanced Theory On ICT Breaker

To confirm your bias or add to existing positions, it is essential to explore various points of reference. ICT mentions the concept of "order blocks" and how they can be used as reference points for trading.

These order blocks, also known as ICT Breakers, can be identified by observing the high and low points of a given range. By measuring the range and analyzing the gradients within it, you can determine potential entry and exit points.

Why did I say order block is breaker? Because a Breaker Block is OB broken through by a powerful impulse, without bouncing from it. The main condition for the formation of a breaker block is that the high or low is broken depending on the trend - that is, that liquidity is taken.

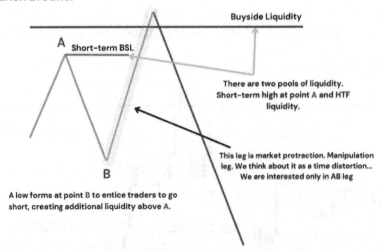

Bearish Breaker

Buyside Liquidity

A
Short-term BSL

There are two pools of liquidity.
Short-term high at point A and HTF
liquidity.

This leg is market protraction. Manipulation
leg. We think about it as a time distortion...
We are interested only in AB leg

B

A low forms at point B to entice traders to go
short, creating additional liquidity above A.

We anticipate the higher time frame to move lower, indicating a sell model.

335

Bearish Breaker

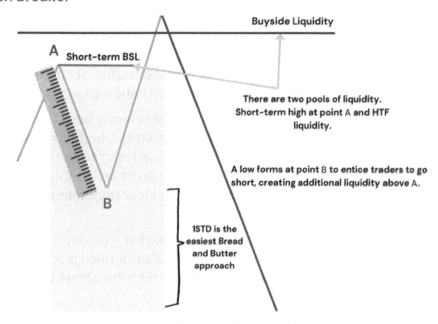

Buyside Liquidity

A — Short-term BSL

There are two pools of liquidity. Short-term high at point A and HTF liquidity.

A low forms at point B to entice traders to go short, creating additional liquidity above A.

B

1STD is the easiest Bread and Butter approach

If we examine the diagram here, we can identify a bearish breaker. It is important to note that this is not a break and retest setup. Instead, it provides a schematic understanding of how liquidity runs and results in a repricing lower. To effectively use the breaker, we need to determine the current liquidity levels.

There are two ways to approach the breaker. In this case, it is a bearish breaker that offers an additional entry point or reference for adding new short positions when we anticipate a market drop.

This particular setup capitalizes on pending orders. It takes advantage of situations where stops are hit, followed by a move in our favor, targeting retail traders who seek trend continuations without considering liquidity and market narrative. These traders often find themselves trapped in unfavorable positions.

To fully understand the breaker, we must consider two stages of liquidity.

The first stage involves short-term buy-side liquidity above the short-term high. However, the breaker pattern seeks to reach higher time frame buy-side liquidity. We observe the market's behavior to determine if it runs away from the initial liquidity pool. Inside the price range from point A to point B, we find our target.

For this model, we utilize the price range from point A to point B. Once the market creates a run and starts to decline, we can take a bearish stance. This means we are expecting lower prices and have already initiated short positions. When the price runs above the buy signal, it may not be our largest position. We might scale in with a larger portion. For example, if we were trading ES, we would start with six contracts

(ICT uses mini, but we consider micro contracts), add three more, and then add one additional contract, resulting in a 10-lot position.

This scaling approach allows us to manage potential drawdowns if the market quickly reverses after reaching our initial target. Please note that this method may not suit everyone, but it aims to enhance understanding of the breaker pattern and counteract misguided teachings prevalent on YouTube and in various courses.

A to B price range: By calculating the Fibonacci levels based on this range, we can determine our entry points. You take that leg from the high down to the low and lay your Fibonacci on it. Taking one standard deviation lower from this range is the easiest and most straightforward approach to using the breaker. This approach applies when we are on the correct side of the trade and have a clear understanding of our objectives and the prevailing market conditions.

If you're on the bullish side and in a bigger market, you don't need it to come down to this level and trade back up. Many times, ICT annotates a breaker and enters at a lower price before it even breaks out, as he is not a breakout trader or a break and retest trader.

Now, let's address the concern of going short here and it is going right up or hitting the stop loss. If that happens, it means the trade didn't work out, and you take a loss.

However, you can consider whether it still wants to go lower. If it does and nothing has changed, you can re-enter with half the position size of your first trade. It's normal to experience losing trades, and you won't be able to avoid them.

If we're bullish, the pattern we're observing could indicate a reversal or continuation in an existing bull market. This can be used on an intraday basis across different time frames, but it's essential to understand where liquidity exists. The best breakers are those that engage two levels of sell-side liquidity, one at the short-term low and another at a higher time frame.

To maximize the effectiveness of this approach, you can combine it with a higher time frame buy model and compare the standard deviations between points A and B with the larger liquidity pool. By understanding the overall market direction and utilizing these patterns, you can enhance your trading strategy.

Bullish Breaker

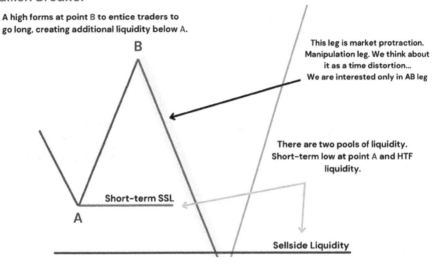

A high forms at point B to entice traders to
go long, creating additional liquidity below A.

B

This leg is market protraction.
Manipulation leg. We think about
it as a time distortion...
We are interested only in AB leg

Short-term SSL

A

There are two pools of liquidity.
Short-term low at point A and HTF
liquidity.

Sellside Liquidity

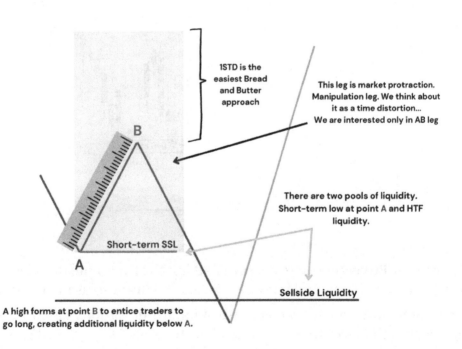

1STD is the
easiest Bread
and Butter
approach

B

This leg is market protraction.
Manipulation leg. We think about
it as a time distortion...
We are interested only in AB leg

Short-term SSL

A

There are two pools of liquidity.
Short-term low at point A and HTF
liquidity.

Sellside Liquidity

A high forms at point B to entice traders to
go long, creating additional liquidity below A.

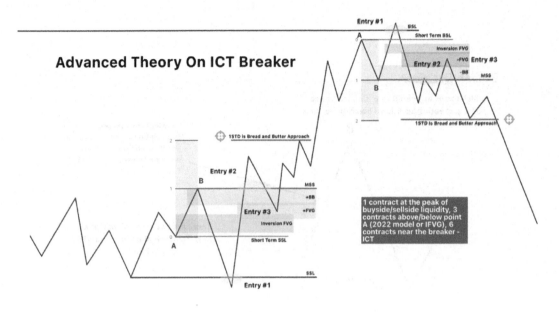

Breaker Block Projection: We measure A-B leg NOT manipulation leg. Measuring AB we can get easiest bread and butter approach. We want to use 1STD as our target.

To determine entry points, we can use standard deviations based on the A to B price leg. Using Fibonacci tools, we can identify areas of interest. For example, in the example below, the one standard deviation below gives us a measured move of 4496.50. This presents an easy bread and butter setup for entry. Additionally, we can focus on the up-close candles within this price leg to further refine our buying strategy.

This approach is commonly seen in ICT recordings when he believes that the price will rise but also may experience a larger retracement.

We aim for a level 1 standard deviation higher/lower than A to B. Additional standard deviations (2, 3, 4, etc.) can be used if HTF liquidity supports it.

Order Block

An Order Block is a candlestick that initiated a move due to the manipulation of the market maker. Up move or down move began with it, and therefore a large number of limit orders of market makers are concentrated around the OB.

The logic of an order block is that a major player moves the price up or down in search of liquidity, actually blocking their positions in the OB area and making them unprofitable. To close a trade in the zone of interest, they need the price to return to the order block, after which it will continue to move in the opposite direction.

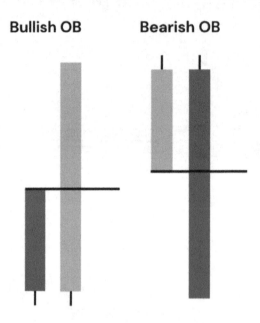

There are two types of order blocks:

1. Bullish order block: This block is determined by move down, followed by price going up.

2. Bearish order block: This block is determined by move up and then price goes down.

For traders, order blocks are necessary for placing limit orders for entry and setting stop losses. It increases the win rate, as it helps to comply with risk management, as well as to open a position more accurately. The correctness of the input depends on the correctness of the block drawing.

Why Order Blocks Work?

Order Blocks work but only if you know how to correctly identify liquidity in the market. On their own, the order blocks have no practical application, since most of them immediately break when activated (price came back to that OB). It is important to be able to initially determine the direction of the market, and only then look for an entry point.

Why does the price bounce off OB? OB is the average price of a big player, if the price goes down below the bullish OB or goes up above the bearish OB, then the big player will be at a loss.

1. Trend . It is necessary to correctly determine where the price is moving, that is, the trend and consider the order blocks in the same direction. If we consider the order block against the trend, then the first liquidity or problem area (another order block) is the target for take profit;

2. Liquidity grab. The order block is formed strictly after the take of liquidity, otherwise what kind of order block is it in which liquidity is not collected, that is, it means that the big player did not actually enter the position and this is a false order block;

3. Structural OB . The order block should have been in the structure where next we update the structure (MSS);

4. Order block with imbalance. A valid order block is the one formed together with the imbalance;

5. You need to look for entry points, and not go right away. That is, let's say we have an order block formed on the higher timeframe (HTF) –4h if we take a trade immediately on 4h , then we will have a big stop loss and there is no confirmation that this is really the order block – no reactions.
To do this, on the lower timeframe (LTF) for 4h OB use 5–15m, we must get a MSS and only then on 5–15m look for entry points.

Order Blocks are based on the lack of market liquidity at the moment when smart capital needs to open a position. As a result, the market maker opens positions in both directions, creating artificial counter liquidity in order to fill the required position volume and deliver the price in the direction it needs.

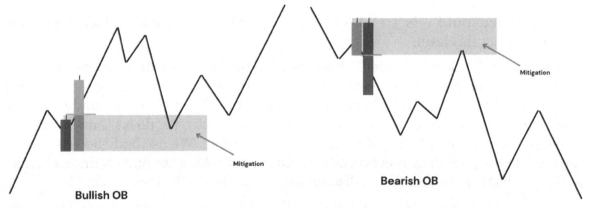

Bullish OB

Bearish OB

MITIGATION OF THE ORDER BLOCK

An order block can be used by traders as a tool for opening a position, since the logic of forming such a model includes the need to mitigate open positions.

Mitigation - the process of closing unprofitable positions with smart capital.

Since the formation of an order block implies the opening of positions in both directions and the subsequent delivery of the price in a specific direction, smart money is faced with the fact that they still have open positions that were used to fill the main volume. Accordingly, after the price has been delivered and the main position has been distributed, the market will most likely try to test the order block, since the market maker is interested in closing its unprofitable positions at breakeven - the prices where they were opened.

How to Find Order Blocks

Order blocks need to be looked for **only at the highs and lows** of the market. You should immediately understand that these are reversal places, where exactly it will form, you can only guess in advance. Your task is to wait for it to form, and then enter the trade when the OB is retested.

> Bullish Order Block – the lowest candle or price bar with a down close that has the most range between open to close and near a support level.

> Bearish Order Block – the highest candle or price bar with a up close that has the most range between open to close and near a resistance level.

Mean threshold – is 50% level of the total range of the order block; we expect price to respect this level.

The Order Block is validated when the high of the lowest down-close candle or the low of the highest up-close candle is traded through by a more recently formed candle. Ideally the best OB will not see the price trade down below the midway point (mean threshold) of the entire body of the candle (bearish). We do NOT use wicks; we measure from the open to the close on the down candle. We use body because wicks can contain the pure data as everyone uses different brokers/exchanges this can make wicks unreliable at times but it is discretionary – wicks can be used.

Price may run away from the OB if it is valid. Often there is a strong reaction so you need to be patient for it to retrace its move and retest the OB. There is an indication

343

that there is a displacement in the marketplace. There is also the evidence in price action that there is institutional sponsorship behind the move. Displacement may also leave behind another POI, the FVG.

Detecting First Order Blocks:

Break of Previous Momentum: An order block is the highest candlestick in the direction of the momentum and opposite to the reversal. It represents the last push of candlesticks in the momentum direction. By identifying the break of previous momentum, we can confirm the presence of an order block.

Differentiating Valid and Invalid Order Blocks: Valid order blocks are backed up by smart money and liquidity, making them reliable for trading decisions. On the other hand, invalid order blocks lack the necessary conditions and should not be considered for trading.

> **Additional conditions and criteria :**
> 1. Preferably a large body and small wicks;
> 2. Updating the high/low at the break of the structure;
> 3. Absorption of impulse candles or impulse reaction;
> 4. Liquidity grab.

Validity of Order Blocks

The order block is validated when the high of the lowest down close candle (for a bullish order block) or the low of the highest up close candle is traded through (for a bearish order block) by a more recently formed candle.

Ideally the best bullish order blocks will not see price trade below the mid-point of the down-close candle, or trade above the up-close candle for the bearish order block.

You can use the Fibonacci tool to measure the open and close of the candle, the mean threshold is, to keep it simple, the 50% of the candle. It is recommended to only use the bodies of the candles and not the wick because bodies are what contains the pure data. As everyone uses different broker and exchanges, wicks can sometimes be unreliable, but it's not always the case - wicks can be used, but in this case, we want the best of the best , so we use bodies.

Impact of price movement on order block validity: Order blocks are the last push of candlesticks in the direction of momentum and opposite to the reversal. They serve as trade targets for Central Banks and also indicate the accumulation of orders in the market. The first and last order blocks in a momentum are considered valid.

Liquidity areas and their significance: Liquidity areas, also known as liquidity zones, are where market makers collect liquidity. These areas are crucial as they can impact the price movement. By identifying these areas, traders can gain insights into the intentions of market makers and make profitable trades.

When price reaches this area, it collects liquidity before making its next move. Retail traders often set their stop orders in this area.

I usually consider liquidity area between 2 OBs close to each other :

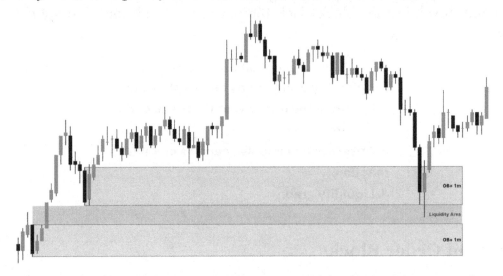

Validity of order blocks based on liquidity collection: To determine the validity of an order block, four conditions must be met. Firstly, the order block should be supported by smart money and liquidity. Secondly, it should be the highest candlestick in the direction of momentum and opposite to the reversal. Thirdly, it should serve as a target for Central Banks. Lastly, it should not have a significant correction afterwards.

Entry and Risk:

When price impulsively moves away from the bullish/bearish OB, it may retrace after the displacement which can offer a buying or selling opportunities as price returns to the open of the bullish/bearish OB candle. Target the buy stops above/sell stops below the marketplace as your first target profit or full target profit. The low of the Bullish OB or high of the Bearish OB is a relatively safe stop loss place.

Bullish OB:

Bullish Order Block

Bullish order block: This block is determined by move down, followed by the price going up.

This up candle must trade through the Bullish OB candle

Trade through this high to consider Bullish OB

Price may run away from the OB if it is valid. Often there is a strong reaction so you need to be patient for it to retrace its move and retest the OB.

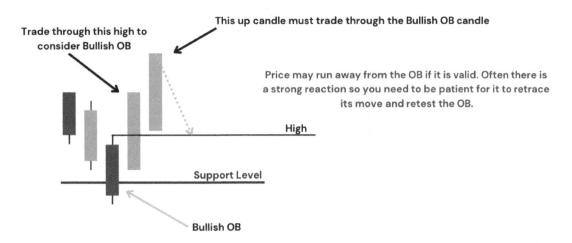

High

Support Level

Bullish OB

Bullish Order Block

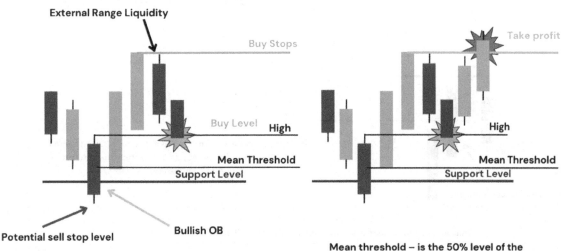

External Range Liquidity

Buy Stops

Buy Level

High

Mean Threshold

Support Level

Potential sell stop level

Bullish OB

Take profit

High

Mean Threshold

Support Level

Mean threshold – is the 50% level of the total range of the order block; we expect price to respect this level.

Bearish OB:

Bearish Order Block

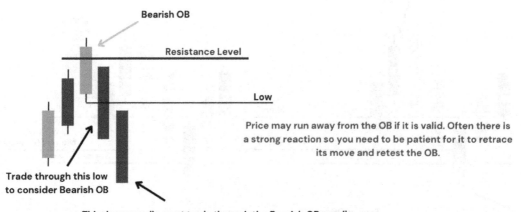

Bearish OB

Resistance Level

Low

Price may run away from the OB if it is valid. Often there is a strong reaction so you need to be patient for it to retrace its move and retest the OB.

Trade through this low to consider Bearish OB

This down candle must trade through the Bearish OB candle

Bearish order block: This block is determined by move up and then goes down.

The Order Block is validated when the high of the lowest down close candle or the low of the highest up-close candle is traded through by a more recently formed candle. Ideally the best OB will not see the price trade down below the midway point (mean threshold) of the entire body of the candle (bearish).

Bearish Order Block

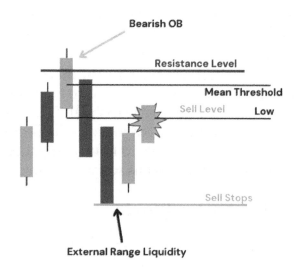

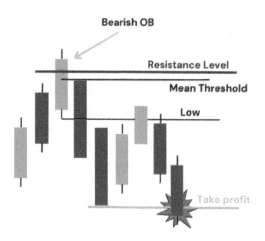

Mean threshold – is the 50% level of the total range of the order block; we expect price to respect this level.

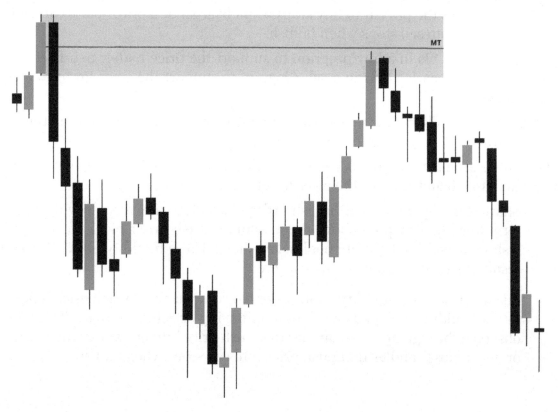

Order Block vs Breaker Block

The LAST BULLISH or BEARISH candle before an IMPULSE up or down, represent Order Block. Order Blocks are one type of supply and demand on the market, you can expect them to act as a support or resistance depending on the impulse after them. OB is where larger players have orders sitting in wait for the price to return to a level they are interested in, so that's how they act as strong supply or demand areas. The last bearish candle before an impulse up is a BULLISH OB. The last bullish candle before an impulse down is a BEARISH OB. Breaker is an OB that fails to hold and the price finally breaks through it. BULLISH BREAKER, when a bearish OB fails to hold as resistance and the price jumps above it, we expect that area to act as support now vice versa with BEARISH BREAKER, when a bullish OB fails to hold as support and the price breaks it to the downside, we expect that area to act as resistance now.

Characteristics of High Probability Order Blocks

- Forming at a key level: High probability order blocks tend to occur at key levels in the market, such as previous swing highs or lows, major liquidity pool levels, or areas where significant buying or selling activity has taken place.

OBs push the price into a liquidity pool causing a purge on stops – an up-close candle that pushes the price into buy stops when bearish or a down-close candle that pushes the price into sell stops when bullish.

Again, bullish OBs in a buy program to support the price higher to a DOL above market price and bearish OBs in a sell program to support the price lower to a DOL below market price.

When we are bullish, down-close candles will act as a roadblocks – when the price moves down into OB and support the price higher.

When we are bearish, up-close candles will act as a roadblocks – when the price moves up into OB and support the price lower.

- Short-term liquidity pool: Bullish order blocks typically form leaving a short-term low liquidity pool above them, while bearish order blocks form leaving a short-term high liquidity pool below them. These liquidity pools can be the result of stop loss orders being triggered.

- Pushing price into liquidity pool: Order blocks are created when price is pushed into a liquidity pool, causing a surge in buying or selling activity. This can be observed through up-close candles that push price into buy stops when bearish, or down-close candles that push price into sell stops when bullish.

Timeframe alignment for OBs

Monthly Level > Daily OBs.
Weekly Level > 4h OBs.
Daily Level > 1h OBs.
4h Level > 15m OBs.
1h Level > 5m OBs

[Weekly chart]

Reclaimed Order Block

When price is dropping and we see a little displacement to the upside, that's smart money with new accumulation of orders of long positions. Then when we get to the HTF PD array that's where the impulsive price action to the upside starts. A lot of people try to get involved in those early rallies while smart money is accumulating end, they end up getting stopped out.

Bullish Reclaimed Order Block – is a candle or bar that was previously used to Buy Price and a short-term bounce confirms minor displacement. In the Buy Side of Curve – these "Old" blocks will be reclaimed longs.

351

Bearish Reclaimed Order Block – is a candle or bar that was previously used to Sell Price and a short-term decline confirms minor displacement. In the Sell Side of Curve – these "Old" blocks will be reclaimed shorts.

Market Maker Buy Model is understanding that the market is going lower to go higher.

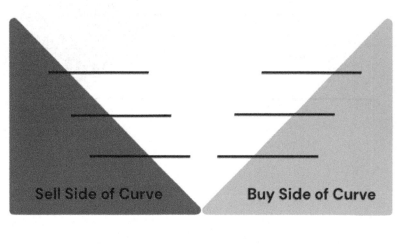

Same goes for the opposite, on the buyside of the curve smart money starts hedging that's why you already see premature bearish order blocks forming.

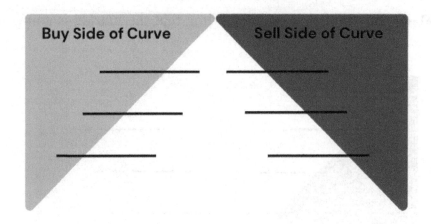

Mitigation Block

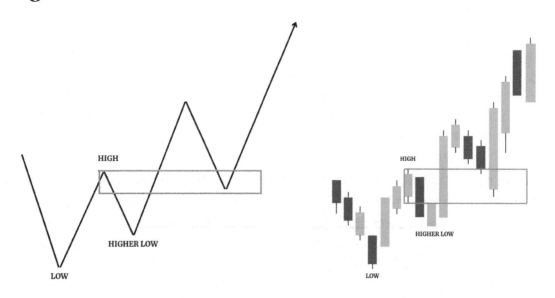

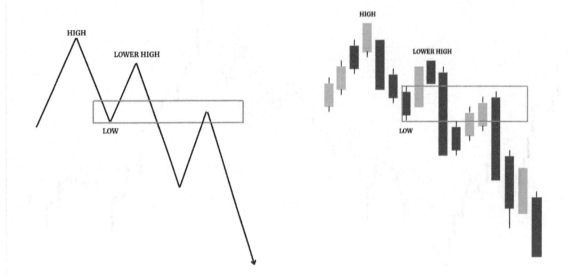

Factors for the formation of mitigation block:

1. No liquidity grab, i.e. no renewal of the high or low before the impulse. There is Break of Structure before a breakout.

2. Impulse breakdown.

A mitigation block is a reversal pattern formed when the market fails to make a higher high or lower low. In simple terms, a mitigation block results from a failure swing in the foreign market. In contrast, a breaker results from a successful swing in the market. This means price will form higher highs, collecting Buyside Liquidity on previous highs or forming lower lows, collecting sell-side liquidity on previous lows if it's a bullish mitigation block.

Consider a bearish example. The market moves up to a potential bearish resistance level (old high, old low, bearish OB, breaker).

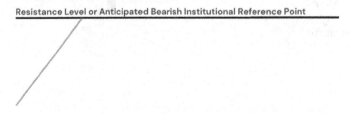

355

We are waiting for confirmation that there are sellers at this level.

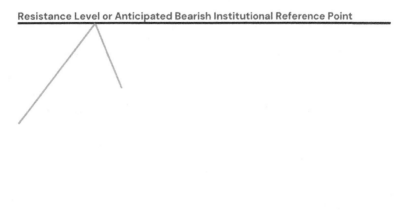

Then wait for the market to go up again and show us further interest in the fall.

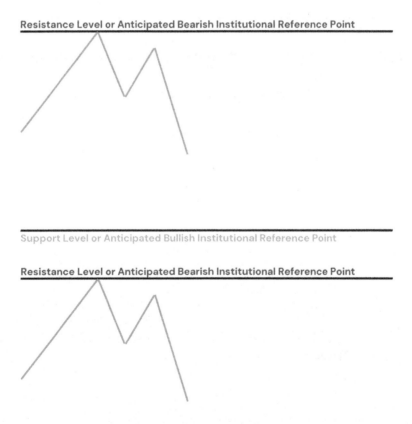

As a result, the market shows us that it really wants to go lower.

This is an 'M' pattern.

When we see that there is a shift in the market structure, the price goes below the previous low => confirmation that the big money wants to lower the price.

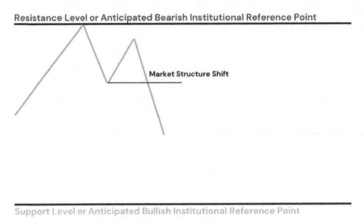

We will consider the range from a short-term low to a short-term high.

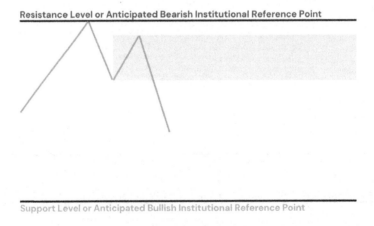

There were buyers inside this range, but now these buyers have gone under water. **This is Mitigation Block.**

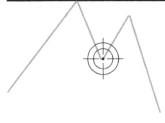

Resistance Level or Anticipated Bearish Institutional Reference Point

Once price posts a market structure shift lower, your attention moves to this specific low in price action.

Support Level or Anticipated Bullish Institutional Reference Point

As soon as price tells us that the market structure is moving down, your attention shifts to that particular low in the price action.

Inside this low, we will focus on the last down candle because that is where the last orders were placed before the short rally up.

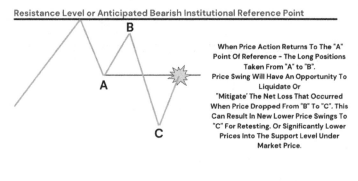

Resistance Level or Anticipated Bearish Institutional Reference Point

B

A

C

When Price Action Returns To The "A" Point Of Reference – The Long Positions Taken From "A" to "B".
Price Swing Will Have An Opportunity To Liquidate Or
"Mitigate' The Net Loss That Occurred When Price Dropped From "B" To "C". This Can Result In New Lower Price Swings To "C" For Retesting. Or Significantly Lower Prices Into The Support Level Under Market Price.

Support Level or Anticipated Bullish Institutional Reference Point

Resistance Level or Anticipated Bearish Institutional Reference Point

Short Setup

Support Level or Anticipated Bullish Institutional Reference Point

That is, it is an opportunity for short positions. We can use the same principle further if we believe that the price will fall further to some level of support.

We also note a short-term rally and focus on the last down candle.

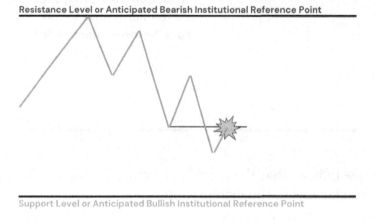

Once price reaches the support level we expect (old high, old low, bullish OB, etc.), we close our trade.

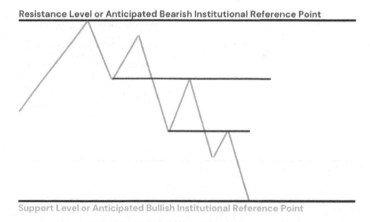

We see how the classic broken support turns into resistance every time the price returns to the old low. This is called "buyers' remorse".

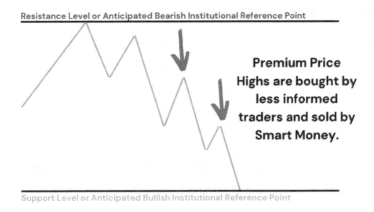

Resistance Level or Anticipated Bearish Institutional Reference Point

Premium Price Highs are bought by less informed traders and sold by Smart Money.

Support Level or Anticipated Bullish Institutional Reference Point

Price highs are bought by less informed traders and sold by smart money.

ICT uses the actual low of the down candle, not just the body, but also the low of the wick. The entire down candle is a mitigation block.

Thus, we can be a seller at the lowest point of the candle, at the wick. And our stop loss could be at the highest point of the down candle given the wick.

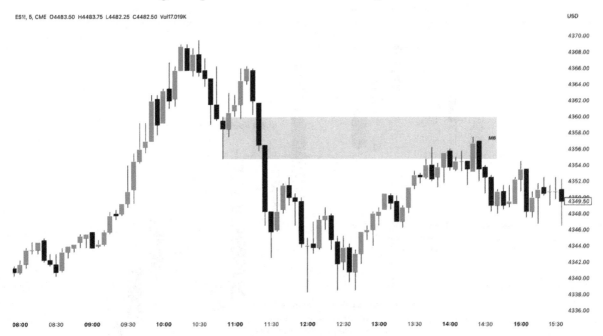

Breaker Block vs Mitigation Block

A Breaker forms a higher high, while a Mitigation Block forms a lower high. When these unfold, we are looking for trading opportunities in the market. A breaker will collect Buyside Liquidity on the previous high creating a new higher high, while a mitigation block will fail to collect Buyside Liquidity forming higher lows. A mitigation block is a result of a failure swing. In comparison, a breaker results from a successful swing in the market.

Difference between Mitigation Block and Breaker Block – Mitigation Block has a failure swing whilst on breakers there is stop run.

In the example below, we can see when price action breaks down and returns to reference point '1', the long positions from the '1' to '2' price swing will have an opportunity to mitigate their loss that occurred when price fell from '2' to '3'. This can lead to new lower price swings to retest '3' or even lower towards the HTF Support level under market price.

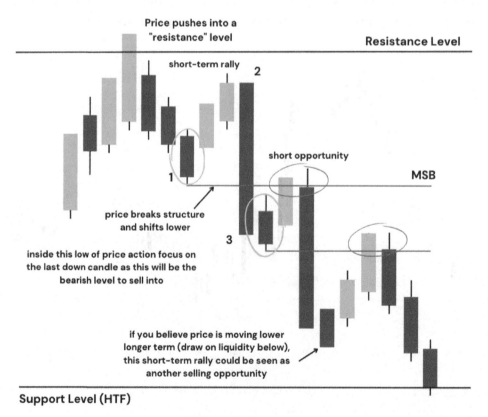

[credit to @luciusthe3rd]

Rejection Block

Every time a new high or low is formed we anticipate some sort of rejection, that is the first anticipatory price skill set you should be working on because it is the hardest.

Bearish Rejection Block is when a High has formed with long wicks on the high(s) of the candlestick(s) and price reaches up above the body of the candle(s) to run Buy Side Liquidity out before price declines.

Bullish Rejection Block is when a Low has formed with long wick(s) on the low(s) of the candlesticks) and price reaches down below the body of the candle(s) to run Sell Side Liquidity out before price rallies higher.

This is when we move into a PD array, in this case Premium array. It's also a bull flag. Price does not need to make a higher high to make a failure swing.

All you need to know about price action is basically the open high low and close, and if you follow the swing highs and lows, and you chart the open high low and close and deal specifically with the open and closes you'll be able to figure out what distribution and accumulation takes place at these turning points.

While not really focusing on the wicks, they highlight the idea of the pattern forming. Instead, look for the highest close or open at the swing high that forms. It doesn't matter if the highest candle closed bullish or bearish. We see the wick as a Bearish Order Block.

This is one of the few times where ICT uses selling on a stop order as an entry pattern, you could also immediately enter on the close in this case or wait for it to trade trough it a bit, or like ICT does a sell stop where it trades above the close and you place a sell stop at the close to sell it on when it goes back down again.

It can form over multiple candles; it's not limited to 1 candle.

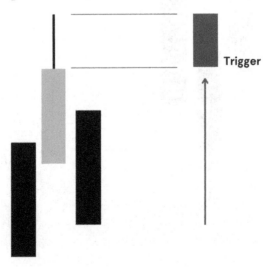

Trigger

On a bullish rejection block it's the opposite, so we take the lowest open (in case of a bullish candle) and the lowest wick and that is in theory our bullish order block, the wick.

The key is it must be a swing low/high that has a wick or wicks.

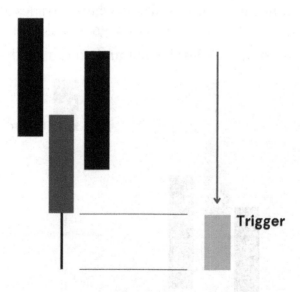

Trigger

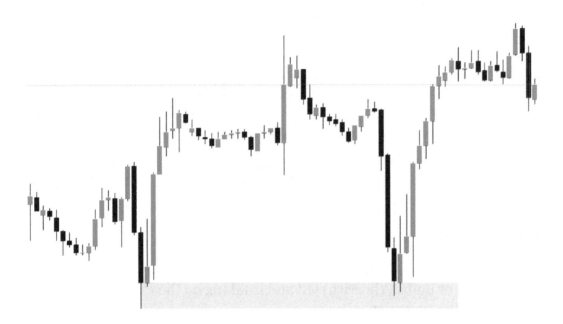

Example of the bearish Rejection Block.

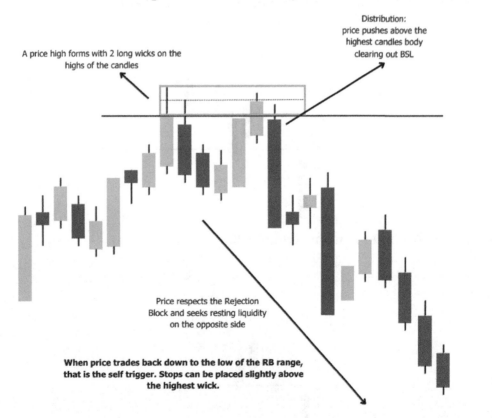

A price high forms with 2 long wicks on the highs of the candles

Distribution: price pushes above the highest candles body clearing out BSL

Price respects the Rejection Block and seeks resting liquidity on the opposite side

When price trades back down to the low of the RB range, that is the self trigger. Stops can be placed slightly above the highest wick.

[credit to @luciusthe3rd]

To identify rejection blocks, traders typically begin by analyzing price action on the higher time frame charts, such as the daily or 4-hour chart. They look for areas where price has consistently bounced off a certain level or has been unable to break through a certain level. These levels are often referred to as "key support and resistance levels".

Once the key levels have been identified, traders will then move down to lower time frames, such as the 1-hour or 15-minute chart, to identify potential entry and exit points for their trades.

Propulsion block

Propulsion Block is a candle or bar that has previously traded down (up) into a down (up) candle or bullish (bearish) OB and is taking on the role of price support for higher (lower) price movement.

We have a descending candle, which shows the willingness of the price to move higher, and there is a candle that is trading directly in the OB:

This candle becomes a propulsion block.

This new so-called OB will be very sensitive, it should never see the mean threshold exceeded, 50% of the body. Most of the time it will trade back to the high of the candle and then immediately we will see a reaction.

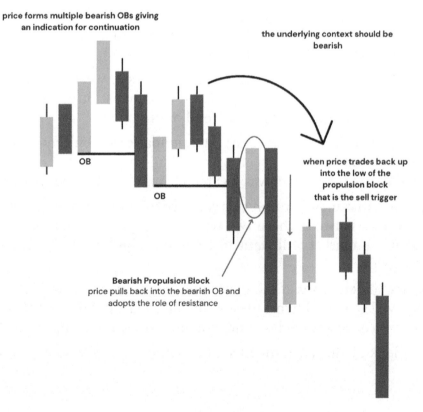

[credit to @luciusthe3rd]

Vacuum Block

A bullish and bearish vacuum blocks are "gaps" created in price action as a result of some volatile event. The gap is formed due to the "vacuum" of liquidity, directly related to the event. For example, NFP [Nonfarm Payroll] can create a vacuum block or session opening.

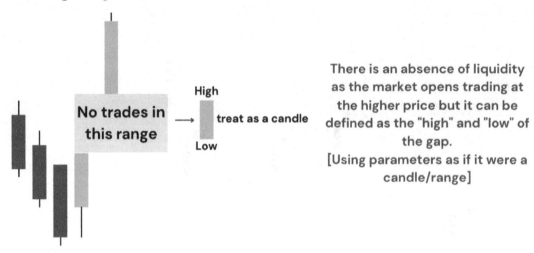

When traders see this gap, they think that prices will continue to rise. Sometimes it will.

If the price has already been rising for several days or weeks, the market has been in a prolonged uptrend => then this is probably an exhaustion gap. An exhaustion gap is essentially the last impulse of a major trend or direction.

A vacuum block is best when we are in a pullback in a bull market or if we have been in a down market and are expecting some bullish news. That is, we will leave the Discount zone, where the market was located => we expect higher prices.

It is important to remember that this space between the two candles is important. There are no trades between these two points => liquidity vacuum. There is a high probability that the market will want to come back and close this and deliver both buyside and sellside.

And we have to determine if the market will continue to move higher, leaving the gap open. Or it will go back down and close in that range. If it doesn't close in the range => how far can we expect it to close and look for a potential setup inside that range.

We would look at the Vacuum Block the same way we would look at any other candle.

If the price is trading lower, consider scenarios:

1. If we were waiting for an up move, is there any bullish OB that would make the gap not want to fill completely. We can expect to continue going long, leaving the gap open. Here we should see an immediate backlash.

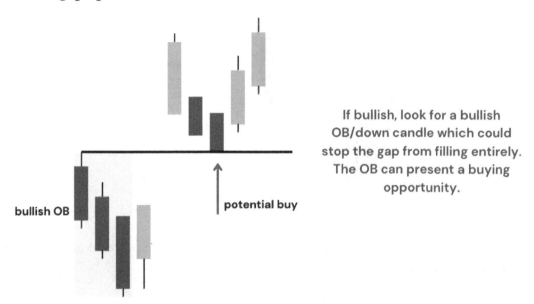

If bullish, look for a bullish OB/down candle which could stop the gap from filling entirely. The OB can present a buying opportunity.

bullish OB

potential buy

2. If the price is trading lower and we don't want to buy the OB, let's say we have a stronger belief that the price will trade until the very last up candle before the gap. The reason for such a wait, for example, depends on the time of day. If this is just the beginning of New York, then New York will probably fill the gap. If the gap was late in the evening, it will most likely leave a gap open. So, if the time of day allows, then it will most likely fill the gap.

This gap most often occurs during news events in New York and is highly unlikely to occur in the London session.

If it's the end of the day and the gap remains open, then this will give us FVG for a later time and we'll expect price to come back here later and close it.

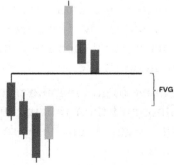

FVG

3. Fully rebalanced, this could be a blue arrow buy if we expect higher prices.

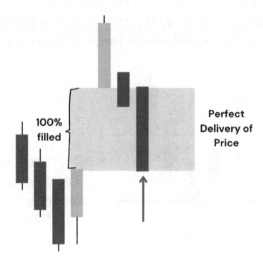

When we close a gap and see a rally up, we don't want the price to go back below the level that closed the gap.

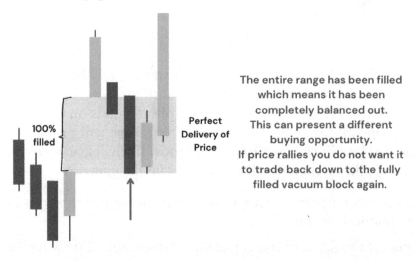

So, a vacuum block is nothing more than a breakout gap, that creates a liquidity vacuum. Not all gaps are filled completely. If we had a bullish OB, the price might just want to come to it inside this gap and then move higher. In this case, a small gap remains, and we can use it later in our trade.

And if we were expecting a move to go long and price filled the gap, which means we had a gap up and then selling and then rallying up, so we had both selling and buying happening in the area of the gap, then there are no reasons for the price to fall below this low of the first up candle.

369

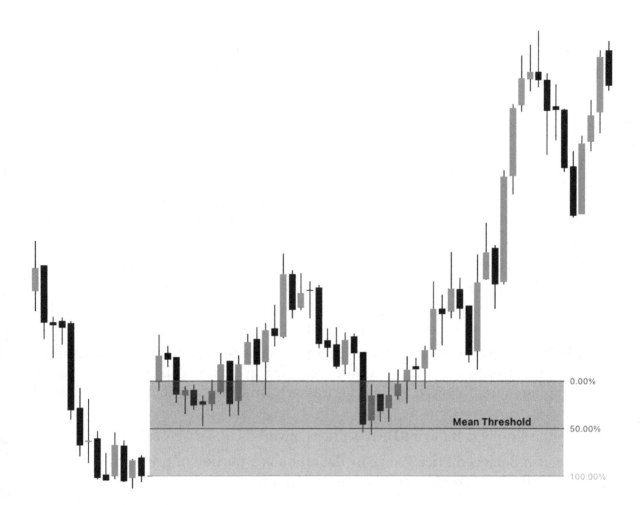

0.00%

Mean Threshold

50.00%

100.00%

Chapter 30

Breakaway Gaps and the Redelivered Rebalanced PD Array

credit to the MMXM Trader

A Breakaway Gap refers to a gap in price action that occurs after a period of consolidation. It signifies a significant shift in market sentiment and often marks the beginning of a new trend. On the other hand, a Balanced Price Range refers to a portion of price action that has experienced both buying and selling pressure, resulting in a period of equilibrium.

The Redelivered Rebalanced PD array is defined as a price range that has experienced both buying and selling pressure, resulting in a balanced market.

A bullish Balanced Price Range by definition is a portion of price action that has delivered buyside -> sellside and then buyside again.

A bullish Balanced Price Range is a portion of price action that demonstrates a specific pattern of movement: up, down, and then up again. This indicates a period of buying pressure, followed by selling pressure, and then another surge in buying activity.

To put it simply, a Bullish RDRB is price delivered UP, DOWN & UP AGAIN.

A bearish Balanced Price Range by definition is a portion of price action that has delivered sellside -> buyside and then sellside again.

A bearish Balanced Price Range is a portion of price action that follows a specific pattern of sell side, buy side, and sell side again. This pattern can be summarized as "down, up, and down again." It is called a balanced price range because it represents a period of equilibrium between buyers and sellers, where both sides have had their chance to influence the price.

To put it simply, a Bearish RDRB is price delivered DOWN, UP & DOWN AGAIN.

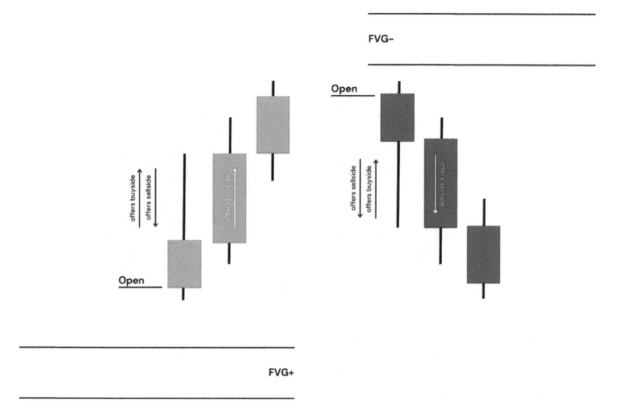

The FVG will stay open because there is a balanced price range above/below it. The Redelivered Rebalanced PD Array. This FVG that will stay open is a Breakaway Gap.

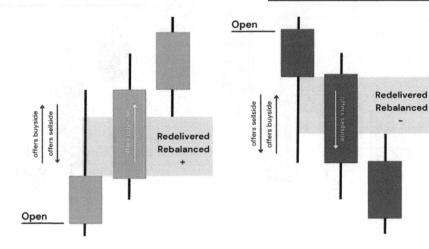

FVG−

Open

Redelivered
Rebalanced
−

offers sellside

offers buyside

offers sellside

Open

offers buyside

offers sellside

offers buyside

Redelivered
Rebalanced
+

FVG+

RDRB+

+FVG

RDRB

Chapter 31

Central Bank Dealers Range

The Central Banks Dealing Range occurs from 14:00 - 20:00 NY Time and it will continue into Asian session.

By using 1h chart, mark the high and low of 14:00 – 20:00 NY Time (mark the body of the candles and ignore the wicks).

Within that specific time, you can find the lowest low and highest high. If the range is less than 20-25 points (ES/SP500), it will give you a better understanding of where the banks will most likely price the London high or London low. This range needs to be used in conjunction with DAILY BIAS. Using Standard deviations up to 4 (above and below) will give you a range to work with.

Mark the middle of the range (sellers will be below the middle of the range and buyers will be above it).

Draw the deviations of above the range and below the range and extend horizontal lines at every deviation.

For a sell trade expect a high at 1 deviation above the flout. After high is made, the market will fall 2 deviations below the flout. Consider the high to form in London.

For a buy trade is the opposite. Expect the flout to occur between Monday, Tuesday, and Wednesday.

Sometimes price will go a little bit above/below the flout.

To put it simple, measure the number of points from the low to high of 14:00 – 20:00 NY Time range. For a sell trade, the high of the day will form at same number of points above the 14:00 – 20:00 NY Time range (1 deviation). For example, if the flout range is 15 points (ES/SP500), the high of the day will form at 15 points (ES/SP500) above the flout. Target or low of the day will form at 15 times 2 below the flout (2 deviations), that will be 30 points (ES/SP500) below the 14:00 – 20:00 NY Time range.

For a buy trade is the opposite of the above. The ideal high/low of the day will form at 1 deviation above/below the flout but it can go up to 2 deviations for Reversal market profile (London Close/New York open reversal – earlier in this book).

The ideal take profit is 2 deviations but it can go up to 3.

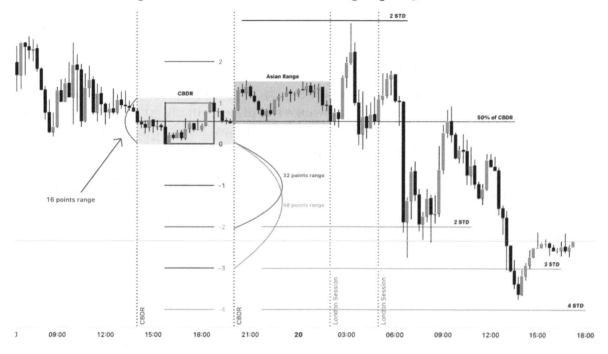

For a high probability London Normal Protraction sell day, the CBDR should be less than 20 points (ES/SP500), and the Asian session range should be between 10 to 15 points (ES/SP500). The market can move one to two standard deviations of the CBDR during the protractionary stage or Judas Swing.

The CBDR also can be used to identify potential trading opportunities and market movements during specific time periods.

High impact news will cause larger standard deviations to be reached. The CBDR is helpful with anticipating the LOD or HOD selection.

Using the CBDR is more accurate Tuesday – Thursday. That is where we see most of the volume of the week. This does not mean it could not occur on Monday .

Ideal Sell days Create HOD	
4 Standard Deviation	
3 Standard Deviation	
2 Standard Deviation	
1 Standard Deviation	
CBDR	
1 Standard Deviation	Ideal Buy days Create LOD
2 Standard Deviation	
3 Standard Deviation	
4 Standard Deviation	

The market is more likely to expand 4 standard deviation is going to be on very high impact news. Or price can go to the 4th deviation to create a New York Session market reversal profile.

We can use the wicks as well; ICT prefers to use only bodies . Just because we use the bodies, we still must look at the wick ranges every time. We can't use the CBDR criteria for day trading on this day, we can look at scalping.

The daily candle is around 40-50 points (ES/SP500) generally. We must have a bias, what will the next 3 days likely do, what's the price is likely going to do this week, where we are at seasonally, where we at quarterly, do we have a quarterly shift, do we have IPDA PD arrays that haven't been met yet?

So, if we come into a premium array on the daily and we expect bearishness price, then we can look at London open for 1-2 or maybe 3 standard deviations higher to create the high of the day. Also add seasonal tendency to it. When we blend all this together, it becomes higher probability.

Chapter 32

High Probability Daytrade Setups

 Ideally, choose a setup on the HTF. This is the main function of high probability trading. We need to look at the higher timeframe chart to predict direction, support and resistance ideas, institutional order flows.

What makes a setup "worthwhile":

- Large institutions and banks analyze charts on Day => Week => Month TFs.

- We determine price levels that correspond to the Institutional Order Flow. This is key.

- HTFs form slowly and allow enough time for planning.

What can we do to reduce the risk of a trade?

- HTF puts a lot of emphasis on price, so we focus on it.

- The conditions that provide a setup on a higher timeframe can be refined on a LTF.

- Moving the levels of the HTF to the LTF is important so we can reduce our risk (stops).

The Highest Importance is placed on the HTF Daily or 4h direction.

When Daily and or 4h direction is Bullish:

1. Use Previous Day's Low to High for Retracement Entries.

2. Use Previous Day's NY Session Low to High for Retracement Entries.

3. Use Previous Day's Low for Sell Stop Raid to accumulation longs.

4. Focusing on the anticipated move from HTF Discount to Premium PD Arrays.

When Daily and or 4h direction is Bearish:

1. Use Previous Day's High to Low for Retracement Entries.

2. Use Previous Day's NY Session High to Low for Retracement Entries.

3. Use Previous Day's High for Buy Stop Raid to accumulate shorts.

4. Focusing on the anticipated move from HTF Premium to Discount PD Arrays.

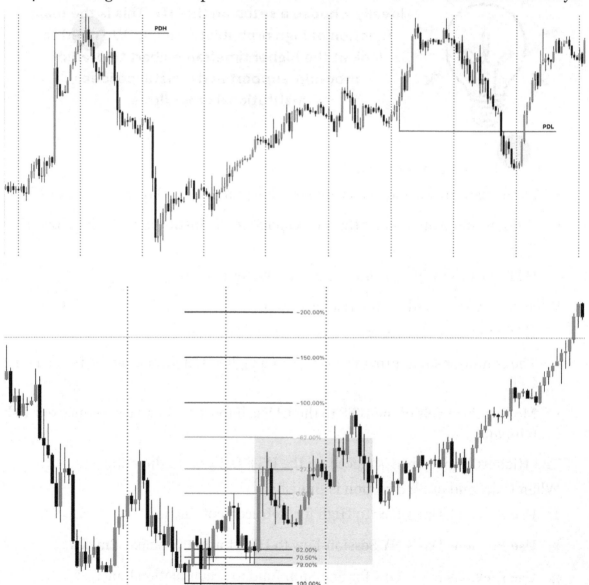

When Do We Need to look to buy?

- Ideally in seasonally Bullish periods of the year. *Not required.

- When the current Quarter or new Quarter is expected Bullish.

- After the Daily chart has reacted positively on a Discount PD Array.

- When Price has a clear unobstructed path to an opposing Premium Array.

- The Ideal Days of the Week buying Monday, Tuesday, and Wednesday.

- Refer to the CBDR and determine if it is less than 20 points (ES/SP500) ideally.

- Determine the Asian Range be in a 10-15 points (ES/SP500) range ahead of Frankfurt Open.

- Buying between 2:00am to 4:00am EST seeking LOD.

- Buy 1-2 STD of CBDR and or Asian Range coupled with Discount PD Array.

- Timeframe to execute on 5 or 15m chart

FVG below a short-term low from previous days NY session obviously has to line up with other things as well, like the CBDR, Asian range etc. And time of day, during London open.

If we have rallied right after MNO and didn't get any retracement then at 2:00am EST we buy the first bullish order block on the retracement on a 15m or 5m timeframe.

Where do we look to buy?

- Under Asian Range plus 2-5 points (ES/SP500).

- FVG below a Short-term low from Previous Day's NY Session.

- Bullish OB below a Short-term low either Previous Day or today.

- 1 STD with any Discount PD Array in London Killzone.

- Inside the Protraction lower post 12:00am to 2:00am EST with PD Array.

- Filling Liquidity Void that completes under a Short-term low.

- If after rally post 12:00am – Buy the 1st retrace into 5 or 15m +OB.

- 1-2 STD in Asian Range coupled with Discount PD Array.

- If Short-term low is taken out twice with no buyside taken – buy the Turtle Soup.

On the LTF we look for the same things we looked for on the HTF in the previous months. These criteria is not every possible scenario, these are the things ICT looks every single day when the conditions are right.

Measure the London session range to right before the New York open the extreme high and low, that's important to know before the New York session: if were bearish then that range is going to help find the next trading day retracement up. During the protractionary state, that move up is going to be a retracement into that London session range from London going into the beginning of New York, so 2am to 7am.

Also, measure the New York session range high and low, that will also many times give the setup frame for the next day's high or low, there will be a retracement inside that range.

Look for the previous day's high and low to look for stop raids, generally you're going to see those scenarios occur when there is an end to a most recent move, in other words when we've seen several days go up its going to go up into a premium array and it's probably going to trade above an old high then look for a buy stop run there and then go short the next day, vice versa when the market has been trading lower into a discount array and we look for the market to trade down below a previous day's low then buy the sell stops and use that as a daytrade.

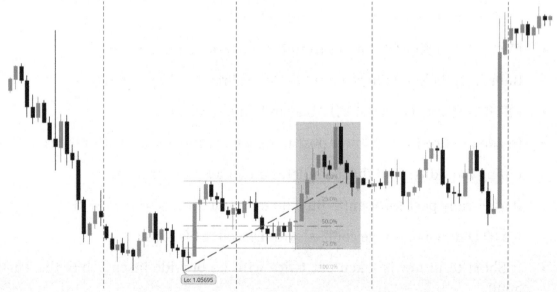

Placing Stop Losses In Buy Daytrades?

Whatever you use as the initial Stop loss - Do Not Rush to move it.

I have utilized the ES (E-mini S&P 500) as an example to explain this topic. However, please note that when applying these points to your own trading strategy, make necessary adjustments based on the instruments and assets you use in your trades.

If you are Trading the CBDR overlap with PDA - Stop is 15 points (ES/SP500) under. If you are Trading a Run under the Asian Range - Stop is 20 (ES/SP500) points under. If you are Trading ANY Sell Stop Raid - 15 points (ES/SP500) under the low/entry.

If you are Trading the 1st retracement into +OB - 5 points (ES/SP500) under LOD. If you are Trading 2nd return for Sell Stops - 15 points (ES/SP500) under the LOD .

If you are Trading any other setup not described above - use 50% ADR of the last 5 days subtracted from the Asian Range Low.

London can come back with a double pass, might knock you out at BE and you miss the move, so don't rush moving your SL. Leave it until you get at least 40-50% of the daily range and then put it at BE.

If you are trading 2nd return for sell stops, that's when we have a move lower and then it moves lower one more time and takes out the sell stops; your stop has to be below that with 15 points.

Again that one is if you don't see any move right away after MNO. If it's only been a straight down move and then it goes down one more time below the low, it formed initially your stop has to be 15 points below that if you're buying that as a turtle soup.

Assume we have a 50 points (ES/SP500) ADR over the last 5 days, take 25 points (ES/SP500) minus the Asian range low. Whatever that price is that's what your stop loss has to be.

Taking Profits In Buy Daytrades

Always try to take something off in gain at 10-15 points (ES/SP500).

Look to Scale something off every 2 STD of the Asian Range or CBDR.

Take something off at the Previous Day's High +2 - 7 points (ES/SP500). Take something off at 50% of the Price Range you are trading inside 1h. Take or have 60-80% off at 5 day ADR projections.

If trading higher than Previous Trading Week High - take something off. If trading higher than Previous Month High - take something off.

In Time Of Day - scale out at 5:00am NY Time a portion. In Time Of Day - scale out at Short Term High prior to 7:00am NYO. In Time Of Day - scale out at 10:00am to 11:00am NY time in rally.

Ideally any of the above scenarios coupled with a Premium PD Array.

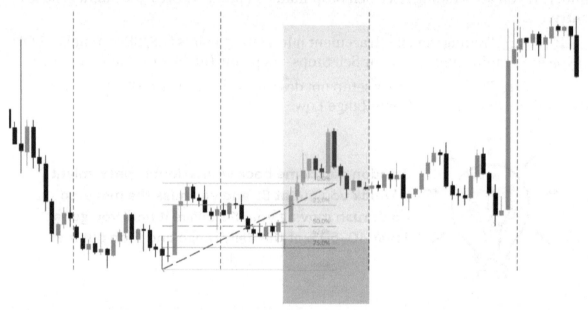

When Do We Need to Look to Short?

- Ideally in seasonally Bearish periods of the year. *Not required.

- When the current Quarter or new Quarter is expected Bearish.

- After the Daily chart has reacted positively on a Premium PD Array.

- When Price has a clear unobstructed path to an opposing Discount Array.

- The Ideal Days of the Week selling Monday, Tuesday, and Wednesday.

- Refer to the CBDR and determine if it is less than 20 points (ES/SP500) ideally.

- Determine the Asian Range be in a 10-15 points (ES/SP500) range ahead of Frankfurt Open.

- Shorting between 2:00am to 4:00am EST seeking HOD.

- Sell 1-2 STD of CBDR and or Asian Range coupled with Premium PD Array.

- Timeframe to execute on 5 or 15m chart.

Where Do We Look to Short?

- Above Asian Range plus 2-5 points (ES/SP500).

- FVG above a Short-term high from Previous Day's NY Session.

- Bearish OB above a Short-term high either Previous Day or today.

- 1 STD with any Premium PD Array in London Killzone.

- Inside the Protraction higher post 12:00am to 2:00am EST with PD Array.

- Filling Liquidity Void that completes above a Short-term high.

- If after drop post 12:00am – Buy the 1st retrace into 5 or 15m -OB.

- 1-2 STD in Asian Range coupled with Premium PD Array.

- If Short-term high is taken out twice with no downside – sell Turtle Soup.

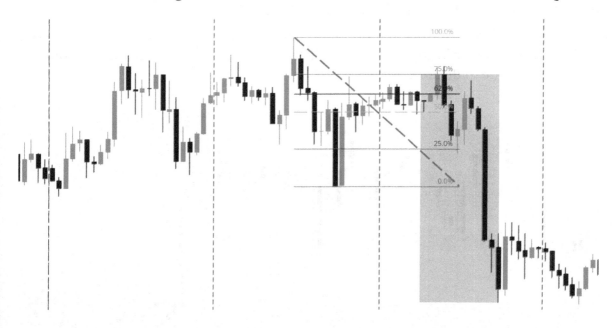

Placing Stop Losses In Short Daytrades

Whatever you use as the initial Stop Loss - Do Not Rush moving it.

If you are Trading the CBDR overlap with PDA - Stop is 15 points (ES/SP500) above. If you are Trading a Run above the Asian Range - Stop is 20 points (SP500) above. If you are Trading ANY Buy Stop Raid - 15 points (ES/SP500) above the high/entry.

If you are Trading the 1st retracement into -OB - 5 points (ES/SP500) above HOD. If you are Trading second return for Buy Stops - 15 points (ES/SP500) above the HOD.

If you are Trading any other setup not described above - use 50% ADR of the last 5 days added to the Asian Range High.

Taking Profits In Short Daytrades

Always try to take something off in gain at 10-15 points (ES/SP500).

Look to Scale something off every 2 STD of the Asian Range or CBDR.

Take something off at the Previous Day's Low - 2 - 7 points (ES/SP500). Take something off at 50% of the Price Range you are trading inside 1h. Take or have 60-80% off at 5 day ADR projections... Always.

If trading lower than Previous Trading Week Low - take something off. If trading lower than Previous Month Low - take something.

In Time Of Day - scale out at 5:00am NY Time a portion. In Time Of Day - scale out at Short Term Low prior to 7:00am NYO . In Time Of Day - scale out at 10:00am to 11:00am NY time in decline.

NYO could be a reversal, or a retracement into the CME opening, so we want to see profit taking ahead of 7:00am EST.

***Don't try to pick tops and bottoms.

The 1st question is, what is the current market narrative? What is it likely going to do now? Is it going up for stops or lower for stops? Is it going higher or lower to rebalance?

As we have already discussed, every time price rebalances a FVG that swing that did that is an ITH/ITL. Typically, an ITL will have a higher STL to the left and right. Between 2 STH will be an ITH. Use market structure within a HTF premise.

You can go hunting for FVGs in the ITH leg while the STH is in the making to the right of the ITH and under the ITH. Mark everything on the TF you're trading on, don't go too low that's an overkill Daily FVG -> 1h structure -> 15m entries for example.

LTH and LTL is generally going to be linked to a daily chart. The daily chart is what institutions and banks work off of. Daily is the most important, bias is found off daily limit your forecast to a 5 day time horizon. A break above/below an ITH/ITL is a significant break in market structure. Draw FIB from LTL to ITH when bearish, -1.5 is a standard deviation. Cause that's where the swing starts.

If the ITH is not higher than 2 STH that means the market is weak/bearish vice versa for bullish.

In bearish conditions, all up close candles should be respected vice versa when bullish. If that doesn't happen, it's only allowed if there's a STH above it, then it's likely a liquidity grab.

The high/low that rebalances a FVG should not get taken out, otherwise you might have the wrong bias.

The ITH/ITL shouldn't be violated, it's a key high/low if the ITH/ITL gets broken wait on the sidelines and observer. If you think price can go either way and have no clear bias then that's low probability, if you can see it clearly go in 1 direction then that's high probability.

When price is close to the objective it doesn't like to retrace before reaching the target, price might engineer EQL/EQH before taking it out. Remember that often the initial move when market opens at 9:30am is a Judas Swing. Pyramiding is adding on entries with lower risk each time, you want to risk the most on the initial move/entry, on the continuation entries you want to risk less. ITL/ITH should not be breached until the objective is met.

High Probability Scalps

Focus:

- Learn directional bias for HTF institutional sponsorship.

- Determine highest probable times of the day.

- Framing high probability setups for runs on liquidity.

- 5 – 10 points (ES/SP500) swings.

- There will be times scalping setups will overlap with longer term conditions.

- Running out previous day's highs / lows:

    - Targeting buy stops above previous day's high or 1 / 2 days ago: Always going to be looking previous 3 days as your range (counting current day as day 1).

    - Reason for 3 days is because every swing high / low consists of 3 individual bars.

1h CHART:

1. Highlighted individual daily highs + lows.

2. Use Daily TF to determine bias.

3. Use H1 TF to look for draws on liquidity.

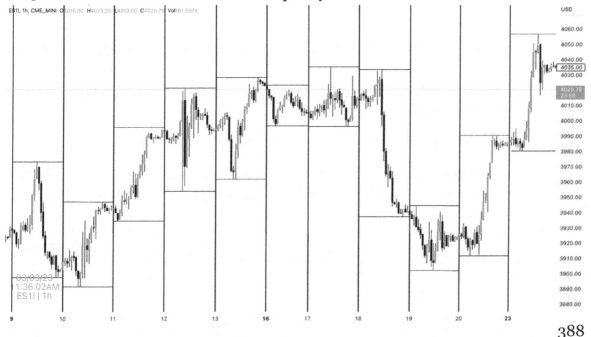

If we are bullish - seek to run previous day(s) highs / old high (vice versa for bearishness):

1. Known as drawn on liquidity (DOL).

2. Going to be in the form of buyside liquidity or buy stops.

3. Market will be drawn to that level and dip into liquidity pool.

Any of the 3 candles for swing points can be up or down close. Formation is most important - only 3 candles needed to form this pattern:

• Daily swing low should have the middle candle being the lowest low and higher lows to the left and right.

• Daily swing high should have the middle candle being the highest high and lower highs to the left and right.

Bullish scenario:

Only interested in looking for a daily swing low after a daily swing high has been broken:

1. Once the highest high of the daily swing high is traded through - this indicates bullish momentum.

2. Wait for a swing low to form to show oversold conditions.

3. After a swing low forms, we wait for the last swing candle of the 3 to be violated to the upside -> We play the pullback and target previous day(s) highs.

Bearish scenario:

Only interested in looking for a daily swing high after a daily swing low has been broken:

1. Once the lowest low of the daily swing low is traded through - this indicates bearish momentum.

2. Wait for a swing high to form to show overbought conditions.

3. After a swing high forms, we wait for the last swing candle of the 3 to be violated to the downside -> We play the pullback and target previous day(s) lows.

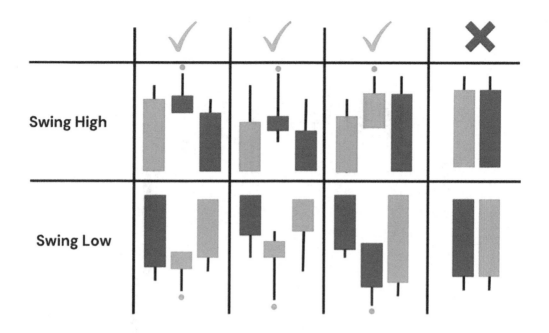

	✓	✓	✓	✗
Swing High				
Swing Low				

Swing Low

Implementing daily bias

*Referring to daily chart

Bullish scenario:

- Wait for a swing high on the daily to be broken = Bullish stage:

    - Swing high = Candle with lower highs to both sides.

    - We anticipate buying opportunities in the future.

- When price retraces, look for a swing low to form but does not break a recent swing low:

    - Swing low = Candle with higher lows to both sides.

When swing low forms - anticipate the 3rd daily candle high (last candle of the swing low formation) to be raided or traded through the following day:

- The candle that opens after this should preferably open below the 3rd candle's high.

- Look for previous day highs to be raided each day until a swing high on the daily forms or price reaches a key S&R level.

Swing High Broken = Bullish Stage

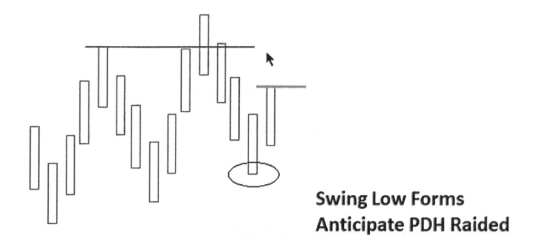

**Swing Low Forms
Anticipate PDH Raided**

[Circle is swing low Blue line is 3rd daily candle expected to be raided or traded through].

Bearish scenario

- Wait for a swing low on the daily to be broken = Bearish stage:

    - Swing low = Candle with higher lows to both sides.

    - We anticipate selling opportunities in the future.

- When price retraces, look for a swing high to form but does not break a recent swing high:

    - Swing high = Candle with lower highs to both sides.

When swing high forms - anticipate the 3rd daily candle's (last candle of the swing high formation) low to be raided or traded through the following day:

- The candle that opens after this should preferably open above the 3rd candle's low.

- Look for previous day lows to be raided each day until a swing low on the daily forms or price reaches a key S&R level.

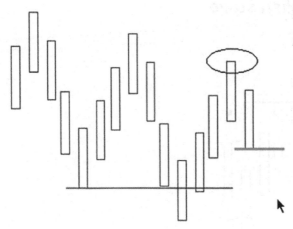

**Swing High Forms
Anticipate PDL Raided**

Swing Low Broken = Bearish Stage

When daily bias is bullish: 3 components that make up generic price action:

- Accumulation phase - longs or shorts accumulated.

- Manipulation phase - price goes opposite direction to what intended future direction will be.

- Range expansion / Distribution.

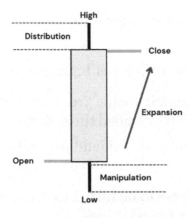

Guide:

1. Confirm London session was bullish:

   - Measure of bullishness after an attempt to go lower was rejected and price has seen a rally + Daily bias bullish.

2. Wait for 7am NY time to stalk for longs.

3. Between 7am – 9am NY time, setup will typically form.

4. After 7am NY time, wait for price retracement lower.

5. NY session will typically retrace from a swing high intraday that was formed for daily high or a short term high during London session.

6. Ideally select retracements of at least 7-10 points (ES/SP500) lower.

7. If no retracement of 7-10 points (ES/SP500) forms by 9AM - don't take anything.

8. If it does form - enter on 62% fib as it drops.

9. Expect price to retest high of day or previous day's high -> Look for targets 1 & 2 on the fib.

[ES – 5m]

When daily bias is bearish: 3 components that make up generic price action:

- Accumulation phase - longs or shorts accumulated.

- Manipulation phase - price goes opposite direction to what intended future direction will be.

- Range expansion / Distribution.

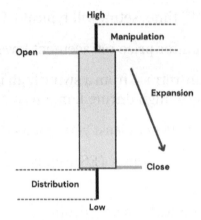

Guide:

1. Confirm London session was bearish:

    - Want to see price move above opening price at midnight NY time then rejects and go lower -> Should anticipate idea of NY session continuing in bearish conditions.

2. Wait for 7am NY time to stalk for shorts.

3. Between 7am-9am NY time, setup will typically form.

4. After 7am NY time, wait for price retracement.

5. NY session will typically retrace from a swing low intraday that was formed for daily low or a short-term low during London session.

6. Ideally select retracements of at least 7-10 points (ES/SP500) higher.

7. If no retracement of 7-10 points (ES/SP500) form by 9AM- don't take anything.

8. If it does form - enter on 62% fib as it rallies.

9. Expect price to retest current low of day or previous day's low -> Look for targets 1 & 2 on the fib.

When to Expect Reversals

- When H1 chart trades to an obvious old high or old low that has shown a clear willingness to reverse price before - this will likely repeat.

- Sometimes price will not respect an old high or low and those generic S&R levels will give way and we never know for sure.

- Far better to expect them to cause a reaction than not to -> Plenty of moves and price swings between these key HTF price points to never have to worry about them.

Chapter 33

Quarterly Shifts & IPDA Data Ranges

Quarterly shifts refer to the concept that every three months or so, the markets tend to form an intermediate-term turning point. These shifts are crucial for finding the next explosive market moves and are influenced by factors such as institutional order flow and seasonal tendencies.

Quarterly shifts apply to every market. It happens because the market needs to create new interest. Always look at price on a macro level, monthly weekly and daily timeframe. Every 3 or 4 months there's a market shift, it may cause a consolidation or a retracement of whatever price swing had been evolving.

If the market is in a strong uptrend, you will likely not see a retracement but more a consolidation, Smart Money will capitalize new longs that way and they might take a short-term low on the daily to then go higher.

IPDA is Interbank Price Delivery Algorithm. It plays a role in seeking new levels in price for liquidity and moving the price to an area of new liquidity.

IPDA helps traders forecast the direction of the weekly candle and the potential for higher or lower prices in relation to PD arrays and IPDA data range

IPDA delivers price quotes to global financial institutions and banks, determining the trading range within a day, week, month, season, year.

Is it good or bad? Manipulation in the market is a forced necessity for a market maker who, following the main rule of preserving and increasing capital, must perform a certain sequence of asset management actions in order to continue to stay in the game.

How does it help in trading?

Firstly, it allows smart money traders to determine a trading pattern, which will allow them to develop an optimal trading strategy based on the structure of consolidation within a period.

Secondly, by understanding the trading pattern, a trader has the most important knowledge of when to trade and when it is better to stay away.

In the era of digitalization, the only way to teach a neural network to trade is to define instructions according to the initial data, the main ones being time and price. The price displays the liquidity pools where the trading volume is most likely to be, and the time is the reference points for the periods of formation of such liquidity. Understanding these two components of the market mechanics puts the trader at the top of Maslow's market pyramid - you are no longer a retailer; you are a smart money.

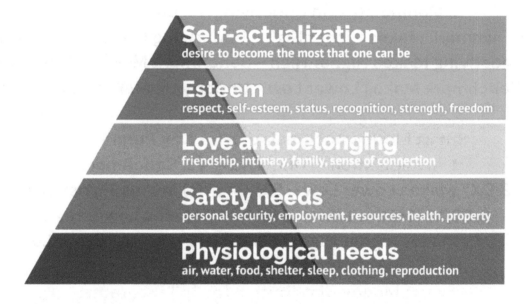

IPDA Data Ranges:

3-4 Month Major Market Shifts

Smart Money Accumulation for Buy Programs:
1. Manipulation In Underlying Vs. Benchmark
2. Benchmark Makes Lower Low – Underlying Makes Higher Low
3. Underlying Makes Lower Low – Benchmark Makes Lower High
4. Benchmark Makes Higher High – Underlying Makes Higher Low

Smart Money Distribution for Sell Programs:
1. Manipulation In Underlying Vs. Benchmark
2. Benchmark Makes Higher High – Underlying Makes Lower High
3. Underlying Makes Higher High – Benchmark Makes Higher Low
4. Benchmark Makes Lower Low – Underlying Makes Lower High

Smart Money Accumulation for Buy Programs:
1. Manipulation In Underlying Vs. Benchmark
2. DXY Makes Lower Low – ES/YM (NQ) Makes Higher Low
3. ES/YM Makes Lower Low – DXY Makes Lower High
4. DXY Makes Higher High – ES/YM (NQ) Makes Higher Low

Smart Money Distribution for Sell Programs:
1. DXY Makes Higher High – NQ/YM (ES) Makes Lower High
2. NQ/YM (ES) Makes Higher High – DXY Makes Higher Low
3. DXY Makes Lower Low – ES/YM (NQ) Makes Lower High

When things like this happen, you can anticipate it being a turtle soup on the daily. If the old low/high has a lot of long wicks then you'll be looking for a rejection block. Instead of a sweep of the wicks, it will be a sweep of the bodies.

The Quarterly Shift

The Look Back:

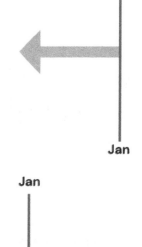

1. 60 – 40 – 20 Trading Days
2. Identify Institutional Order Flow
3. Refer to Recent Institutional Reference Points:
   Old Price High
   Old Price Low
   Bearish OB
   Bullish OB
   Fair Value Gap or Liquidity Void

4. Anchor Vertical Line to Previous Market Shift

The Cast Forward:

1. Anticipate Market Shift In 20 to 60 Trading Days
2. Cast Forward 20 Days When Last Shift Was 40 Days Ago
3. Cast Forward 40 Days When Last Shift Was 20 Days Ago
4. Projected 3 Month Limit

ICT suggests that by having IPDA data ranges on your chart, you can look backwards and forwards for the most recent 20-day, 40-day, and 60-day buy and sell stops.

After they have been cleared out on both sides of the marketplace, once they have been wiped out and we're in equilibrium, you have to look at where the next range high and low is outside of the last 60 days. That will tell you where the next big significant move is going to be. By combining this with weekly and monthly charts, you can anticipate a significant move 20 days from the new market delineation. You can identify where significant short-term and intermediate-term highs and lows are by looking at the last range of 20 days behind us and 20 days casting forward, expecting a new high or a new low to form. Therefore, you can use the most obvious buy stops and sell stops to look for the near-term high and low in the last 20 days, the short-term high and low in the last 40 days, and the intermediate-term high and low in the last 60 days.

The algo will do a shift between 60 and 20 days in the look forward phase. We expect a setup in the next 60 trading days, you don't have to trade the daily if it doesn't suit you, this also helps with daily bias context.

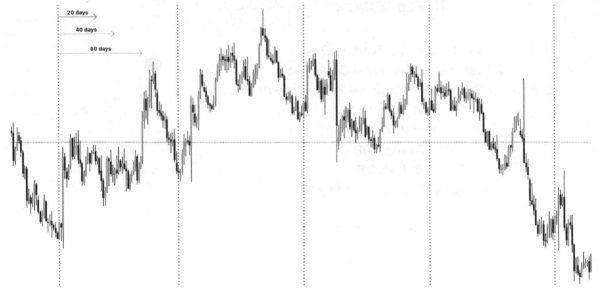

This will help map out WHEN the setups occur, time is very important. The algo will seek to do something in the first 20 days, 40 days, 60 days after the most recent market structure shift.

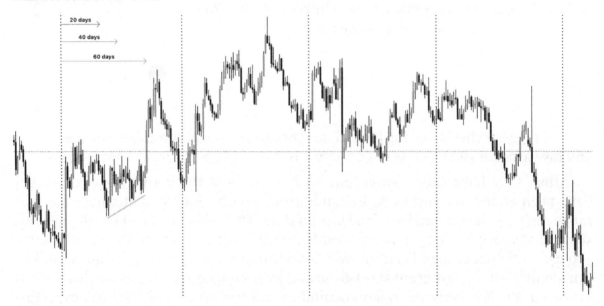

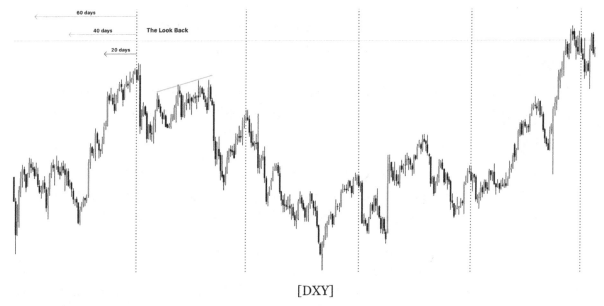

[DXY]

SMT between DXY and ES, the underlying is making higher lows and the benchmark is making higher highs. And its occurring within the 3/4 months and within the 60 days look forward phase.

There's a rhythm behind price Every 3/4 months there's a sentiment shift to cause interest.

To conclude, we know that there is a quarterly shift in the market. This market is not random, and if they were nobody would have gained many profits consistently. The market is controlled to the exact point as an exit or target.

1. Build your IPDA Data Range annotations:

   - Use the Daily Time Frame ONLY

   - Do not include the weekends, just the week days when counting back (Mon. - Fri.)

   - Look for the highest high and lowest low within each look back range (20, 40, 60)

   - Look for certain PD Arrays like Old Monthly, Weekly, 4H, lows, highs, Gaps, Liquidity Voids, ICT Order Blocks etc.

   - Find the highest high and lowest low within the last 60 days and cut that range in half.

   - Locate all obvious premium and discount arrays within the respected trading range you cut in half.

When should a trader use IPDA?
It should be used on the first trading day of every month.

Where should a trader use IPDA look back data ranges?
Traders should be using it on the Daily Time frame (1 candle = 1 trading day).

Why should a trader be using IPDA?
IPDA gives a better reference point as to where the markets might reach throughout the new trading month.

Main idea of the concept: The markets will make a quarterly shift every 3, 4, or 6 months. This sets traders up to anticipate if we get a higher time frame market structure shift. Finding these highs and lows and PD arrays allow us to have more trading context without any indicators.

Disclosure: IPDA look back data ranges alone does not tell you where to buy and sell. There needs to be a blend of concepts, mainly time and price.

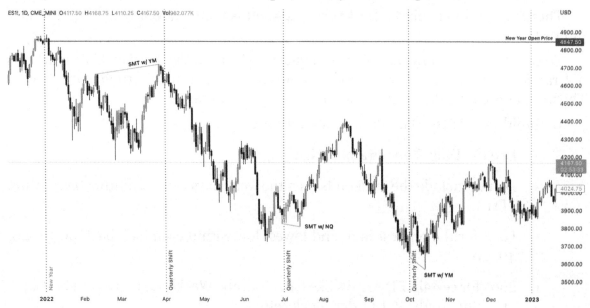

Dear Reader,

As we reach the final page of this book, I want to extend my heartfelt gratitude to you for taking the time to explore the ICT concept and ideas that have filled these pages. It has been a privilege to have you as a reader, and I hope you found inspiration, knowledge, or simply an enjoyable experience within these words.

Your curiosity and dedication to learning are truly commendable. If you have any questions, thoughts, or feedback, I would love to hear from you. Please don't hesitate to reach out to me on Twitter: **@LumiTraders**, or email at **info@lumitraders.com** Your insights and questions are invaluable to me, and I look forward to connecting with you.

If you're interested in joining my community and becoming part of my team, please visit www.LumiTraders.com. We're always on the lookout for passionate individuals who share our vision and values. Together, we can continue to learn, grow, and make a positive impact on the world.

Thank you once again for being a part of this journey. Your support means the world to me, and I'm excited to see where our paths may lead.

LumiTraders ✓
@LumiTraders

Elisabeth
@no_hay_calor

@lumi_traders

@no_hay_calor

lumitraders.com

Made in the USA
Las Vegas, NV
07 February 2024

85352217R00223